MANPOWER AND HUMAN RESOURCES STUDIES

NO. 7

THE AVAILABILITY OF MINORITIES AND WOMEN FOR PROFESSIONAL AND MANAGERIAL POSITIONS 1970-1985

by

STEPHEN A. SCHNEIDER

With the Assistance of

MARTHA B. PREISS and ROBERT W. SHANGRAW

INDUSTRIAL RESEARCH UNIT
The Wharton School, Vance Hall/CS
University of Pennsylvania
Philadelphia, Pennsylvania 19104
U.S.A.

Foreword

The administration and enforcement of civil rights legislation and executive orders have progressed from equal opportunity to affirmative action. Affirmative action requires that companies take action to seek out and to employ minority and female employees. This presupposes that such employees either have the requisite skills and training or can be easily, or at least reasonably quickly, trained. Inadequate consideration is usually given by governmental enforcement agencies to the possibility that (1) for some skills, minorities or women may simply not be available; or (2) when they are not available, the job requires more than casual preparation and training.

The need for realistic appraisal of the availability of women and minorities assumes even greater significance when one considers professional and managerial positions. Not only are the professions important in themselves, but they are, as well, the stepping stones to managerial positions. Consequently, it is important to understand how minorities and women have participated in the professions in the past, what is their present status, and what are their prospects for the future in the key professions of engineering, law, accounting, other business related areas, chemistry, physics, medicine, and dentistry. This is what has been accomplished by Professor Stephen A. Schneider and his associates.

The results of the study show that, by 1985, there will be substantial improvement in minority and female participation in most all the professions studies herein, but not in all; and that progress will vary considerably from one profession to another. Moreover, it will obviously be many years before parity is achieved in any of the professions, either by minorities or by women.

The findings and estimates of Professor Schneider and his associates raise many questions about the enforcement of civil rights legislation and executive orders. Many years of very limited participation cannot be quickly overcome. Progress may be great, but even a 1,000 percent increase in entrance ratios cannot induce parity if the base is only 2 percent.

It should also be obvious that the very concept of numerical parity in all fields is totally unrealistic. People seek different outlets and aspirations and do not go proportionately into various occupations, and this in turn varies among the races, sexes, and ethnic groups. The closer that we push toward quota employment, the more clear it should be that quotas do not fit the labor force.

Second, it would seem that practicing affirmative action against employers, at least for the professions, is both a misapprehension of the problem and a misdirection of the remedy. It is a misapprehension because the problem is not discrimination, but training and development. Blacks and females are given special incentives to enter college. Black and female professionals and professional school graduates are today's superstars, sought after by industry and often paid a premium over and above their white male counterparts. What is needed is not more pressure on industry but better motivation, schooling, and counseling, especially of blacks, to induce women and minorities to take the hard study road through college, professional, and graduate training. The jobs and potentially great careers are there for the taking, but preparation is necessary. By concentrating our emphasis on discrimination and affirmative action, the real problems of education, training, and entrance into the professions receive less emphasis, and availability remains low.

A special problem of women involves high departure rates from professions, undoubtedly because of continued family commitments. Again this should be recognized as a fact of life by compliance agencies when assessing equal employment performance and the availability of women for such positions.

*   *   *   *

Professor Schneider's work (No. 55 of the Major Industrial Research Unit Studies) is published in the Manpower and Human Resources Studies series. This series was inaugurated as part of the Industrial Research Unit's commitment to support the type of research which dates back to the forming of the Unit in 1921 and which was continued in later years in the thirty-one monographs of the Racial Policies of American Industry series and the seven volumes of the Studies of Negro Employment. Recent studies and monographs published in this series include: *Educating the Employed Disadvantaged for Upgrading*, by Richard L. Rowan and Herbert R. Northrup (1972); *Manpower in Homebuilding*, by Howard G. Foster (1974); the encyclopedic analysis of government manpower activity, *The Impact of Government Manpower Programs*, by Charles R. Perry, Bernard

E. Anderson, Richard L. Rowan, and Herbert R. Northrup
(1975); *Manpower and Merger*, by Steven S. Plice (1976); and
The Opportunities Industrialization Centers, by Bernard E. Anderson (1976).

The principal author of this work, Dr. Stephen A. Schneider,
Assistant Professor of Management and Industrial Relations,
The Wharton School and Senior Faculty Research Associate in
the Industrial Research Unit, received his undergraduate and
Master of Business Administration degrees at the University
of Cincinnati and the Ph.D. degree in Industrial Relations at
the University of Pennsylvania. He was assisted by Martha
B. Preiss, who researched the literature and drafted the summaries of that body of knowledge, and by Robert W. Shangraw,
who handled the data processing. Martha B. Preiss performed
these activities while a candidate for the Master of Business
Administration degree at the Graduate Division of The Wharton
School; Robert W. Shangraw is a candidate for a Master of
Science in Accounting at the University of Pennsylvania. Roy
S. Neff, Ronald C. Smeder, and Vincent Cuiule also contributed
to the project while Master of Business Administration
candidates.

The manuscript was edited by the Industrial Research Unit's
chief editor, Mr. Robert E. Bolick, Jr., and by Mr. David O. Northrup who also made up the index. It was typed by Miss Mary McCutcheon and Mrs. Bonnie J. Petrauskas. Mrs. Margaret E. Doyle
handled the administrative matters. Dr. Donald F. Morrison,
Professor of Statistics, provided valuable counsel in the development of the study.

Funds for the project were provided by grants from E.I.
duPont de Nemours and Company and Appalachian Power Company. Publication costs were provided through the unrestricted
grants to the Industrial Research Unit by the Rollin M.
Gerstacker Foundation, the Gulf Oil Foundation, and Hercules,
Inc. The senior author is fully responsible for the research and
the views expressed, which should not be attributed to the
grantors nor to the University of Pennsylvania.

HERBERT R. NORTHRUP
Industrial Research Unit
Philadelphia   The Wharton School
May 1977   University of Pennsylvania

TABLE OF CONTENTS

LIST OF TABLES

FIGURE

CHAPTER II

CHAPTER I

Introduction

The broad civil rights advancements of the past fifteen years have opened new job vistas for minorities and women. A key to their success in achieving economic equality is how much they will participate during the next decade in the prestigious professional and managerial positions. Against the backdrop of past experience, this study will examine the current status of women and minorities in professional and managerial positions and what can be forecast for the situation in the years ahead to 1985. The purpose of this study is to provide meaningful information to corporate and government administrators concerned with developing realistic equal employment opportunity programs based on reasonable estimates of available minorities and women in occupational categories.

Changing Labor Force Participation

Today women workers comprise more than one-third of the world's labor force. The attachment of women to the labor force in the United States has grown stronger as a result of legislation prohibiting employment discrimination based on sex, changing attitudes toward careers for women outside the home, and the increasing numbers of households headed by women. In the United States, the proportion of women in the work force increased from 34 percent to 40 percent between 1962 and 1975. Moreover, women now constitute a larger portion of workers in every major occupational group with the exception of farm laborers than they did in the early 1960s. To evaluate effectively the progress of women in the job market, it is necessary to examine their participation not only in major groupings of the labor force, such as "professional and technical workers," but also their participation in specific occupations. The implications are much different if the increase in the proportion of women in

1

the "professional and technical" group of the labor force resulted from employment increases in occupations in which women have been traditionally employed, such as nursing and elementary teaching, than if the increases occurred in occupations in which women were underrepresented in the past.

The increased participation of blacks in the labor force has not been as substantial as that of women in recent years. Between 1962 and 1974 the proportion of blacks employed increased from 10 percent to 11 percent. Black workers have, however, experienced improvement in occupational status as they moved into higher skilled and more highly paying jobs and as black employment in undesirable job groups fell. For the same reasons discussed previously in regard to women, to evaluate effectively the advancement of blacks and other minorities in the job market, it is necessary to study the participation of these groups in specific occupations.

Study Organization

The occupations chosen for this study include the principal engineering subfields, accounting, business administration, law, chemistry, physics, medicine, and dentistry. These professions were selected on the basis of relevance to the business community and of availability of information related to the subject matter.

The past and present experience of minorities and women in these occupations is examined by drawing together a comprehensive review of the related literature and statistical materials. The assessment of the future experience for each occupation is based on the results of a mathematical model of the labor supply creation process. This model produces estimates of the future racial and sexual composition of each occupational labor force under varying conditions.

Chapter II of the study will describe the methodology used to assess the experience of minorities and women in the future. A generalized model of the labor supply process will be discussed with data sources and the format for presentation of the model output.

Chapters III through VIII will examine each occupation individually. Chapter III will examine the entire occupational field of engineering including its major subfields (industrial, chemical, electrical, and mechanical).

Chapter IV and Chapter V both relate to the status of minorities and women in accounting and business. Chapter IV will be concerned with accountancy while Chapter V will cover the all-inclusive managerial and administrative classification associated with graduates of colleges of business administration.

Chapter VI will examine the experience in law, and the subject of Chapter VII will be the scientific professions of chemistry and physics. Chapter VIII will discuss the status of minorities and women in the health fields of medicine and dentistry.

The final section, Chapter IX, a summary and comparison of the findings, will draw conclusions about the rate of increase of black and female participation in these occupations based on the previous chapters.

CHAPTER II

The Labor Supply Process

In this study the quantitative analysis of the availability of minorities and women in professional, technical, and managerial occupations are the results of a computer simulation and sensitivity analysis of the process that creates the labor supply of an occupation. A discussion of the generalized model of the labor supply process, the sources of data common to all the occupations in this study, and the format for presenting the analysis output will follow.

THE GENERALIZED MODEL [1]

Because a continuous flow of workers into and out of an occupation is taking place, the underlying assumption of the generalized model used in this study is that the supply of workers in a particular occupation is not static. Ideally, entrants into an occupation include the following: (1) persons entering directly after completion of a training program designed to prepare them for that occupation; (2) persons entering directly after completion of a training program designed to prepare them for some other occupation; (3) persons other than students who are not in the civilian labor force, including housewives, retired persons, and those in the Armed Forces; (4) persons employed in other occupations; and (5) immigrants. Occupational losses include an estimate of the number of workers in an occupation who will die or retire during the projection period, those who will leave the civilian labor force for some other reason, those who will transfer to other occupations, and those who will emigrate. The flow of manpower into and out of an occupation is illustrated in Figure II-1.

---

[1] The material in this section is based upon U.S. Department of Labor, Bureau of Labor Statistics, *Tomorrow's Manpower Needs*, Bulletin No. 1606 (Washington, D.C.: U.S. Department of Labor, 1969), pp. 59-63.

FIGURE II-1

THE STREAM OF MANPOWER INTO AND OUT OF AN OCCUPATION

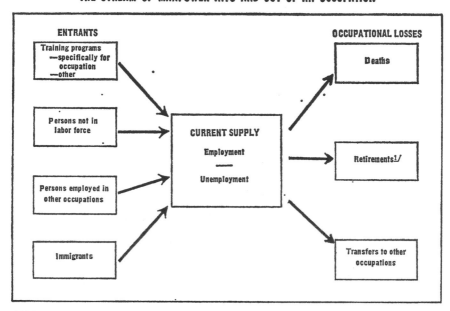

1/ Includes all workers who leave the civilian labor force or who emigrate.

Source: U.S. Department of Labor, Bureau of Labor Statistics, *Tomorrow's Manpower Needs*, Bulletin No. 1606 (Washington, D.C.: U.S. Department of Labor, 1969), p. 60.

The procedure followed in developing supply estimates consists of three basic steps. First, a current supply estimate is established as the base of the simulation. Then, the annual number of entrants from all sources is developed for the period that the estimation will cover. Third, the base current supply is aggregated with an estimate of the annual number of entrants, and annual occupational losses are deducted.

The use of this method is limited to relatively few occupations. The occupations for which sufficient information is available to develop a projected supply estimate are primarily those in the professional and technical occupational groups which have a specific training requirement. Most are in the scientific, engineering, health, and teaching fields.

Methodology for Projection of Labor Supply for a Specific Occupation

The inflows and outflows of an occupation are illustrated in the following formula which indicates the changes in supply from period N to N + 1: supply in the future period equals current supply plus entrants minus occupational losses between the two periods.

$$(E + UE)_{N+1} = (E + UE)_N +$$
$$(TP_S + TP_O + OC + NLF + I)_{N \to N+1} -$$
$$-(D + R + T + OL)_{N \to N+1}$$

where E = Employment

UE = Unemployed workers seeking work in occupation

TP_S = Entrants from training programs designed to prepare workers specifically for the occupation

TP_O = Entrants from training programs designed to prepare workers for other occupations

OC = Entrants from other occupations

NLF = Entrants from outside the labor force

I = Immigrants entering the occupation

D = Deaths

R = Retirements

T = Transfers

OL = Other losses (e.g., emigrants)

Each of the steps involved in using this formula to project supply in period N + 1 is discussed below. Each variable identified in the above formula is described with regard to the availability of data, limitations of usefulness, and the assumptions which were made for this study.

Current Supply. Current supply, when defined as the sum of the employed and unemployed, is different from potential supply, which would include all workers who could perform a certain type of work regardless of their decision to work in another occupation or not to work at all. In general, because of the multiplicity of skills possessed by individuals, the number of persons qualified for employment in any occupation will always be larger than the number actually employed. Many of those qualified, but not currently employed in an occupation, are employed in other occupations, and some are persons not economically active (e.g., retired persons). The labor supply for an occupation, therefore, may be viewed as elastic to some extent.

The current supply estimates used in this project were extracted from 1970 Census data.[2] Tables 5 and 6 in *Occupational Characteristics* provide estimates of the experienced civilian labor force by detailed occupation, years of school completed, race, and sex. These data, partitioned to include only those individuals with four or more years of college (five or more years for dentistry, medicine, and law), were used for the base period estimates of current supply in this study. The experienced civilian labor force includes both those persons currently employed in an occupation and those unemployed who had previously been employed in that occupation.

New Entrants. Entrants into the labor force come from a variety of sources. College graduates from United States schools will make up, by far, the largest portion of new entrants into professional, managerial, and technical positions in the United States. The estimates of the number of college graduates who enter the labor force are based on three factors: (1) projections of new college graduates in each field; (2) estimates of the proportion of new college graduates in each field who work in that field immediately after receiving their degrees; and (3) estimates of the proportion of these graduates who are employed in a certain field at the time they received their degrees.

Projections of the number of graduates in individual fields of study have been made by the National Center for Educational Statistics (NCES) of the United States Office of Education, Department of Health, Education and Welfare, on the basis of the continuation of past trends in the proportion of the total school population graduated in each field. These projections assume that the propensity of students to enroll and to graduate in the various fields will follow past trends and will not be affected by changes in student vocational preferences resulting from vocational guidance or the publication of information on employment opportunities. They also assume that schools will continue to

---

[2] *1970 Census of Population Subject Report, Occupational Characteristics,* PC(2)-7A (Washington, D.C.: U.S. Department of Commerce, 1973), pp. 12-27, Table 2.

expand their facilities for teaching each field in line with past trends and will not take into account, any more than in the past, projections of manpower needs in the various occupations.

Although projections of the number of earned degrees by NCES have been made on the basis of sex, they are not utilized in this study. The published statistics have been aggregated to reflect only the total number of degrees for each field. (For a more detailed description of the methodology used to project degrees by the NCES, see Appendix A of the NCES publication, *Projections of Educational Statistics to 1984-85*.[3] Rather, partitioning of degree earners among race and sex groups is achieved by a procedure that relies on historical data. The proportions of men and women receiving degrees were taken from the NCES records. Data on the racial composition of degree earners were developed from an exhaustive search of sources, including professional associations and journals, and public and private documents. This is described in a technical note at the end of this chapter.

Not all graduates obtain jobs in the field of their training. Some mathematics graduates, for example, obtain positions in engineering, and conversely, some persons with degrees in engineering follow a career in mathematics. Some graduates with bachelors' degrees begin professional training in other fields such as medicine or business management. Some graduates with degrees in science or engineering take jobs that do not directly use their technical knowledge (e.g., clerical, sales, etc.). Therefore, estimates of the proportion of students in each degree field who will work in the field in which they were trained immediately after graduation are necessary. Such estimates can be made by analyzing the type of work obtained by college graduating classes in the past. For example, graduating classes of 1960, 1965, and 1970 have been followed up by the College Placement Council and other organizations.[4] Furthermore, these follow-up studies have

---

[3] U.S. Department of Health, Education and Welfare, National Center for Educational Statistics, *Projections of Educational Statistics to 1984-85* (Washington, D.C.: Government Printing Office, 1976), pp. 109-149.

[4] Three publications are available which provide data in developing such estimates: Helen Astin and Ann Bisconti, *Career Plans of College Graduates of 1965 and 1970*, Report No. 2 (Bethlehem, Pa.: CPC Foundation, 1973); and *Career Plans of Black and Other Non-White College Graduates*, Report No. 3 (Bethlehem, Pa.: CPC Foundation, 1973); *IEEE Manpower Report 1973: Career Outlook in Engineering* (New York: The Institute of Electrical and Electronic Engineers, Inc., 1973), p. 79, Table 4-II.

been made with breakdowns by race and sex for the 1960, 1965, and 1970 classes. Unfortunately, these data have not been used in this study because of their lack of occupational detail. In almost all simulations (with exceptions as noted), a labor force accession rate of 80 percent was used for bachelor degree recipients, 90 percent for master degree earners, and 100 percent for individuals receiving a doctorate. An accession rate of 100 percent was used for the first professional degrees of law, medicine, and dentistry. In addition, the same rates were applied across race and sex lines.

A final step in preparing estimates of the accession of new entrants with United States college degrees into a particular occupation was to determine the proportion of graduates in the corresponding field of study who were already employed in that occupation at the time they received their degrees. Because of the lack of data in this area, this study does not account for graduates previously employed. Thus, there will undoubtedly be some double-counting of persons in the years immediately following 1970.

Other Entrants. In addition to new United States college graduates, persons enter scientific and engineering professions from other areas. Technicians and other persons without college degrees are upgraded, for example, to science and engineering positions; workers in other occupations who have college degrees transfer to science or engineering; many persons transfer from one science field to another; and others enter from outside the labor force. In addition, immigrants add to the supply of scientists and engineers.

Unfortunately, very little information is available for any of these sources of other entrants. Moreover, techniques have not been adequately developed to convert the limited data which is available into useful estimates of labor force entrants. Thus, it has been assumed in this study that transfers into and out of an occupation will offset each other—that is, that no occupation among those studies will gain or lose persons because of transfers among occupations. It was further assumed that there would be no upgrading of persons from lower level occupations to higher level ones. These assumptions were necessary for the aforementioned reasons and constitute limitations of this study.

Several assumptions were made in order to implement the model. It was generally assumed that all college graduates who did not begin an advanced degree program would enter the labor force, the occupation entered being dependent on the field of study. This assumption is supported by the observation that persons of both sexes and all races exhibit very high rates of labor force participation upon graduation (see Table II-1). Furthermore, this assumption helps to offset to some degree the assumption that no one would enter the occupations studied in a given year who were not graduates of a degree program in that year. The assumption will, at least in part, correct for the inestimable number of persons who entered the labor force that year from the outside.

It was assumed that net migration was zero each year through 1985. The model which was used does account for foreigners who enter the labor force upon graduation from United States colleges and universities. There is no adjustment, however, for those foreigners who leave the United States upon graduation or thereafter.

Losses to Supply. In estimating the supply of workers in a future year, an estimate is needed of new entrants and of losses of supply in the base year occurring because of deaths, retirements, persons leaving the labor force for other reasons, transfers out of the occupation, and persons migrating to other areas.

The Bureau of Labor Statistics has published separation rates by detailed occupation and sex which have been used to calculate estimates for men and women of annual separations from the labor force because of death, retirement, disability, or temporary withdrawal for personal reasons.[5] These rates, which are based on "tables of working life," reflect the attrition from the labor force caused by withdrawals from the labor force as well as by mortality. Tables of working life, which have been set upon an actuarial basis for men and women, account for deaths and retirements (separately) at each age level.

Although men usually remain in the labor force until retirement or death, women often withdraw temporarily because of marriage, children, or other family considerations. Many women who leave the labor force for such reasons reenter after their children reach school age or after their husbands' deaths. Therefore, temporary and permanent withdrawals or retirements have been considered in tables of working life for women.

---

[5] U.S. Department of Labor, Bureau of Labor Statistics, *Tomorrow's Manpower Needs*, Supplement No. 4 (Washington, D.C.: U.S. Department of Labor, 1974).

TABLE II-1

Labor force status of July 1971 to June 1972 recipients of baccalaureate and advanced degrees, by selected characteristics, October 1972

[Numbers in thousands]

Characteristic	Total degree[1] recipients	In labor force					Not in labor force
		Total	Labor force participation rate	Employed	Unemployed		
					Number	Rate	
All persons	812	751	92.5	681	70	9.3	61
AGE							
Under 25 years	485	441	90.9	383	58	13.2	44
Under 22 years	58	51	87.9	43	8	15.7	7
22 to 24 years	427	390	91.3	340	50	12.8	37
25 to 29 years	177	168	94.9	163	5	3.0	9
30 to 34 years	77	75	97.4	73	2	2.7	2
35 years and over	73	67	91.8	62	5	7.5	6
SEX AND MARITAL STATUS							
Men	475	451	94.9	414	37	8.2	24
Married, spouse present	264	260	98.5	252	8	3.1	4
Single[2]	211	191	90.5	162	29	15.2	20
Women	337	300	89.0	267	33	11.0	37
Married, spouse present	161	131	81.4	118	13	9.9	30
Single[2]	176	169	96.0	149	20	11.8	7
RACE							
White	781	722	92.4	656	66	9.1	59
Negro and other races	31	29	(3)	25	4	(3)	2
TYPE OF DEGREE							
Baccalaureate	600	546	91.0	482	64	11.7	54
Master's	160	156	97.5	152	4	2.6	4
All other degrees	52	49	94.2	47	2	(3)	3
MAJOR FIELD OF STUDY							
Business or commerce	120	115	95.8	109	6	5.2	5
Education	246	223	90.6	206	17	7.6	23
Humanities	103	91	88.3	77	14	15.4	12
Social sciences	128	119	93.0	100	19	16.0	9
All other fields	215	203	94.4	189	14	6.9	12

[1] Persons 16 years old and over who received degrees between July 1971 and June 1972, were in the civilian noninstitutional population and were not enrolled full time in a college or university as of October 1972.

[2] Includes some persons who were widowed, divorced, or separated, not shown separately.

[3] Percent not shown where base is less than 50,000.

NOTE: Because of rounding, sums of individual items may not add to totals.

Source: Anne M. Young, "Labor Market Experience of Recent College Graduates," *Monthly Labor Review*, Vol. 97 (October 1974), p. 34.

The Bureau of Labor Statistics (BLS) cites several limitations in using the separation rates in *Tomorrow's Manpower Needs*. One limitation is that the 1985 rates are based on 1970 Census occupational age distributions which are assumed to remain constant over the fifteen-year period. Another limitation is the lack of working life tables by occupation. The same age-specific separation rates are applied to the age distributions as if mortality and retirement do not differ by occupation. The nature and environment of work, coverage and provisions of pension plans, opportunities for employment, and other factors influence retirement patterns and mortality trends among occupations.

Although working life tables are not available on the basis of race, differences may exist in the separation rates exhibited by the white and black members of an occupation because of differences in their respective age distributions. This may be expected because the bulk of minorities in the occupations included herein should be newcomers to the labor force and, on the average, should be younger than their white counterparts. Accordingly, separation rates for black men and women were calculated using the same method incorporated in the BLS statistics.

ANALYSIS FORMAT

Each of the chapters that follow examines the availability of minorities and women in the specific professional, technical, and managerial occupations included in this study. The integration of the simulation results with the qualitative material on the past and present status of minorities and women is similar for each occupation group. To avoid duplication, the common format is explained in this section. Any exceptions are discussed in the individual chapters.

A direct application of the generalized model described in this chapter could be used to make forecasts of the future occupational labor supplies. We have chosen, however, to implement a simulation of the labor supply process to produce sets of projections. Two reasons underlie this decision. First, the quality of the available data is not consistent with the connotation of a prediction. Certain assumptions were necessary because of missing, incomplete, or inappropriate data. Certain concepts, such as the relationship between entry and separation rates and the state of the economy, are not incorporated into the methodology. The second reason for adopting the simulation mode is that it permits a sensitivity analysis of the labor supply process. This exercise allows the introduction of adjustments in the basic determinants of the process by a wide range of values and by the resulting changes in the composition of the labor supply. This circumvents the questionable nature of some of the data.

A summary table of input data is provided for each of the occupations. Included in the table for an occupation is the supply base, the entry and separation rates, and the partition rates used to classify the NCES degree projections into racial and sexual groups. The data in this form are used to produce the following base line projections of new labor force entrants and the labor supply. Additional tables show the results and impact of altering the racial and sexual distribution of degree recipients on the labor supply. In most cases these tables show the effects of achieving a 100 percent increase in the number of minority and female degree recipients by 1985 from the base line projections for 1985, which are based on historical data and on prorating the increase over the 10-year period from 1975 to 1985.

TECHNICAL NOTE:
RACIAL AND SEXUAL PARTIONING PROCEDURE

The procedure used to partition degree recipients into racial and sexual groups is straightforward and based on accounting identities. The interaction of two dichotomous variables, race, (white-black) and sex (male-female), produces four subgroups: white male, black male, white female, and black female. Since the value of each variable is the proportion of degrees awarded to that subgroup in one particular year, the sum of the male and female values must equal 100 percent as must the sum of the black and white values. In order to determine subgroup values, racial and sexual compositions are assumed to be independent so that the racial compositions of the male and female groups are the same.

The projection of the partitions begins with the marginal male-female breakdown. The group which exhibits a downward sloping trend over time (usually males) is regressed against time using a logarithmic relationship ($Y = a + b$ log time), and the derived coefficients are used to project future values for the group. The logarithmic relationship is employed in order to insure that the projected values are not less than zero. The values for the complementary group (females) can be determined by subtraction from 100 percent. The same routine is applied to the black-white dichotomy.

The projected values for the four subgroups are determined by identifying the subgroup with the most downward sloping trend over time. The values for this subgroup are regressed against time using the logarithmic relationship, and projected values are calculated using the derived coefficients. Complementary values are determined by subtraction. For example, values for the white male group are found by the regression relationship and are subtracted from the previously determined white values to derive the projections for white females and are subtracted from male values to determine black males. Values for black females can be determined by substracting black male values from black values or by subtracting white female values from female values.

CHAPTER III

Minorities and Women in Engineering

Engineering is a key occupation, not only because of its importance as a profession, but also because it is frequently a means of entry into management positions. In this chapter we shall first assess the information available in the literature on the participation of minorities and women and, then, taking these findings into account, utilize our model to predict the supply of minority and female engineers in the years ahead.

THE PROBLEM

Engineering is one occupation that has traditionally been conspicuous for its lack of minorities and women. Census data on experienced occupational engineers from 1940 to 1970, which are shown in Table III-1, readily illustrate the dominance of white males in the engineering profession. In 1970, 2.8 percent of the engineers in the United States were black, Chicano (Mexican-American), Puerto Rican, or American Indian, although these four minorities represented 14.4 percent of the nation's population at the time.[1] Women that same year constituted 51.3 percent of the United States population, but only 1.6 percent of those were in the engineering occupation.[2]

Engineering is often an entry profession to leadership positions in industrial research, corporate management, education, and government. The small number of women and minorities in managerial and professional positions is attributable in part to the inadequate supply of women and minorities having the education to compete successfully for such positions. As the trend toward more engineers moving into executive positions has de-

---

[1] The Planning Commission for Expanding Minority Opportunities in Engineering, *Minorities in Engineering: A Blueprint for Action* (New York: The Alfred P. Sloan Foundation, 1974), p. 1.

[2] John D. Alden, "Women and Minorities in Engineering," *IEEE Transactions on Education*, Vol. E-17 (February 1974), p. 6.

TABLE III-1

*Number of Experienced Civilian Engineers by Sex and Race,
1940-1970*

Sex and Race	1940	1950	1960	1970
Engineering Total	255,480	527,190	869,716	1,256,935
Male Engineers	255,480	520,530	862,002	1,236,160
White	255,160	517,800	849,807	1,199,811
Negro	320 [a]	1,620	4,174	14,198
Other Races		1,110	8,021	22,151
Males with 4 or more years of college	155,760	279,030	479,899	725,308
White	155,580	277,710	472,513	
Nonwhite	180	1,320	7,386	6,989 [b]
Female Engineers	—	6,660	7,714	20,775
White	—	6,510	7,552	19,697
Negro	—	150	102	757
Other Races	—	—	60	321
Females with 4 or more years of college	—	2,640	2,830	9,069
White	—	2,610	2,788	
Nonwhite	—	30	42	229 [b]

Sources: *Sixteenth Census of the United States: 1940 Population, The Labor Force, Occupational Characteristics* (Washington, D.C.: Government Printing Office, 1943), pp. 59-70 passim, Table 3.
United States Census of Population 1950, Occupational Characteristics, P-E No. 1B (Washington, D.C.: Government Printing Office, 1956), pp. 29, 107, 115, Tables 3, 10, 11.
United States Census of Population 1960, Occupational Characteristics, PC(2)-7A (Washington, D.C.: U.S. Department of Commerce, 1961), pp. 21, 116, 123, 130, 137, Tables 3, 9, 10.
1970 Census of Population Subject Report, Occupational Characteristics, PC(2)-7A (Washington, D.C.: U.S. Department of Commerce, 1973), pp. 12, 59, 73, 87, 101, Tables 2, 5, 6.

[a] Only nonwhite data available.
[b] Only Negro data available.

veloped in recent years, minorities and women, who have been continually underrepresented in the engineering professions, have not shared in the advancement.

J. Stanford Smith, then Senior Vice President of General Electric Company and now Chairman of International Paper Company, introduced the goal of a tenfold increase in minority engineering graduates in a decade with his address to the Engineering Education Conference on July 25, 1972. He said:

> . . . I repeat the real problem today, in professional and managerial levels, is not one of demand, but of supply.
>
> Of 43,000 engineers graduated in 1971, only 407 were black and a handful were other minorities or women. One percent. It takes about fifteen to twenty-five years for people to rise to top leadership positions in industry. So if industry is getting one percent minority engineers in 1972, that means that in 1990, that's about the proportion that will emerge from the competition to the top leadership positions in industry. Not five percent, or ten percent, or seventeen percent, but one percent.
>
> Gentlemen, this is a formula for tragedy. Long before the year 1990, a lot of minority people are going to feel that they have been had. Already there are angry charges of discrimination with regard to upward mobility in industry, whereas the real problem, clearly visible today, is that there just aren't enough minority men and women who have taken the college training to qualify for professional and engineering work.
>
> To put the challenge bluntly, unless we can start producing not 400, but 4,000 to 6,000 minority engineers a year within the decade, industry will not be able to achieve its goals of equality, and the nation is going to face social problems of unmanageable dimensions.
>
> The only acceptable solution is to take bold, innovative, all-out action to increase the supply of minority engineering graduates not by a few percentage points, but ten- or fifteen-fold, and to get it done within the decade. This is the only way we can expect to see acceptable proportions of minority men and women in the top ranks of industry by the end of the century.[3]

Background

The Minority Engineering Education Effort (ME[3]) Task Force was formed in December of 1972 to increase the number of minority engineering students. Comprised of the Engineers' Council for Professional Development (ECPD), the American Society for Engineering Education (ASEE), the National So-

---

[3] J. Stanford Smith, "Needed: A Ten-Fold Increase in Minority Engineering Graduates," Address to Engineering Education Conference, Crotonville, New York, July 25, 1972.

ciety of Professional Engineers (NSPE), the American Society of Mechanical Engineers (ASME), national associations representing guidance counselors and math and science teachers, community liaison groups, an educational media organization, and industry, the Task Force's objective was "to identify, motivate and equip minority students at all pre-engineering school grade levels to pursue engineering careers and to help bring them and engineering schools together." [4]

The three basic goals adopted by ME[3] were a 50 percent increase in minority engineering freshmen in fall 1973, a 100 percent increase in minority engineering freshmen in fall 1974, a tenfold to fifteenfold increase in minority engineering graduates in the mid-1980s (relative to the 1972 enrollments and graduates). Efforts of the Task Force in the spring of 1973 resulted in identifying 8,000 1973 high school graduates and 2,350 community college graduates interested in engineering or related fields. Lists of these 10,000 minority students were distributed to 115 engineering schools that had previously shown interest in recruiting minority students.

The National Academy of Engineering (NAE) was another group that responded to the need for increased numbers of minority engineers. In May 1973 NAE conducted a two-day symposium in Washington, D.C., which was attended by 250 engineers, educators, and university and industrial leaders. The dominant topics were the recruitment, training, and financial support of minority engineering students. Representatives to the symposium agreed on setting the target of "a tenfold increase in the nation's minority engineers within a decade by raising the annual number of graduates in the field from 500 to 5,000 . . . provided the necessary resources could be marshalled at the national and local levels." [5]

In order to accomplish their goal, in 1974 NAE established the National Advisory Council on Minorities in Engineering (NACME), composed of minority group representatives and leaders in industry, government, and education. The NACME is organized to mobilize resources and advise on minority engineering activities. Moreover, the NAE established the Com-

---

[4] Calvin H. Conliffe, "Formula for Action: ME[3]=Minority Engineering Education Effort," *IEEE Transactions on Education*, Vol. E-17 (February 1974), p. 38.

[5] *Committee on Minorities in Engineering, 1975-1976* (Washington, D.C.: Assembly of Engineering National Research Council, n.d.), pp. 3-4.

mittee on Minorities in Engineering (COME) in April 1974 as a professionally staffed working committee for the purpose of providing national leadership and coordinating efforts to advance the participation of black, Mexican-American, Puerto Rican, and American Indian students in the engineering profession.

Census Data

John Alden, Executive Secretary of the Engineering Manpower Commission of the Engineers' Joint Council, suggests that the difficulty with national statistics on engineers is a result of the different definitions used by various data-collecting groups.[6] The Bureau of the Census records engineers according to those who list engineering as their occupation. Obviously, not all "occupational engineers" have engineering degrees. Educational agencies report the number of engineering degrees awarded; however, not all degreed engineers are currently working in that occupation. Professional organizations represent the third engineering group, and although most individuals with professional membership are degreed engineers, they may have moved into managerial or other related occupations. Consequently, occupational, educational, and professional data on engineers make it difficult to reconcile statistics on the profession.

BLACKS

Before World War II, black students were choosing professions that had been highly visible in their environment; these included careers in theology, law, and medicine.[7] Engineering was not an occupation chosen by a significant number of blacks in this early period. Consequently, it was not until the mid-1950s that a definitive survey was done of the relationship of blacks to the engineering profession.

Kiehl's Studies

Dr. Robert Kiehl of the Newark College of Engineering conducted studies on black participation in engineering in 1955-56, 1961-62, and 1969-70. The last of these contains summaries of the first two studies and also comparisons of the 1969-70 data

---

[6] Alden, "Women and Minorities in Engineering," p. 3.

[7] H. A. Young, J. R. Hill, and E. J. Hayes, "Role Models for Blacks in Engineering," *Engineering Education*, Vol. 66 (January 1976), p. 337.

with that of 1955-56 and 1961-62. Since statistics for past years of black engineering education are incomplete, Kiehl's work provides the primary data for examination of black engineering students of the past.[8]

Kiehl showed that the ratio of Negro students to all others in the freshman enrollment in 1955-56 was 1:102, and in 1961-62 it was 1:92 (see Table III-2). There are two lines of ratios for 1969-70. The first does not include the freshman enrollment of two additional predominantly Negro colleges that emerged during the seven-year interval; however, the last line does include the enrollment of those two Negro colleges. The ratio improvement for the black engineering student demonstrates the impact of the predominantly Negro college.

Kiehl estimated that in 1969-70, 2.0 percent of the United States engineering students were black, and that about 45 percent of the black graduates in spring 1970 would be from predominantly Negro schools. The survey showed electrical engineering to be the most popular branch of study, the percentage of blacks in that field being higher than that of whites. In chemical engineering, however, the white percentage was considerably higher than that of blacks. The representation of black women engineering students was found to be 2.0 percent. Kiehl found bachelor of science degrees distributed among specialties in the following manner:

Engineering Specialty	As Percent of All Black Engineering Specialties
Electrical	47
Mechanical	24
Civil	13
Chemical	6
All other	10

According to Kiehl's 1969-70 study, lack of familiarity with engineering and the employment discrimination before World War II were the primary reasons for Negroes' lack of interest in the engineering profession. In responding to Kiehl's survey, however, black engineering graduates and engineering school deans maintained that there were good employment opportunities available to black engineers. The obvious conclusion to this

---

[8] Robert Kiehl, *Opportunities for Blacks in the Profession of Engineering* (Newark, N.J.: Foundation for the Advancement of Graduate Study in Engineering, 1970), pp. 7-14.

TABLE III-2

Enrollment of College Students in Engineers' Council for Professional Development (ECPD) Accredited Engineering Colleges Showing Ratio of Negro to All Other Students and Comparing the Figures for the Academic Years 1955-56, 1961-62, and 1969-70

Year and Ratio	1st year	2nd year	3rd year	4th year
1955-56				
ratio of Negro students to all other students	1/102	1/168	1/210	1/236
1961-62				
ratio of Negro students to all other students	1/92	1/94	1/97	1/102
1969-70 without Greensboro and Tuskegee				
ratio of Negro students to all other students	1/46	1/64	1/92	1/117
1969-70 including Greensboro and Tuskegee				
ratio of Negro students to all other students	1/36	1/45	1/61	1/72

Source: Robert Kiehl, *Opportunities for Blacks in the Profession of Engineering* (Newark, N.J.: Foundation for the Advancement of Graduate Study in the Profession of Engineering, 1970), p. 23, Table 2.

study was that programs for black engineers had to be initiated: time alone would not increase the entry of blacks into engineering at an acceptable rate.

Alden Study

John Alden estimates that presently blacks represent 1.2 percent of this country's engineers, and that they are concentrated in the three largest branches of engineering—electrical, mechanical, and civil (see Table III-3).[9] Considering that blacks comprise 11.1 percent of the United States population, it is obvious that today blacks are seriously underrepresented in the engineering profession. Engineering Manpower Commission (EMC) data show an increase in black freshman engineering enrollment from 1.32 percent in 1969-70 to 3.86 percent in 1974-75 and an increase in black bachelor engineering graduates from 0.88 in 1969-70 to 1.92 percent in 1974-75 (see Table III-4). Nevertheless, even this growth rate cannot provide the number of black engineers necessary for a 10-fold increase in minority engineering graduates by the mid-1980s, the ME[3] objective.

Future Trends

As mentioned previously, blacks have historically chosen careers in health care, social work, and education. Growing up in a society void of engineers, blacks lack information and understanding of the engineering profession. Furthermore, teachers, counselors, and parents who are in a position to influence the child's career choice are also often unaware of the opportunities available in the field. One current article in *Engineering Education* states:

> . . . [M]obilization of large groups of blacks towards engineering must be preceded by a program geared towards conveying to guidance counselors and high school science teachers at predominantly black high schools and the parents of the students the dire need for large numbers of black engineers and—most important of all—that one does not need to be an "A" student in high school to "make it" in engineering.[10]

Once minority students are enrolled in the engineering program, the concern is for retention of these students. Retention

[9] Alden, "Women and Minorities in Engineering," p. 6.

[10] Satinderpaul S. Devgan and Mohammed H. Baluch, "Minority Enrollment: Averting the 'Formula for Tragedy,'" *Engineering Education*, Vol. 66 (February 1976), p. 437.

TABLE III-3

Estimated Representation of Women and Minorities in Engineering

Sex and Race	% in U.S. Population	% in Engineering Occupation	Number in Engineering Occupation	Number with Engineering Degrees
Women	51.3	1.6	19,600	3,500
Negro	11.1	1.2	14,800	8,100
Spanish	4.4	1.6	20,000	15,000
American Indian	0.39	0.55	6,800	5,500
Japanese	0.29	0.42	5,200	4,400
Chinese	0.21	0.63	7,800	6,600
Filipino	0.17	0.50	6,200	5,300
Asian Indian & Other	0.35	1.34	16,700	14,200

Source: *Statistical Abstract of the United States, 1972*, cited by John D. Alden, "Women and Minorities in Engineering," *IEEE Transactions in Education*, Vol. E-17 (February 1974), p. 6, Table 2.

is most difficult during the first year of study, particularly retention of those students not adequately prepared. Some assistance for such students can be provided with preenrollment summer sessions. Since, however, the preparation for engineering study involves course selections that begin in the eighth and ninth grades, it will take several years to establish an adequate pool of minority students who are prepared for engineering study.[11]

Programs initiated to increase black students' interest in an engineering career need to be aimed at the elementary and junior high schools. Evidence from the study "Profile of Black American Doctorates in Natural Sciences" shows that black children who are going to be scientists and engineers make that decision as early as age fourteen.[12]

OTHER MINORITIES

Unfortunately, data on the racial and ethnic composition of the engineering profession are scarce. It is only within the

---

[11] Raymond B. Landis, "Improving the Retention of Minority Engineering Students," *Engineering Education*, Vol. 66, No. 7 (April 1976), p. 737.

[12] Young, "Role Models for Blacks in Engineering," pp. 337, 339.

TABLE III-4

Engineering Enrollments and Bachelor Engineering Degrees Granted for Women and Blacks in U.S. Engineering Schools, 1969-70 through 1974-75

Sex and Race	1969-70	1970-71	1971-72	1972-73	1973-74	1974-75
Total Freshman Year, Full-time	74,113	71,661	58,566	52,100	51,925	63,444
Blacks	977	1,424	1,289	1,477	2,106	2,447
percent of total	1.32	1.99	2.20	2.83	4.06	3.86
Women	1,181	1,457	1,541	1,542	2,417	4,266
percent of total	1.59	2.03	2.63	2.96	4.65	6.72
Total Undergraduate, Full-time	233,530	231,730	210,825	194,727	186,705	201,099
Blacks	2,757	3,753	4,136	4,356	5,528	6,319
percent of total	1.18	1.62	1.96	2.24	2.96	3.14
Women	3,061	3,569	3,983	4,487	6,064	9,828
percent of total	1.31	1.54	1.89	2.30	3.25	4.89
Total Bachelor Degrees Granted	42,966	43,167	44,190	43,429	41,407	38,210
Blacks	378[a]	407[a]	579	657	756	734
percent of total	0.88	0.94	1.31	1.51	1.83	1.92
Women	358[a]	353[a]	525	624	744	878
percent of total	0.83	0.82	1.19	1.44	1.80	2.30

Sources: Betty M. Vetter and Eleanor L. Babco, *Professional Women and Minorities: A Manpower Resource Data Service* (Washington, D.C.: Scientific Manpower Commission, 1975), pp. 317, 318, 325, 329, Tables E-6, E-23, E-4, and E-15.
John Alden, "Engineering and Technology Enrollments, Fall, 1974," *Engineering Education*, Vol. 66 (October 1975), p. 47.

[a] Totals for women and blacks in these years include only members actually reported. The totals would be higher if all institutions had reported all categories.

past four or five years that information on racial and national origin has been reported; consequently, there is no historical data base for comparison. As a result, only the current status of the Spanish-surnamed, Oriental, and American Indian minorities in the engineering profession will be discussed.

Spanish-surnamed Americans

This minority group includes people of Mexican, Cuban, Puerto Rican, or Spanish origin. Alden estimates that in 1974 there were 9,000 Spanish-speaking engineers in the United States as a result of immigration alone.[13] Within the Latin American countries, engineering has always been a highly regarded profession, so it is understandable that a substantial number of immigrants from those countries are engineers.

Data found in a 1974 study on minorities in engineering indicate that Chicanos and Puerto Ricans rank far below the United States average of educational attainment, and below the averages of other Spanish Americans.[14] It follows that if these two groups fall so far below in college education, they must be seriously underrepresented in engineering education. Table III-5 shows the number of engineering degrees awarded to Spanish-surnamed Americans in recent years.

If engineering school administrators are serious about recruiting Spanish-surnamed minorities, they must understand the true bilingual and bicultural human being. Moreover, this understanding needs to be reflected in the development of new engineering programs.

Counseling is a critical factor to the development of the Spanish-speaking student. These counselors need not only to be fluent in the language, but also to understand the cultural factors of the student. Forty-five percent of all the Spanish-speaking students enrolled in secondary schools do not complete the twelfth year; furthermore, 95 percent of all Spanish-speaking students who enter college drop out before completing their fourth year.[15] It is time for schools, colleges, and univer-

---

[13] Alden, "Women and Minorities in Engineering," p. 5.

[14] The Planning Commission for Expanding Minority Opportunities in Engineering, *Minorities in Engineering*, p. 3.

[15] Pepé Barren and Alfredo De Los Santos, Jr., "Are Chicanos Attending Universities?," *IEEE Transactions on Education*, Vol. E-17, No. 1 (February 1974), pp. 11-12.

TABLE III-5

*Number of Engineering Degrees by Minority Group and Degree Level,
1972-73 through 1974-75*

Degree Level and Year	Total		Spanish-Surname		Asiatics		American Indians	
	Number	Percent	Number	Percent	Number	Percent	Number	Percent
Bachelor								
1972-73	43,429	100	866	2.0	684	1.6	46	0.1
1973-74	41,407	100	1,037	2.5	957	2.3	32	0.07[a]
1974-75	38,210	100	1,060	2.8	883	2.3	44	—[a]
Master								
1972-73	17,152	100	139	0.8	261	1.5	15	0.09[a]
1973-74	15,885	100	192	1.2	425	2.7	4	0.02
1974-75	15,773	100	185	1.2	482	3.1	3	0.02[a]
Doctorate								
1972-73	3,587	100	12	0.3	55	1.5	1	0.03[a]
1973-74	3,362	100	20	0.6	106	3.2	0	—[a]
1974-75	3,039	100	28	0.9	141	4.6	2	—[a]

Source: Betty M. Vetter and Eleanor L. Babco, *Professional Women and Minorities: A Manpower Data Resource Service* (Washington, D.C.: Scientific Manpower Commission, 1975), p. 325, Table E-16.
[a] Percentages not considered reliable because of small numbers involved.

sities to adjust to their students instead of insisting that the students adjust to their programs.

Oriental Americans

Oriental Americans include those people of Chinese, Japanese, Filipino, and Asian-Indian origin. Between 1965 and 1972, 27,000 Oriental engineers immigrated to this country.[16] Both the engineering profession and a college education are highly regarded by Orientals; therefore, these people have long been prominent in the profession of engineering. The number of degrees awarded to Oriental students is shown in Table III-5.

Alden's estimate that 2.9 percent of the United States engineers are Oriental compared with the minority's 1.0 percent distribution in the 1970 United States population shows that Oriental Americans are not underrepresented in engineering. Therefore, the opportunity for engineering educations and careers is available and being used by Oriental minorities in this country.

American Indians

Little data are available on the number of American Indians in engineering. Alden's table shows that American Indians represent 0.55 percent of those in the engineering occupation. He notes, however, "the favorable showing of American Indians is at variance with conventional wisdom and therefore somewhat surprising. It could, of course, be the result of weakness in the statistics from which the estimate is derived." [17] The number of American Indians graduating with engineering degrees in 1973, 1974, and 1975 is shown in Table III-5.

Like blacks, American Indians receive inadequate preparation for the study of engineering. Historically, Indians have lived in harmony with the land and have shunned those aspects of engineering technology which are destroying or polluting the environment. Furthermore, the traditional rearing of an Indian, stressing cooperation and development of strong interpersonal ties, is in conflict with the competitive emphasis of American education.[18] In light of this, one of the few American Indians'

---

[16] Alden, "Women and Minorities in Engineering," p. 5.

[17] *Ibid.,* p. 6.

[18] The Planning Commission for Expanding Minority Opportunities in Engineering, *Minorities in Engineering,* pp. 57-59.

associations with civil engineering, for example, is a result of the Mohawk Indians' involvement in the construction industry. Thus, efforts to recruit American Indian engineering students will require significant changes in the educational system to prepare them adequately in elementary school and high school.

WOMEN

Between 1949 and 1961, women received 0.3 percent of the bachelor degrees, 0.3 percent of the master's degrees, and 0.9 percent of the doctoral degrees awarded in engineering. By 1974-75 those percentages had increased to 2.3 percent of bachelor degrees, 2.4 percent of master degrees, and 1.1 percent of doctoral degrees.[19] Although the past 25 years have shown a significant increase in the percentage of engineering degrees awarded to women, there remains a tremendous demand for female engineers in the labor force.

Women have often been deterred from engineering by peers, parents, and teachers because of the unfeminine aspect of the profession. Historically, women have entered nursing, education, and social work careers.

Just as they are unaware of the demand for black engineers, counselors are frequently unaware of the demand for women engineers and are responsible for counseling students with aptitude for successful engineering study into other fields. Studies have shown that 40 percent of the high school students with aptitude for engineering are female. Although black women may receive encouragement from their parents to attend college and enter a well-paying profession, white women are more likely to major in liberal arts or one of the traditional female professions.[20]

Present Opportunities

Government equal opportunity and affirmative action policies and the equal rights movement among women have raised the aspirations and increased the percentages of women entering professional schools; however, the demand for female engineers is

[19] Betty A. Sproule and Harold F. Mathis, "Recruiting and Keeping Women Engineering Students: An Agenda for Action," *Engineering Education*, Vol. 66 (April 1976), p. 745, Table 1.

[20] Martha E. Sloan and Irene C. Peden, "Some Comparisons between Women and Ethnic Minority Engineers," *IEEE Transactions on Education*, Vol. E-17 (February 1974), p. 8.

far greater than the number of women engineering graduates. In 1952 women received 0.17 percent of the total engineering bachelor degrees, and by 1975 that percentage had increased to 2.3 percent.[21] Yet 2.3 percent represents only 878 graduates out of a total of 38,210, which is much less than the hiring demand of engineering schools and industry. Even though female full-time undergraduate enrollment in engineering schools has increased from 3,061 in fall 1969 to 9,828 in fall 1974 (from 1.31 percent to 4.89 percent), this is still below what is needed (see Table III-4). A survey taken by the Society of Women Engineers (SWE) in the summer of 1974 reports the specialization of its membership. The results of this survey are presented in Table III-6.

Future Outlook

Because of the disparity between the percentage of women in the engineering occupation, 1.6 percent, and the percentage of women in the United States labor force, 40 percent, special programs are necessary to make women aware of the opportunities available in engineering. Engineering schools, industry, and engineering professional societies are committing themselves to increasing the number of female engineers. These programs will be discussed in a later section of this study; nevertheless, it is obvious that the major need is for communicating to women the career opportunities available in engineering.

SPECIFIC ENGINEERING BRANCHES

The specialized fields of engineering examined in this study are chemical, electrical, mechanical, and industrial. Data in Tables III-7 and III-8 show the distribution of minority groups in these engineering subfields according to the 1970 labor force data gathered by the Bureau of the Census and according to the data on earned engineering degrees gathered by EMC.

Chemical Engineering

Data from the American Chemical Society show that work in this occupation is performed primarily by those with chemical engineering degrees: 86 percent of those in the field have chemical

---

21 Betty M. Vetter and Eleanor L. Babco, *Professional Women and Minorities: A Manpower Data Resource Service* (Washington, D.C.: Scientific Manpower Commission, May 1975), p. 317, Table E-5.

TABLE III-6

Field of Specialization of Women Engineers

Specialization	As a Percent of Total SWE Survey[a]
Aerospace Engineering	9
Mechanical Engineering	7
Computers/Mathematics	7
Communications	6
Electrical Engineering	6
Civil Engineering	6
Management/Business Administration	5
Environmental/Sanitary Engineering	5
Chemical Engineering	5
Electronics Engineering	4
Engineering, General	4
Systems Engineering	4
Industrial Engineering	3
Basic Science	3
Product Engineering	3
Engineering Sciences	2
Metallurgical Engineering	2
Nuclear Engineering	2
Plant/Facilities Engineering	2
Other	14

Source: *A Profile of the Woman Engineer* (New York: Society of Women Engineers, n.d.), p. 7, Figure 7.

[a] Categories comprising less than 1.0 percent included Naval Architecture/ Marine Engineering, Agricultural Engineering, and Other Engineering.

engineering degrees and an additional 7 percent have chemistry majors.[22] The poor employment market for chemical engineers in 1970 and 1971 is evidenced in the declining freshmen enrollments in the field in 1971 and 1972; however, this

[22] Office of Manpower Studies of American Chemical Society, *Professionals in Chemistry, 1975* (Washington, D.C.: American Chemical Society, 1976), p. 8.

TABLE III-7
Number of Engineering Degrees in Selected Subfields by Minority Status, 1974

Subfield	Total Degrees	Women		Blacks		Spanish		Oriental		Indian	
		Number	Percent	Number	Percent	Number	Percent	Number	Percent	Number	Percent
Chemical											
B.S.	3,523	111	3.2	29	0.8	39	1.1	60	1.7	5	0.1
M.S.	1,053	33	3.1	6	0.6	11	1.0	38	3.6	0	0.0
Ph.D.	403	7	1.7	1	0.3	3	0.7	9	2.2	0	0.0
Electrical											
B.S.	11,347	118	1.0	265	2.3	176	1.6	347	3.1	3	0.3
M.S.	3,702	61	1.7	36	1.0	46	1.2	122	3.3	0	0.0
Ph.D.	700	4	0.6	3	0.4	1	0.1	25	3.6	0	0.0
Industrial											
B.S.	2,510	46	1.8	76	3.0	45	1.8	36	1.4	2	0.1
M.S.	1,502	41	2.7	9	0.6	21	1.4	18	1.2	2	0.1
Ph.D.	119	1	0.8	1	0.8	2	1.7	3	2.5	0	0.0
Mechanical											
B.S.	7,612	54	0.7	154	2.0	106	1.4	170	2.2	6	0.1
M.S.	1,999	20	1.0	15	0.8	20	1.0	62	3.1	0	0.0
Ph.D.	446	5	1.1	1	0.2	2	0.4	20	4.5	0	0.0

Source: John D. Alden, "Women and Minority Engineering and Technology Graduates, 1974," memo to Industrial Corporate Affiliates of Engineers' Joint Council, 1975.

TABLE III-8

Number of Women and Selected Minorities in Selected Subfields of Engineering Labor Force, 1970 [a]

Subfield	Total	Women		Black		American Indian		Oriental	
		Number	Percent	Number	Percent	Number	Percent	Number	Percent
Chemical	54,217	579	1.1	389	0.7	87	0.2	860	1.6
Electrical	290,185	4,948	1.7	4,130	1.4	238	0.1	5,373	1.9
Industrial	195,060	5,826	3.0	2,144	1.1	126	0.1	741	0.4
Mechanical	185,406	1,830	1.0	1,927	1.0	101	0.05	2,396	1.3

Source: *1970 Census of Population Subject Report, Occupational Characteristics,* PC(2)-7A (Washington, D.C.: U.S. Department of Commerce, 1973), p. 12, Table 2.

[a] Spanish-surnamed American data not available in 1970 census.

decrease in supply combined with the need for engineers in energy and environmental-related research has created a strong present demand for chemical engineers.[23] According to the Bureau of Labor statistics cited by the Institute of Electrical and Electronic Engineers, chemical engineering can expect "moderate growth, due to expansion of chemical industry and increasing expenditures for R & D; some opportunities in environmental control." [24]

The recent increase in chemical engineering enrollments is causing concern that another oversupply of chemical engineers may evolve. Following a 40.2 percent increase between 1973 and 1974, freshmen enrollments in chemical engineering for 1975 were up 34 percent over 1974 according to the Engineering Manpower Commission. A survey taken by the American Institute of Chemical Engineers shows a 43.8 percent increase in freshmen chemical engineering enrollments. The overall freshmen engineering enrollment increased 18.7 percent between 1974 and 1975. The increase of students pursuing chemical engineering is, in part, due to the positive condition of the chemical engineering job market *versus* the negative condition of related fields. For example, employment prospects for pure science graduates are relatively low. There is growing concern on the part of educators about placement of the upcoming chemical engineering graduates. Some department heads are even initiating enrollment restrictions to reduce the number of chemical engineering students.[25]

Electrical Engineering

The Institute of Electrical and Electronics Engineers predicts continued growth in the electrical electronics field; however, caution is given regarding occasional fluctuations in the job market. Electrical engineers will need to remain flexible to accommodate the changes in focus and demand of the economy, business, and technology. According to the BLS cited by the Institute, the prospects in electrical engineering are for "very rapid

---

[23] "While Some Sing the Blues, Engineers Call the Tune," *Chemical Week*, Vol. 115, No. 15 (October 9, 1974), pp. 12-13.

[24] The Institute of Electrical and Electronic Engineers, Inc., *IEEE Manpower Report 1973: Career Outlook in Engineering* (New York: The Institute of Electrical and Electronic Engineers, Inc., 1973), p. 213.

[25] Betty Vetter, ed., *Scientific, Engineering, Technical Manpower Comments*, Vol. 13 (September 1976), p. 7.

growth, due to increased demand for automation equipment, such as computers and numerical controls, and for electrical and electronic consumer goods." [26]

Industrial Engineering

The outlook is for very rapid growth of employment in this field of engineering because of industry's growth, expanding automation, and the increasing complexity of industrial operations. Realization of the impact of scientific management and safety engineering on increasing productivity and reducing costs will provide further impetus to employ industrial engineers.

Mechanical Engineering

Growth of the nation's industry and the resulting need for machine tools and industrial machinery and processes constitute a promising outlook for mechanical engineering. Furthermore, research and development in new areas such as environmental control, atomic energy, and aerospace technology will provide additional positions for mechanical engineers.

CURRENT PROGRAMS

Much has happened since 1973 when ME[3] set as its goal a ten- to fifteen-fold increase in minority engineering graduates within ten years. The offensive force to increase the number of minority engineers now consists of a cross section of industry, engineering schools, state and federal governments, task forces, professional engineering societies, foundations, and minority groups.

In an effort to learn of programs that appear critical to increasing minority participation in engineering, the Committee on Minorities in Engineering (COME) conducted a survey of colleges and universities, which focused on those schools with the largest minority enrollments. In 1974 these schools made up over 50 percent of the total undergraduate minority engineering enrollment and included the 6 traditionally black schools along with 45 predominantly white schools. This and the following information on minority engineering programs are taken from that COME survey.[27]

---

[26] The Institute of Electrical and Electronic Engineers, Inc., *IEEE Manpower Report 1973*, p. 212.

[27] Committee on Minorities in Engineering, *Building Effective Minority Programs in Engineering Education* (Washington, D.C.: National Academy of Sciences, September 1975), pp. 1-26.

COME Survey Results

The major problems in minority engineering programs are how to identify and motivate minority youth to choose engineering careers; how to recruit successfully minority youth; how to assist those with weak scholastic backgrounds; and how to support enrolled students financially, academically, and socially so that they can obtain an engineering degree. The University of Kansas was found to have one of the most comprehensive programs. The University's Student Council for Recruiting, Motivating and Educating Black Engineers (SCoRMEBE) raises funds, recruits students and staff, and plans, implements, and evaluates program activities.

The California Consortium for Minorities in Engineering, which consists of academic, professional, and community group members, focuses on a minority population of over two million in the Los Angeles metropolitan area. Industry plays a key role in Oklahoma State University's Council of Partners to Increase Black Graduates in Engineering, Technology and Architecture. The Committee on Institutional Corporation (CIC) Consortia represents thirteen midwestern schools and works to increase the pool of midwest minority secondary school students motivated and capable of entering engineering colleges.

Efforts are also being made to work directly with high school students to inform them of engineering career advantages and to build their science and math skills. The Minority Introduction to Engineering (MITE) program sponsored by the Engineers' Council for Professional Development and also by Purdue, Stevens Institute, Tulane, and Wayne State conducts summer programs to expose minority high school students to engineering. Illinois Institute of Technology and Pratt Institute operate Saturday programs involving preengineering and pre-science education.

Almost 40 percent of the colleges surveyed conduct prematriculation summer programs for minority students. North Carolina A & T University operates its summer program of mathematics review and practice in solving engineering problems entirely by mail with no cost to the student. The University of Bridgeport and Wayne State University coordinate their summer programs with work experience which often evolves into co-op situations.

Eighty percent of the schools surveyed maintain postmatriculation support programs for minority students. This support is evidenced in tutoring, counseling and advising, flexible curriculum, and minority student organizations.

Other Programs

The Minority Manpower Resources Project was established in 1963 by Dr. B. A. Turner of Texas Southern University to assist NASA Mission Control Center in hiring ethnic minority employees. Success has broadened the program to the point that now high school seniors are given the opportunity to work during the summer for participating companies such as the DuPont Company, Dow Chemical, the American Oil Company, NASA, and Shell Oil. Between 1965 and 1973, 149 students participated in this program.

The Delaware Program for Black Engineers, established in June 1972, is sponsored by the DuPont Company in cooperation with the University of Delaware's College of Engineering, the Delaware State College, the Delaware Technical and Community College, and the public and private schools of New Castle County. The program's objective is to help over a period of five years about one hundred high school black students prepare for engineering careers.

The Dual Degree programs, or 3-2 plans as they have been called in the past, look to black liberal arts colleges for prospective engineering students. Under this program, students spend 3 years at a liberal arts college taking one-half of the course content of a normal engineering curriculum and, then, transfer to an engineering college for the final 2 years of required engineering curriculum.

Georgia Institute of Technology's Dual Degree Program, which received significant funding in 1969 from Olin Charitable Trust Fund, is recognized as one of the prominent programs of this type and shows promise of contributing substantially to the increase of minority engineering graduates.

The National Consortium for Graduate Degrees for Minorities in Engineering, composed of 19 colleges and universities and 8 research centers, has set a goal "to increase by 100 the annual number of minority students receiving masters degrees in engineering." [28] Chosen after their junior year of undergraduate study, students will be offered 3 years of summer employment at 1 of the participating research centers and will receive scholar-

---

[28] Leonard A. Eiserer, ed. and pub., "National Consortium Formed to Increase Minorities in Engineering," *Fair Employment Report*, Vol. 14, No. 14 (July 12, 1976), p. 110.

ship support including living expenses for up to 2 years of graduate study at 1 of the universities participating in the consortium.

International Business Machines and Standard of California provide financial assistance for a four-week summer program for female high school students at the University of Idaho's College of Engineering. Designed to attract young women into the engineering curriculum and eventually into engineering careers, the program provides participants a weekly stipend to offset the loss of summer job income.

In 1972 Kaiser Engineers in Oakland, California, initiated a program to bring minority high school students in contact with engineers. Students with demonstrated math and science ability are chosen to participate in Kaiser's familiarization study, which meets each week for nineteen weeks during their junior high school year. Not only are students able to see the engineering environment, but they also receive guidance in developing their high school academic programs for later engineering study.

Eight professional engineering societies in the San Francisco area have formed the Bay Area Engineering Societies' Committee on Manpower Training (ESCMT), which has placed over 125 para-professional trainees with over 80 firms through a 42-week program that is federally assisted. ESCMT also has summer placement programs for minority engineering students and scholarship programs for trainees interested in further education.

Investments have been made in diverse media to communicate the need and work of engineers. Films providing information about engineering are available from the Engineers' Council for Professional Development, Consulting Engineers' Council, and the American Society of Chemical Engineers. Furthermore, General Electric's mobil van called "Expo-Tech" provides math and science exhibits for junior high students to encourage a better understanding of engineering.

Programs currently in operation to increase the number of minorities and women in engineering are too numerous to describe adequately here; however, the *Directory of Organibations in Engineering Programs for Minorities,* which is available from COME, does provide a more complete listing of these programs.[29]

---

[29] Committee on Minorities in Engineering, *Directory of Organizations in Engineering Programs for Minorities* (Washington, D.C.: National Academy of Sciences, 1976).

PREDICTING THE NUMBERS OF MINORITIES
AND WOMEN IN ENGINEERING

With this background of the meager past supply of minorities and women in engineering and the attempts under way to increase this supply, we now turn to our predictive model in order to estimate future supply. This model, which was described in the previous chapter, was used to develop five projections of the engineering labor force. The first of these produces a base line projection of new labor force entrants and the resulting engineering labor force from 1970 through 1985. The remaining four simulations comprise a sensitivity analysis showing the impact that altering the racial and sexual distribution of degree recipients has on the labor supply. These last four projections show that because of the large number of white males and the small number of black males and females in engineering, even a large increase in the number of black male and female entrants into engineering will produce only a minor change in the engineering labor force distribution. This conclusion holds for total engineering and for the five subfields included in this report. Comments on and tables for each of the five projections appear in this section.

Base Line Projections

The results of the labor supply model for the total engineering group and for each of the five subfields of industrial, chemical, electrical, mechanical, and other engineering are shown in Tables III-9 through III-26. The basic input data used in the model exercise are provided, followed by the projections of new labor force entrants and projections of the total labor force field by field.

Tables III-9, III-10, and III-11 are concerned with the total engineering group. Most of the information presented in Table III-9 has already been discussed in the methodology chapter. The figures in the table that enumerate the percent of total engineering degrees awarded to blacks were taken from reports of the Engineering Manpower Commission as reported in *Professional Women and Minorities: A Manpower Data Resource Service.*[30]

---

[30] Vetter, *Professional Women and Minorities*, p. 325, Table E-15.

TABLE III-9

Input Data for Simulation
of the Total Engineering Labor Force to 1985

	MALE	FEMALE
SEPARATION RATE		·WHITE
1970	0.0147	0.0554
1985	0.0132	0.0569
	BLACK	
1970	0.0091	0.0509
1985	0.0079	0.0521
ENTRY RATE .		
BACHELOR	0.8000	0.8000
MASTER	0.9000	0.9000
DOCTOR	1.0000	1.0000
SUPPLY BASE — 1970		
TOTAL	725308	9069
BLACK	6989	229

	DEGREES AWARDED	
	% FEMALE	% BLACK
BACHELOR		
1969	0.72	0.79
1970	0.77	0.88
1971	0.80	0.94
1972	1.03	1.31
1973	1.20	1.51
1974	1.58	1.83
1975	2.16	1.92
MASTER		
1969	0.74	0.11
1970	1.12	0.32
1971	1.13	0.29
1972	1.60	0.45
1973.	1.67	0.61
1974	2.31	0.99
1975	2.44	0.89
DOCTOR .		
1969	0.35	0.06
1970	0.65	0.03
1971	0.63	0.22
1972	·0.60	0.34
1973	1.55	0.36
1974	1.66	0.36
1975	2.12	0.55

TABLE III-10
United States
New Labor Force Entrants, by Occupation,
Race, and Sex, 1970 to 1985

ENGINEERING

YEAR	TOTAL	WHITE MALE	WHITE FEMALE	BLACK MALE	BLACK FEMALE
1970	52214	·51443	425	344	3
1971	52970	52057	504	406	4
1972	54287	53080	658	543	6
1973	53191	51797	759	626	9
1974	51408	49758	902	735	13
1975	49297	47500	1037	744	16
1976	49765	47785	1117	844	19
1977	52187	49882	1292	988	25
1978	57013	54246	1535	1198	33
1979	58189	55123	1701	1325	40
1980	58878	55531	1858·	1443	47
1981	59369	55750	2009	1556	54
1982	60143	56229	2171	1680	63
1983	60411	56233	2317	1790	72
1984	60044	55648	2437	1879	80
1985	59493	54896	2546	1963	.88

Percentage Distribution of
New Labor Force Entrants, by Occupation,
Race, and Sex, 1970 to 1985

ENGINEERING

YEAR	TOTAL	WHITE MALE	WHITE FEMALE	BLACK MALE	BLACK FEMALE
1970	100.00	98.52·	0.81	0.66	0.01
1971	100.00	98.28	0.95	0.77	0.01
1972	100.00	97.78	1.21	1.00	0.01
1973	100.00	97.38	1.43	1.18	0.02
1974	100.00	96.79	1.76··	1.43	0.02
1975	100.00	96.35	2.10	1.51	0.03
1976	100.00	96.02·	2.24	1.70	0.04
1977	100.00	95.58	2.47	1.89	0.05
1978	100.00	95.15	2.69	2.10	0.06
1979	100.00	94.73·	2.92	2.28	0.07
1980	100.00	94.32	3.15	2.45	0.08
1981	100.00	93.90	3.38	2.62	0.09
1982	100.00	93.49	3.61	2.79	0.10
1983	100.00	93.08	3.83	2.96	0.12
1984	100.00	92.68	4.06	3.13	0.13·
1985	100.00	92.27	4.28	3.30	0.15

TABLE III-11
United States
Projection of Labor Force, by Occupation,
Race, and Sex, 1970 to 1985

ENGINEERING

| YEAR | TOTAL | WHITE | | BLACK | |
		MALE	FEMALE	MALE	FEMALE
1970	734377	718319	8840	6989	229
1971	776303	759897	8853	7332	221
1972	819013	801969	9019	7809	216
1973	860086	842231	9276	8366	214
1974	898863	879960	9660	9027	216
1975	935052	914982	10158	9692	221
1976	971272	949886	10706	10452	228
1977	1009482	986493	11397	11351	241
1978	1052059	1027053	12292	12453	262
1979	1095292	1068031	13301	13674	288
1980	1138690	1108961	14408	15003	320
1981	1182057	1149663	15603	16435	358
1982	1225682	1190410	16891	17981	402
1983	1269059	1230733	18250	19626	453
1984	1311564	1270058	19651	21347	509
1985	1353029	1308239	21078	23141	571

Percentage Distribution of
Projection of Labor Force, by Occupation,
Race, and Sex, 1970 to 1985

ENGINEERING

| YEAR | TOTAL | WHITE | | BLACK | |
		MALE	FEMALE	MALE	FEMALE
1970	100.00	97.81	1.20	0.95	0.03
1971	100.00	97.89	1.14	0.94	0.03
1972	100.00	97.92	1.10	0.95	0.03
1973	100.00	97.92	1.08	0.97	0.02
1974	100.00	97.90	1.07	1.00	0.02
1975	100.00	97.85	1.09	1.04	0.02
1976	100.00	97.80	1.10	1.08	0.02
1977	100.00	97.72	1.13	1.12	0.02
1978	100.00	97.62	1.17	1.18	0.02
1979	100.00	97.51	1.21	1.25	0.03
1980	100.00	97.39	1.27	1.32	0.03
1981	100.00	97.26	1.32	1.39	0.03
1982	100.00	97.12	1.38	1.47	0.03
1983	100.00	96.98	1.44	1.55	0.04
1984	100.00	96.84	1.50	1.63	0.04
1985	100.00	96.69	1.56	1.71	0.04

The number of new entrants to the total engineering labor force will grow from approximately 52,200 in 1970 to 59,500 in 1985, as shown in Table III-10. Although this increase in annual entrants is modest, the representation of females among new entrants will increase by 1985 to almost 5.5 times their 1970 representation level of 0.82 percent. A similar improvement is projected for the proportion of blacks which will grow from less than 0.7 percent to almost 3.5 percent over the 15-year period.

The total engineering labor force will grow by about 84 percent from its 1970 level of 734,000 people. The gains in black and female representation among new entrants, however, will not translate into comparable improvement in labor force penetration because of the size of the labor force relative to the number of new entrants. The proportion of women in the engineering labor force, as shown in Table III-11, will increase to 1.6 percent, only 0.4 percentage points from its 1970 level of 1.2 percent, if these projections are achieved. The representation of blacks will grow to almost 1.8 percent of the labor force in 1985 from the 1970 participation level of less than 1.0 percent.

Base Line Projections: Engineering Subfields

The input data for the five engineering subfields are provided in Tables III-12, III-15, III-18, III-21, and III-24. Data on the percentage of black degree recipients by subfield are available from the Engineering Manpower Commission for only two years, 1974 and 1975. Comparable data points by subfield for 1969 through 1973 were created by calculating the average ratio of the percentage of black degree earners in each subfield for 1974 and 1975 to the corresponding figures for total engineering and by applying those ratios to the percentage of total engineering degrees awarded to blacks in 1969 through 1973.

Industrial Engineering. The black and female representations among new entrants to the industrial engineering labor force in 1970 were approximately 0.7 percent for each group, as shown in Table III-13, and are projected to increase to 5.1 percent for women and 3.8 percent for blacks in 1985. Because their representations among new entrants are less than their respective proportions of the relevant labor force (Table III-14), little progress can be seen in the black and female labor force projections to 1985. The proportion of women in the industrial engineering labor force is projected to decline from 1.8 percent

TABLE III-12
Input Data for Simulation
of Industrial Engineering Labor Force to 1985

	MALE	FEMALE
SEPARATION RATE	WHITE	
1970	0.0142	0.0546
1985	0.0127	0.0563
.	BLACK	
1970	0.0069	0.0434
1985	0.0058	0.0454
ENTRY RATE		
BACHELOR	0.8000	0.8000
MASTER	0.9000	0.9000
DOCTOR	1.0000	1.0000
SUPPLY BASE – 1970		
TOTAL	90728	1648
BLACK	970	71

	DEGREES AWARDED	
	% FEMALE	% BLACK
BACHELOR		
1969	0.54	0.99
1970	0.66	1.10
1971	0.60	1.18
1972	1.03	1.63
1973	0.81	1.89
1974	1.50	2.29
1975	2.06	2.40
MASTER		
1969	0.55	0.06
1970	0.96	0.19
1971	1.20	0.17
1972	1.44	.0.27
1973	1.82	0.36
1974	2.60	0.59
1975	3.32	0.53
DOCTOR		
1969	0.01	0.07
1970	0.01	0.04
1971	2.16	0.26
1972	0.01	0.40
1973	2.31	0.42
1974	1.37	0.42
1975	4.20	0.65

TABLE III-13
United States
New Labor Force Entrants, by Occupation,
Race, and Sex, 1970 to 1985

INDUSTRIAL ENGINEERING

YEAR	TOTAL	WHITE		BLACK	
		MALE	FEMALE	MALE	FEMALE
1970	4247	4187	30	31	0
1971	4405	4328	41	36	0
1972	4670	4561	56	53	1
1973	4332	4214	59	58	1
1974	4003	3866	76	59	1
1975	3453	3314	84	54	1
1976	3381	3234	88	58	1
1977	3724	3543	106	73	2
1978	4598	4351	138	106	3
1979	4688	4413	154	118	3
1980	4755.	4454	169	128	4
1981	4797	4470	184	138	5
1982	4854	4500	200	149	6
1983	4870	4492	214	158	6
1984	4845	4446	226	166	7
1985	4793	4376	236	173	8

Percentage Distribution of
New Labor Force Entrants, by Occupation,
Race, and Sex, 1970 to 1985

INDUSTRIAL ENGINEERING

YEAR	TOTAL	WHITE		BLACK	
		MALE	FEMALE	MALE	FEMALE
1970	100.00	98.57	0.70	0.72	0.00
1971	100.00	98.25	0.93	0.82	0.01
1972	100.00	97.67	1.19	1.13	0.01
1973	100.00	97.29	1.37	1.33	0.02
1974	100.00	96.59	1.91	1.48	0.02
1975	100.00	95.97	2.44	1.55	0.03
1976	100.00	95.65	2.60	1.72	0.04
1977	100.00	95.14	2.84	1.97	0.05
1978	100.00	94.62	3.00	2.32	0.06
1979	100.00	94.14	3.28	2.51	0.07
1980	100.00	93.66	3.56	2.69	0.09
1981	100.00	93.18	3.84	2.87	0.10
1982	100.00	92.71	4.12	3.06	0.12
1983	100.00	92.24	4.39	3.24	0.13
1984	100.00	91.77	4.66	3.42	0.15
1985	100.00	91.30	4.92	3.62	0.17

TABLE III-14
United States
Projection of Labor Force, by Occupation,
Race, and Sex, 1970 to 1985

INDUSTRIAL ENGINEERING

YEAR	TOTAL	WHITE MALE	WHITE FEMALE	BLACK MALE	BLACK FEMALE
1970	92376	89758	1577	970	71
1971	95419	92820	1532	999	68
1972	98696	96082	1503	1045	66
1973	101599	98960	1480	1096	64
1974	104145	101460	1475	1148	62
1975	106116	103384	1478	1194	60
1976	107999	105212	.1484	1244	59
1977	110210	107335	1507	1310	58
1978	113275	110247	1561	1408	58
1979	116398	113194	1628	1517	59.
1980	119556	116154	1707	1635	61
1981	122724	119102	1796	1763	63
1982	125915	122054	1895	1901	66
1983	129090	124971	2003	2047	69
1984	132208	127817	2116	2201	73
1985	135242	130570	2233	2362	78

Percentage Distribution of
Projection of Labor Force, by Occupation,
Race, and Sex, 1970 to 1985

INDUSTRIAL ENGINEERING

YEAR	TOTAL	WHITE MALE	WHITE FEMALE	BLACK MALE	BLACK FEMALE
1970	100.00	97.17	1.71	1.05	0.08
1971	100.00	97.28	1.61	1.05	0.07
1972	100.00	97.35	1.52	1.06	0.07
1973	100.00	97.40	1.46	1.08	0.06
1974	100.00	97.42	1.42	1.10	0.06
1975	100.00	97.43	1.39	1.13	0.06
1976	100.00	97.42	1.37	1.15	0.05
1977	100.00	97.39	1.37	1.19	0.05
1978	100.00	.97.33	1.38	1.24	0.05
1979	100.00	97.25	1.40	1.30	0.05
1980	100.00	97.15	1.43	1.37	0.05
1981	100.00	97.05	1.46	1.44	0.05
1982	100.00	96.93	1.51	1.51	0.05
1983	100.00	96.81	1.55	1.59	0.05
1984	100.00	96.68	1.60	1.66	0.06
1985	100.00	96.55	1.65	1.75	0.06

TABLE III-15
Input Data for Simulation
of Chemical Engineering Labor Force to 1985

		MALE	FEMALE
SEPARATION RATE		WHITE	
	1970	0.0116	0.0746
	1985	0.0103	0.0754
		BLACK	
	1970	0.0087	0.1369
	1985	0.0075	0.1404
ENTRY RATE			
	BACHELOR	0.8000	0.8000
	MASTER	0.9000	0.9000
	DOCTOR	1.0000	1.0000
SUPPLY BASE – 1970			
	TOTAL	46607	472
	BLACK	227	22

		DEGREES AWARDED	
		% FEMALE	% BLACK
BACHELOR			
	1969	1.44	0.44
	1970	1.43	0.46
	1971	1.76	0.53
	1972	2.04	0.74
	1973	2.35	0.85
	1974	3.35	1.03
	1975	4.40	1.08
MASTER			
	1969	0.79	0.08
	1970	1.72	0.23
	1971	2.36	0.21
	1972	2.43	0.32
	1973	2.00	0.44
	1974	2.97	0.71
	1975	2.53	0.64
DOCTOR			
	1969	0.73	0.02
	1970	0.01	0.01
	1971	0.49	0.08
	1972	0.25	0.12
	1973	0.50	0.12
	1974	2.50	0.12
	1975	1.16	0.19

in 1970 to a low of 1.4 percent in 1977 and then increase to 1.7 percent in 1985. Black penetration in the labor force will increase minimally from the 1970 level of 1.1 percent to 1.8 percent in 1985. Of special interest is that in 1970 women had their greatest representation in the industrial engineering labor force of the 5 subfields included in this study.

Chemical Engineering. The chemical engineering subfield has the distinction of having the greatest proportion of women among new entrants to its labor force of the 5 subfields. Women claimed almost 1.4 percent of new entrants in 1970 and are projected to increase their presence to almost 7.6 percent in 1985, as the figures in Table III-16 indicate. In 1970, blacks made up 0.4 percent of the pool of new chemical engineering labor force members and will improve their representation to almost 2.1 percent by the end of the 15-year period. The chemical engineering labor force was 1.0 percent female and more than 0.5 percent black in 1970 (Table III-17). Given the trends in the race and sex composition of new entrants, the projections indicate female participation in the labor force could increase by 1.5 percentage points to 2.5 percent from 1970 to 1985, and black penetration could double over that interval.

Electrical Engineering. Of the 5 engineering subfields, this engineering subfield has the largest proportion of blacks in the new entrants pool and the labor force. As the data in Table III-19 show, the new entrants pool in 1970 was 0.9 percent black and less than 0.6 percent female. Black representation among those entering the labor force will increase to almost 4.8 percent in 1985, and women will improve their presence in the pool by 1.3 percentage points over the 15 years. Because women make up a smaller proportion of new entrants than their representation in the 1970 labor force, the projections of the labor force, shown in Table III-20, indicate a net decline in female participation from the 1970 level of 1.3 percent to 1.1 percent in 1985. The pattern in the figures shows a decline in the proportion of women to less than 1.0 percent in 1977 and then an increase to 1.1 percent over the next 8 years. The proportion of blacks in the electrical engineering labor force is projected to increase steadily from its 1970 level of 1.3 percent to more than 2.3 percent in 1985.

Mechanical Engineering. The proportions of new entrants to the mechanical engineering labor force claimed by women and blacks in 1970 were 0.4 percent and 0.8 percent, respectively. As

TABLE III-16
United States
New Labor Force Entrants, by Occupation,
Race, and Sex, 1970 to 1985

CHEMICAL ENGINEERING

| YEAR | TOTAL | WHITE | | BLACK | |
		MALE	FEMALE	MALE	FEMALE
1970	4331	4256	59	16	0
1971	4259	4165	75	19	0
1972	4333	4218	90	25	1
1973	4205	4078	98	28	1
1974	4059	3901	124	33	1
1975	3795	3630	131	33	1
1976	4038	3846	151	39	2
1977	4359	4126	183	48	2
1978	5258	4945	245	65	3
1979	5364	5017	272	71	4
1980	5430	5051	297	77	5
1981	5471	5062	320	83	6
1982	5535	5093	346	90	6
1983	5568	5096	369	96	7
1984	5535	5038	388	100	8
1985	5484	4964	406	105	9

Percentage Distribution of
New Labor Force Entrants, by Occupation,
Race, and Sex, 1970 to 1985

CHEMICAL ENGINEERING

| YEAR | TOTAL | WHITE | | BLACK | |
		MALE	FEMALE	MALE	FEMALE
1970	100.00	98.27	1.36	0.37	0.01
1971	100.00	97.78	1.77	0.44	0.01
1972	100.00	97.35	2.07	0.57	0.01
1973	100.00	96.98	2.33	0.68	0.02
1974	100.00	96.11	3.05	0.81	0.03
1975	100.00	95.65	·3.46	0.86	0.03
1976	100.00	95.24	3.74	0.98	.0.04
1977	100.00	94.66	4.19	1.10	0.05
1978	100.00	94.04	4.67	1.23	0.06
1979	100.00	93.53	5.07	1.33	0.08
1980	100.00	93.02	5.46	1.43	0.09
1981	100.00	92.52	5.85	1.52	0.10
1982	100.00	92.01	6.25	1.62	0.12
1983	100.00	91.52	6.63	1.72	0.13
1984	100.00	91.02	7.02	1.81	0.15
1985	100.00	90.53	7.40	1.91	0.16

TABLE III-17
United States
Projection of Labor Force, by Occupation, Race, and Sex, 1970 to 1985

CHEMICAL ENGINEERING

YEAR	TOTAL	WHITE		BLACK	
		MALE	FEMALE	MALE	FEMALE
1970	47079	46380	450	227	22
1971	50766	50011	492	244	19
1972	54485	53657	545	266	17
1973	58037	57127	602	293	16
1974	61403	60385	681	323	15
1975	64468	63341	761	353	14
1976	67742	66485	855	389	14
1977	71301	69880	973	434	14
1978	75718	74062	1146	495	15
1979	80189	78278	1331	563	17
1980	84672	82489	1528	636	20
1981	89142	86672	1733	714	22
1982	93623	90850	1949	798	26
1983	98082	94994	2171	888	29
1984	102456	99045	2396	982	33
1985	106727	102990	2621	1079	38

Percentage Distribution of
Projection of Labor Force, by Occupation, Race, and Sex, 1970 to 1985

CHEMICAL ENGINEERING

YEAR	TOTAL	WHITE		BLACK	
		MALE	FEMALE	MALE	FEMALE
1970	100.00	98.52	0.96	0.48	0.05
1971	100.00	98.51	0.97	0.48	0.04
1972	100.00	98.48	1.00	0.49	0.03
1973	100.00	98.43	1.04	0.50	0.03
1974	100.00	98.34	1.11	0.53	0.02
1975	100.00	98.25	1.18	0.55	0.02
1976	100.00	98.14	1.26	0.57	0.02
1977	100.00	98.01	1.36	0.61	0.02
1978	100.00	97.81	1.51	0.65	0.02
1979	100.00	97.62	1.66	0.70	0.02
1980	100.00	97.42	1.80	0.75	0.02
1981	100.00	97.23	1.94	0.80	0.03
1982	100.00	97.04	2.08	0.85	0.03
1983	100.00	96.85	2.21	0.91	0.03
1984	100.00	96.67	2.34	0.96	0.03
1985	100.00	96.50	2.46	1.01	0.04

TABLE III-18
Input Data for Simulation
of Electrical Engineering Labor Force to 1985

	MALE	FEMALE
SEPARATION RATE	WHITE	
1970	0.0116	0.0580
1985	0.0103	0.0595
	BLACK	
1970	0.0067	0.0357
1985	0.0056	0.0378
ENTRY RATE		
BACHELOR	0.8000	0.8000
MASTER	0.9000	0.9000
DOCTOR	1.0000	1.0000
SUPPLY BASE — 1970		
TOTAL	173519	2301
BLACK	2219	21

	DEGREES AWARDED	
	% FEMALE	% BLACK
BACHELOR		
1969	0.57	1.08
1970	0.56	1.20
1971	0.62	1.29
1972	0.65	1.79
1973	1.28	2.07
1974	1.03	2.51
1975	1.26	2.65
MASTER		
1969	0.55	0.12
1970	0.70	0.35
1971	0.70	0.32
1972	1.24	0.49
1973	1.26	0.66
1974	1.57	1.08
1975	1.67	0.97
DOCTOR		
1969	0.46	0.08
1970	0.01	0.04
1971	0.34	0.28
1972	0.36	0.44
1973	1.14	0.46
1974	1.13	0.46
1975	1.57	0.71

TABLE III-19
United States
New Labor Force Entrants, by Occupation,
Race, and Sex, 1970 to 1985

ELECTRICAL ENGINEERING

YEAR	TOTAL	WHITE		BLACK	
		MALE	FEMALE	MALE	FEMALE
1970	14383	14170	82	130	1
1971	14491	14239	99	152	1
1972	14290	13973	120	196	2
1973	14147	13752	162	230	3
1974	12907	12500	151	253	3
1975	12078	11659	163	252	3
1976	12091	11623	181	283	4
1977	12839	12288	210	336	5
1978	13818	13166	244	402	7
1979	14033	13315	267	443	8
1980	14161	13381	289	481	10
1981	14222	13383	309	518	11
1982	14354	13451	331	559	13
1983	14382	13421	351	595	15
1984	14229	13224	366	623	16
1985	14074	13025	380	651	18

Percentage Distribution of
New Labor Force Entrants, by Occupation,
Race, and Sex, 1970 to 1985

ELECTRICAL ENGINEERING

YEAR	TOTAL	WHITE		BLACK	
		MALE	FEMALE	MALE	FEMALE
1970	100.00	98.52	0.57	0.90	0.01
1971	100.00	98.26	0.68	1.05	0.01
1972	100.00	97.78	0.84	1.37	0.01
1973	100.00	97.21	1.15	1.63	0.02
1974	100.00	96.85	1.17	1.96	0.02
1975	100.00	96.53	1.35	2.09	0.03
1976	100.00	96.13	1.50	2.34	0.03
1977	100.00	95.71	1.63	2.62	0.04
1978	100.00	95.28	1.76	2.91	0.05
1979	100.00	94.88	1.90	3.16	0.06
1980	100.00	94.49	2.04	3.40	0.07
1981	100.00	94.10	2.18	3.64	0.08
1982	100.00	93.71	2.31	3.89	0.09
1983	100.00	93.32	2.44	4.13	0.10
1984	100.00	92.93	2.57	4.38	0.11
1985	100.00	92.55	2.70	4.62	0.13

TABLE III-20
United States
Projection of Labor Force, by Occupation,
Race, and Sex, 1970 to 1985

ELECTRICAL ENGINEERING

YEAR	TOTAL	WHITE MALE	WHITE FEMALE	BLACK MALE	BLACK FEMALE
1970	175820	171300	2280	2219	21
1971	188191	183567	2247	2356	21
1972	200237	195442	2236	2537	22
1973	212020	206978	2268	2750	24
1974	222446	217149	2286	2986	26
1975	231946	226383	2316	3219	28
1976	241372	235498	2361	3481	32
1977	251460	245197	2433	3796	36
1978	262436	255688	2533	4174	42
1979	273527	266236	2651	4592	48
1980	284645	276760	2783	5046	56
1981	295724	287196	2928	5534	66
1982	306837	297614	3086	6061	76
1983	317881	307919	3254	6620	88
1984	328677	317944	3427	7205	101
1985	339228	327694	3603	7815	115

Percentage Distribution of
Projection of Labor Force, by Occupation,
Race, and Sex, 1970 to 1985

ELECTRICAL ENGINEERING

YEAR	TOTAL	WHITE MALE	WHITE FEMALE	BLACK MALE	BLACK FEMALE
1970	100.00	97.43	1.30	1.26	0.01
1971	100.00	97.54	1.19	1.25	0.01
1972	100.00	97.61	1.12	1.27	0.01
1973	100.00	97.62	1.07	1.30	0.01
1974	100.00	97.62	1.03	1.34	0.01
1975	100.00	97.60	1.00	1.39	0.01
1976	100.00	97.57	0.98	1.44	0.01
1977	100.00	97.51	0.97	1.51	0.01
1978	100.00	97.43	0.97	1.59	0.02
1979	100.00	97.33	0.97	1.68	0.02
1980	100.00	97.23	0.98	1.77	0.02
1981	100.00	97.12	0.99	1.87	0.02
1982	100.00	96.99	1.01	1.98	0.02
1983	100.00	96.87	1.02	2.08	0.03
1984	100.00	96.73	1.04	2.19	0.03
1985	100.00	96.60	1.06	2.30	0.03

TABLE III-21
Input Data for Simulation
of Mechanical Engineering Labor Force to 1985

	MALE	FEMALE
SEPARATION RATE	WHITE	
1970	0.0152	0.0612
1985	0.0136	0.0622
	BLACK	
1970	0.0144	0.0817
1985	0.0130	0.0797
ENTRY RATE		
BACHELOR	0.8000	0.8000
MASTER	0.9000	0.9000
DOCTOR	1.0000	1.0000
SUPPLY BASE – 1970		
TOTAL	106561	852
BLACK	651	0

	DEGREES AWARDED	
	% FEMALE	% BLACK
BACHELOR		
1969	0.47	0.88
1970	0.42	0.98
1971	0.46	1.04
1972	0.56	1.45
1973	0.72	1.67
1974	0.81	2.03
1975	1.19	2.13
MASTER		
1969	0.17	0.11
1970	0.52	0.33
1971	0.22	0.30
1972	0.79	0.46
1973	0.89	0.63
1974	1.14	1.02
1975	0.81	0.92
DOCTOR		
1969	0.01	0.05
1970	0.01	0.02
1971	0.01	0.18
1972	0.24	0.28
1973	0.81	0.30
1974	1.56	0.30
1975	1.18	0.45

the data in Table III-22 indicate, the proportion of women should increase to 2.2 percent, or approximately half the level of female representation among new entrants to all engineering disciplines. The percentage of black mechanical engineering labor force entrants should increase to more than 4.0 percent in 1985, which is 5 times their 1970 level of representation.

Changes in the participation of women and blacks in the labor force are shown in Table III-23. The trend indicated for women follows the pattern already described for the various fields in which the proportion of female new entrants is less than their representation in the labor force; *i.e.*, the proportion of women initially drops from 0.8 percent in 1970 to 0.6 percent in 1977 and then climbs to 0.8 percent in 1985. Black representation in the labor force is projected to increase from 0.6 percent in 1970 to approximately 3 times that level, 1.8 percent, in 1985.

Other Engineering. The changes in racial and sexual composition projected for the aggregate group, other engineering subfields, are identical to the levels and changes projected for blacks for total engineering, and advances in representation for women are somewhat better than the average. As shown in Table III-25, women made up almost 1.1 percent of all entrants to these fields in 1970, and this proportion will increase about 4.1 percentage points to 5.2 percent in 1985. Female participation in the associated labor force will initially drop from more than 1.2 percent in 1970 and then increase to more than 1.8 percent in 1985 (Table III-26).

Sensitivity Analysis

Four simulations of the model were implemented to show the impact that altering the racial and sexual distribution of degree recipients has on the labor supply. Simulation I is a doubling of the number of black degree earners by 1985, while maintaining the base number of white degrees awarded. Simulation II is a doubling of the number of degrees awarded to women by 1985, while maintaining the base number of male degree recipients. Simulation III is a doubling of the number of white female and black degree earners by 1985, while maintaining the base number of white male graduates. Simulation IV reflects the goal of the ME[3] Task Force—a tenfold increase in the number of degrees awarded to blacks.

Tables III-27 through III-38 show the 1970, 1975, 1980, and 1985 results of these four simulations of the size of the new

TABLE III-22
United States
New Labor Force Entrants, by Occupation,
Race, and Sex, 1970 to 1985

MECHANICAL ENGINEERING

YEAR	TOTAL	WHITE		BLACK	
		MALE	FEMALE	MALE	FEMALE
1970	9900	9780	41	79	0
1971	9538	9406	43	87	0
1972	9289	9121	58	110	1
1973	9115	8918	69	127	1
1974	8192	7981	73	137	1
1975	7782	7561	81	138	2
1976	7836	7589	88	156	2
1977	8677	8373	108	194	2
1978	9566	9196	129	237	3
1979	9733	9325	142	262	4
1980	9812	9368	155	284	5
1981	9849	9372	166	306	5
1982	9958	9443	179	330	6
1983	9971	9423	190	351	7
1984	9878	9303	199	368	8
1985	9767	9167	208	384	9

Percentage Distribution of
New Labor Entrants, by Occupation,
Race, and Sex, 1970 to 1985

MECHANICAL ENGINEERING

YEAR	TOTAL	WHITE		BLACK	
		MALE	FEMALE	MALE	FEMALE
1970	100.00	98.79	0.41	0.80	0.00
1971	100.00	98.62	0.46	0.92	0.00
1972	100.00	98.19	0.62	1.18	0.01
1973	100.00	97.84	0.76	1.40	0.01
1974	100.00	97.42	0.89	1.67	0.01
1975	100.00	97.16	1.05	1.78	0.02
1976	100.00	96.85	1.13	2.00	0.02
1977	100.00	96.49	1.24	2.24	0.03
1978	100.00	96.13	1.35	2.48	0.03
1979	100.00	95.81	1.46	2.69	0.04
1980	100.00	95.48	1.58	2.90	0.05
1981	100.00	95.15	1.69	3.11	0.05
1982	100.00	94.83	1.80	3.32	0.06
1983	100.00	94.50	1.91	3.52	0.07
1984	100.00	94.18	2.02	3.73	0.08
1985	100.00	93.85	2.13	3.93	0.09

TABLE III-23
United States
Projection of Labor Force, by Occupation, Race, and Sex, 1970 to 1985

MECHANICAL ENGINEERING

YEAR	TOTAL	WHITE MALE	WHITE FEMALE	BLACK MALE	BLACK FEMALE
1970	107413	105910	852	651	0
1971	115290	113718	843	729	0
1972	122813	121134	849	828	1
1973	130062	128250	866	944	2
1974	136293	134337	886	1068	3
1975	142035	139927	913	1191	4
1976	147760	145479	945	1331	6
1977	154257	151749	994	1507	8
1978	161564	158768	1062	1724	10
1979	168946	165832	1139	1962	13
1980	176316	172856	1223	2220	17
1981	183634	179803	1313	2496	21
1982	190973	186743	1411	2793	25
1983	198238	193586	1514	3108	30
1984	205325	200236	1619	3435	36
1985	212220	206679	1726	3774	41

Percentage Distribution of Projection of Labor Force, by Occupation, Race, and Sex, 1970 to 1985

MECHANICAL ENGINEERING

YEAR	TOTAL	WHITE MALE	WHITE FEMALE	BLACK MALE	BLACK FEMALE
1970	100.00	98.60	0.79	0.61	0.0
1971	100.00	98.64	0.73	0.63	0.00
1972	100.00	98.63	0.69	0.67	0.00
1973	100.00	98.61	0.67	0.73	0.00
1974	100.00	98.56	0.65	0.78	0.00
1975	100.00	98.52	0.64	0.84	0.00
1976	100.00	98.46	0.64	0.90	0.00
1977	100.00	98.37	0.64	0.98	0.00
1978	100.00	98.27	0.66	1.07	0.01
1979	100.00	98.16	0.67	1.16	0.01
1980	100.00	98.04	0.69	1.26	0.01
1981	100.00	97.91	0.72	1.36	0.01
1982	100.00	97.79	0.74	1.46	0.01
1983	100.00	97.65	0.76	1.57	0.02
1984	100.00	97.52	0.79	1.67	0.02
1985	100.00	97.39	0.81	1.78	0.02

TABLE III-24
Input Data for Simulation
of Other Engineering Labor Force to 1985

	MALE	FEMALE
SEPARATION RATE	WHITE	
1970	0.0161	0.0584
1985	0.0145	0.0598
	BLACK	
1970	0.0097	0.0554
1985	0.0085	0.0555
ENTRY RATE		
BACHELOR	0.8000	0.8000
MASTER	0.9000	0.9000
DOCTOR	1.0000	1.0000.
SUPPLY BASE – 1970		
TOTAL	307893	5796
BLACK	2922	115

	DEGREES AWARDED	
	% FEMALE	% BLACK
BACHELOR		
1969	0.02	0.79
1970	0.94	0.88
1971	0.91	0.94
1972	1.24	1.31
1973	1.21	1.51
1974	1.84	1.83
1975	2.55	1.92
MASTER		
1969	1.09	0.11
1970	1.54	0.32
1971	1.46	0.29
1972	1.96	0.45.
1973	2.02	0.61
1974	2.81	0.99
1975	3.01	0.89
DOCTOR		
1969	0.32	0.03
1970	1.32	0.01
1971	0.84	0.10
1972	0.91	0.16
1973	2.05	0.17
1974	1.73	0.17
1975	2.62	0.25

TABLE III-25
United States
New Labor Force Entrants, by Occupation,
Race, and Sex, 1970 to 1985

OTHER ENGINEERING

| YEAR | TOTAL | WHITE | | BLACK | |
		MALE	FEMALE	MALE	FEMALE
1970	19353	19027	206	119	1
1971	20277	19893	236	146	2
1972	21705	21177	322	204	3
1973	21392	20794	360	234	4
1974	22247	21472	463	305	6
1975	22189	21307	557	317	8
1976	22419	21456	593	360	10
1977	22588	21513	660	403	12
1978	23773	22534	756	468	15
1979	24371	22993	840	520	18
1980	24720	23212	918	568	22
1981	25030	23395	996	614	25
1982	25442	23669	.1079	665	29
1983	25620	23724	1153	710	33
1984	25557	23557	1217	747	37
1985	25375	23280	1272	781	41

Percentage Distribution of
New Labor Force Entrants, by Occupation,
Race, and Sex, 1970 to 1985

OTHER ENGINEERING

| YEAR | TOTAL | WHITE | | BLACK | |
		.MALE	FEMALE	MALE	FEMALE
1970	100.00	98.31	1.07	0.62	0.01
1971	100.00	98.10	1.17	0.72	0.01
1972	100.00	97.56	1.49	0.94	0.01
1973	100.00	97.21	1.68	1.09	0.02
1974	100.00	96.52	2.08	1.37	0.03
1975	100.00	96.02	2.51	1.43	0.04
1976	100.00	95.70	2.65	1.61	0.04
1977	100.00	95.24	2.92	1.78	0.05
1978	100.00	94.79	3.18	1.97	0.06
1979	100.00	94.35	3.45	2.13	0.07
1980	100.00	93.90	3.71	2.30	0.09
1981	100.00	93.47	3.98	2.45	0.10
1982	100.00	93.03	4.24	2.61	0.11
1983	100.00	92.60	4.50	2.77	0.13
1984	100.00	92.17	4.76	2.92	0.15
1985	100.00	91.74	5.01	3.08	0.16

TABLE III-26
United States
Projection of Labor Force, by Occupation, Race, and Sex, 1970 to 1985

OTHER ENGINEERING

YEAR	TOTAL	WHITE MALE	WHITE FEMALE	BLACK MALE	BLACK FEMALE
1970	311689	304971	3681	2922	115
1971	326839	319987	3702	3040	110
1972	343209	336080	3807	3215	107
1973	359037.	351571	3944	3418	105
1974	375504	367532	4176	3691	105
1975	391686.	383118	4487	3974	107
1976	407875	398651	4816	4297	111
1977	424012	414043	5191	4661	117
1978	441116	430264	5640	5087	125
1979	458586	446743	6146	5561	137
1980	476168	463239	6700	6079	151
1981	493823	479719	7297	6639	168
1982	511653	496279	7942	7246	188
1983	529425	512700	8621	7893	210
1984	546898	528768	9323	8571	236
1985	563962	544381	10038	9280	264

Percentage Distribution of Projection of Labor Force, by Occupation, Race, and Sex, 1970 to 1985

OTHER ENGINEERING

YEAR	TOTAL	WHITE MALE	WHITE FEMALE	BLACK MALE	BLACK FEMALE
1970	100.00	97.84	1.18	0.94	0.04
1971	100.00	97.90	1.13	0.93	0.03
1972	100.00	97.92	1.11	0.94	0.03
1973	100.00	97.92	1.10	0.95	0.03
1974	100.00	97.88	1.11	0.98	0.03
1975	100.00	97.81	1.15	1.01	0.03
1976	100.00	97.74	1.18	1.05	0.03
1977	100.00	97.65	1.22	1.10	0.03
1978	100.00	97.54	1.28	1.15	0.03
1979	100.00	97.42	1.34	1.21	0.03
1980	100.00	97.28	1.41	1.28	0.03
1981	100.00	97.14	1.48	1.34	0.03
1982	100.00	97.00	1.55	1.42	0.04
1983	100.00	96.84	1.63	1.49	0.04
1984	100.00	96.68	1.70	1.57	0.04
1985	100.00	96.53	1.78	1.65	0.05

TABLE III-27
United States
New Labor Force Entrants, by Occupation, Race, and Sex, 1970-1985

Engineering	Year	Total	White		Black	
			Male	Female	Male	Female
Simulation I	1970	52,214	51,443	425	344	3
	1975	49,297	47,500	1,037	744	16
	1980	59,623	55,531	1,858	2,164	70
	1985	61,544	54,896	2,546	3,926	177
Simulation II	1970	52,214	51,443	425	344	3
	1975	49,297	47,500	1,037	744	16
	1980	59,830	55,531	2,786	1,443	70
	1985	62,127	54,896	5,091	1,963	177
Simulation III	1970	52,214	51,443	425	344	3
	1975	49,297	47,500	1,037	744	16
	1980	60,551	55,531	2,786	2,164	70
	1985	64,090	54,896	5,091	3,926	177
Simulation IV	1970	52,214	51,443	425	344	3
	1975	49,297	47,500	1,037	744	16
	1980	65,580	55,531	1,858	7,934	257
	1985	77,956	54,896	2,546	19,630	885

Percentage Distribution of New Labor Force Entrants, by Occupation, Race, and Sex, 1970-1985

Engineering	Year	Total	White		Black	
			Male	Female	Male	Female
Simulation I	1970	100.00	98.52	0.81	0.66	0.01
	1975	100.00	96.35	2.10	1.51	0.03
	1980	100.00	93.14	3.12	3.63	0.12
	1985	100.00	89.20	4.14	6.38	0.29
Simulation II	1970	100.00	98.52	0.81	0.66	0.01
	1975	100.00	96.35	2.10	1.51	0.03
	1980	100.00	92.81	4.66	2.41	0.12
	1985	100.00	88.36	8.20	3.16	0.28
Simulation III	1970	100.00	98.52	0.81	0.66	0.01
	1975	100.00	96.35	2.10	1.51	0.03
	1980	100.00	91.71	4.60	3.57	0.12
	1985	100.00	85.65	7.94	6.13	0.28
Simulation IV	1970	100.00	98.52	0.81	0.66	0.01
	1975	100.00	96.35	2.10	1.51	0.03
	1980	100.00	84.68	2.83	12.10	0.39
	1985	100.00	70.42	3.27	25.18	1.13

entrants labor force and projections of the labor force for total engineering and the subfields of industrial, chemical, electrical, mechanical, and other engineering. The aggregate and each sub-field are discussed separately.

In summary, the sensitivity analyses indicate that substantial changes in the rate of entry of blacks and women into the engineering labor forces yield minimal changes in their penetration of the labor force because of the dominant position occupied by white males. The achievement of a 2-fold increase in the number of engineering degrees awarded to women and blacks by 1985 would, on the average, produce a pool of new entrants to the engineering labor force in 1985 that would be 85 percent white male and 15 percent women and blacks.

Total Engineering. The results of the simulation exercises show that the effect of doubling the numbers of black and/or female degree earners (Simulations I, II, and III) show increases in black and female representation among new labor force entrants of about 10 times their 1970 participation levels and approximately 190 percent of the 1985 base line projections for blacks and women as new entrants to engineering. This can be seen by comparing the results shown in Table III-27 with the base line projections in Table III-10. When these large changes in the composition of new entrants are incorporated into the labor force, the effects are minimal. As the figures in Table III-28 indicate, when compared to the projections in Table III-11, the doubling of black degree recipients produces an increase of 0.6 percentage points in labor force participation over 1985 base line projections and approximately a 1.4 percentage point improvement over 1970 levels. The corresponding changes for women are an increase of 0.8 percentage points from base line projections for 1985 and a 1.2 percentage point addition to 1970 female participation in the total engineering labor force of 1.2 percent. The impact of achieving a 10-fold increase in black graduates by 1985 produces a new entrant pool that is approximately 26 percent black in 1985 with black penetration in the associated labor force at 7.4 percent in that year.

Industrial Engineering. The simulation results for blacks in industrial engineering are similar to the results revealed in the analysis of the total engineering group. A doubling of black graduates, shown in Table III-29, when compared to the information in Table III-13, produces a level of black representation among new entrants that is more than 10 times their repre-

TABLE III-28
United States
Projection of Labor Force, by Occupation,
Race, and Sex, 1970-1985

Engineering	Year	Total	White Male	White Female	Black Male	Black Female
Simulation I	1970	734,377	718,319	8,840	6,989	229
	1975	935,052	914,982	10,158	9,692	221
	1980	1,140,618	1,108,961	14,408	16,877	373
	1985	1,362,242	1,308,239	21,078	32,043	884
Simulation II	1970	734,377	718,319	8,840	6,989	229
	1975	935,052	914,982	10,158	9,692	221
	1980	1,141,030	1,108,961	16,695	15,003	373
	1985	1,363,541	1,308,239	31,278	23,141	884
Simulation III	1970	734,377	718,319	8,840	6,989	229
	1975	935,052	914,982	10,158	9,692	221
	1980	1,142,905	1,108,961	16,695	16,877	373
	1985	1,372,442	1,308,239	31,278	32,043	884
Simulation IV	1970	734,377	.718,319	8,840	6,989	229
	1975	935,052	914,982	10,158	9,692	221
	1980	1,156,041	1,108,961	14,408	31,875	797
	1985	1,435,960	1,308,239	21,078	103,259	3,385

Percentage Distribution of New Labor Force Entrants,
by Occupation, Race, and Sex, 1970-1985

Engineering	Year	Total	White Male	White Female	Black Male	Black Female
Simulation I	1970	100.00	97.81	1.20	0.95	0.03
	1975	100.00	97.85	1.09	1.04	0.02
	1980	100.00	97.22	1.26	1.48	0.03
	1985	100.00	96.04	1.55	2.35	0.06
Simulation II	1970	100.00	97.81	1.20	0.95	0.03
	1975	100.00	97.85	1.09	1.04	0.02
	1980	100.00	97.19	1.46	1.31	0.03
	1985	100.00	95.94	2.29	1.70	0.06
Simulation III	1970	100.00	97.81	1.20	0.95	.0.03
	1975	100.00	97.85	1.09	1.04	0.02
	1980	100.00	97.03	1.46	1.48	0.03
	1985	100.00	95.32	2.28	2.33	0.06
Simulation IV	1970	100.00	97.81	1.20	0.95	0.03
	1975	100.00	97.85	1.09	1.04	0.02
	1980	100.00	95.93	1.25	2.76	0.07
	1985	100.00	91.11	1.47	7.19	0.24

TABLE III-29
United States
New Labor Force Entrants, by Occupation, Race, and Sex, 1970-1985

Industrial Engineering	Year	Total	White Male	White Female	Black Male	Black Female
Simulation I	1970	4,247	4,187	30	31	0
	1975	3,453	3,314	84	54	1
	1980	4,821	4,454	169	192	6
	1985	4,974	4,376	236	347	16
Simulation II	1970	4,247	4,187	30	31	0
	1975	3,453	3,314	84	54	1
	1980	4,842	4,454	254	128	6
	1985	5,037	4,376	472	173	16
Simulation III	1970	4,247	4,187	30	31	0
	1975	3,453	3,314	84	54	1
	1980	4,906	4,454	254	192	6
	1985	5,210	4,376	472	347	16
Simulation IV	1970	4,247	4,187	30	31	0
	1975	3,453	3,314	84	54	1
	1980	5,349	4,454	169	704	23
	1985	6,425	4,376	236	1,733	80

Percentage Distribution of New Labor Force Entrants, by Occupation, Race, and Sex, 1970-1985

Industrial Engineering	Year	Total	White Male	White Female	Black Male	Black Female
Simulation I	1970	100.00	98.57	0.70	0.72	0.00
	1975	100.00	95.97	2.44	1.55	0.03
	1980	100.00	92.38	3.51	3.98	0.13
	1985	100.00	87.97	4.74	6.97	0.32
Simulation II	1970	100.00	98.57	0.70	0.72	0.00
	1975	100.00	95.97	2.44	1.55	0.03
	1980	100.00	91.98	5.25	2.64	0.13
	1985	100.00	86.88	9.37	3.44	0.32
Simulation III	1970	100.00	98.57	0.70	0.72	0.00
	1975	100.00	95.97	2.44	1.55	0.03
	1980	100.00	90.78	5.18	3.91	0.13
	1985	100.00	83.99	9.06	6.65	0.31
Simulation IV	1970	100.00	98.57	0.70	0.72	0.00
	1975	100.00	95.97	2.44	1.55	0.03
	1980	100.00	83.25	3.17	13.16	0.43
	1985	100.00	68.11	3.67	26.98	1.24

sentation in 1970 and an increase of more than 90 percent over
1985 base line projection representation levels. If these results
were achieved, the industrial engineering labor force would be
approximately 2.4 percent black in 1985, as shown in Table III-30,
which is an addition of 1.3 percentage points to the 1970 level
of black penetration and only 0.6 percentage points over the 1985
base line projections (Table III-14). Simulation IV, which shows
the effects of attaining ME³ goals, indicates 1985 black representation in the new entrant pool at more than 28 percent, but less
than 7 percent of the labor force would be claimed by blacks.

Industrial engineering is the engineering subfield with the
greatest labor force representation of women in 1970 and with
no net gain in female presence projected by 1985. When the results of the simulations are compared to the base line projections,
a doubling of the number of women graduates produces a 0.6
percentage point increase in female industrial engineering labor
force participation from 1970 levels and 1985 base line figures,
or approximately 2.4 percent representation.

Chemical Engineering. The chemical engineering subfield has
the greatest representation of women among new labor force
entrants of all the engineering subfields. Implementation of the
simulations involving a doubling of female and/or black graduates reveals, in Table III-31, that the proportions of new entrants
claimed by women and blacks should change from 1.4 percent
and 0.4 percent in 1970, respectively, to 14.1 percent for women
and 4.1 percent for blacks in 1985. These increases of 10 times
the 1970 representation levels are 186 percent for women and
195 for blacks of the 1985 base line projections shown in Table
III-16. When these changes are incorporated into the labor force
accounting, black penetration improves from 0.5 percent to 1.5
percent, from 1970 to 1985, and from 1.0 percent to 3.9 percent
for women over the same time interval. Comparing these simulation projections in Table III-32 to the base line projections in
Table III-17 shows a 1.4 percentage point improvement in the
participation of women in 1985 over the 1985 base and a 0.4
percentage point increase for blacks. A 10-fold increase in the
number of black degree recipients yields a 1985 entrant pool that
is 17.5 percent black and black participation in the chemical
engineering labor force of 5.1 percent.

Electrical Engineering. The results of the analysis for electrical engineering are similar to those already described for the
various engineering subfields. The distinguishing feature of elec-

TABLE III-30
United States
Projection of Labor Force, by Occupation,
Race, and Sex, 1970 to 1985

Industrial Engineering	Year	Total	White		Black	
			Male	Female	Male	Female
Simulation I	1970	92,376	89,758	1,577	970	71
	1975	106,116	103,384	1,478	1,194	60
	1980	119,723	116,154	1,707	1,797	65
	1985	136,057	130,570	2,233	3,149	106
Simulation II	1970	92,376	89,758	1,577	970	71
	1975	106,116	103,384	1,478	1,194	60
	1980	119,765	116,154	1,911	1,635	65
	1985	136,209	130,570	3,171	2,362	106
Simulation III	1970	92,376	89,758	1,577	970	71
	1975	106,116	103,384	1,478	1,194	60
	1980	119,927	116,154	1,911	1,797	65
	1985	136,996	130,570	3,171	3,149	106
Simulation IV	1970	92,376	89,758	1,577	970	71
	1975	106,116	103,384	1,478	1,194	60
	1980	121,059	116,154	1,707	3,096	102
	1985	142,581	130,570	2,233	9,445	333

Percentage Distribution of Projection of Labor Force,
by Occupation, Race, and Sex, 1970-1985

Industrial Engineering	Year	Total	White		Black	
			Male	Female	Male	Female
Simulation I	1970	100.00	97.17	1.71	1.05	.0.08
	1975	100.00	97.43	1.39	1.13	0.06
	1980	100.00	97.02	·1.43	1.50	0.05
	1985	100.00	95.97	1.64	2.31	0.08
Simulation II	1970	100.00	97.17	1.71	1.05	0.08
	1975	100.00	97.43	1.39	1.13	0.06
	1980	100.00	96.98	1.60	1.37	0.05
	1985	100.00	95.86	2.33	1.73	0.08
Simulation III	1970	100.00	97.17	1.71	1.05	0.08
	1975	100.00	97.43	1.39	1.13	0.06
	1980	100.00	96.85	1.59	1.50	0.05
	1985	100.00	95.31	2.31	2.30	0.08
Simulation IV	1970	100.00	97.17	1.71	1.05	0.08
	1975	100.00	97.43	1.39	1.13	0.06
	1980	100.00	95.95	1.41	2.56	0.08
	1985	100.00	91.58	1.57	6.62	0.23

TABLE III-31
United States
New Labor Force Entrants, by Occupation,
Race, and Sex, 1970-1985

Chemical Engineering	Year	Total	White		Black	
			Male	Female	Male	Female
Simulation I	1970	4,331	4,256	59	16	0
	1975	3,795	3,630	131	33	1
	1980	5,471	5,051	297	116	7
	1985	5,598	4,964	406	209	18
Simulation II	1970	4,331	4,256	59	16	0
	1975	3,795	3,630	131	33	1
	1980	5,581	5,051	445	77	7
	1985	5,899	4,964	812	105	18
Simulation III	1970	4,331	4,256	59	16	0
	1975	3,795	3,630	131	33	1
	1980	5,619	5,051	445	116	7
	1985	6,004	4,964	812	209	18
Simulation IV	1970	4,331	4,256	59	16	0
	1975	3,795	3,630	131	33	1
	1980	5,800	5,051	297	426	26
	1985	6,506	4,964	406	1,046	90

Percentage Distribution of New Labor Force Entrants,
by Occupation, Race, and Sex, 1970-1985

Chemical Engineering	Year	Total	White		Black	
			Male	Female	Male	Female
Simulation I	1970	100.00	98.27	1.36	0.37	0.01
	1975	100.00	95.65	3.46	0.86	0.03
	1980	100.00	92.33	5.42	2.12	0.13
	1985	100.00	88.69	7.25	3.74	0.32
Simulation II	1970	100.00	98.27	1.36	0.37	0.01
	1975	100.00	95.65	3.46	0.86	0.03
	1980	100.00	90.51	7.97	1.39	0.13
	1985	100.00	84.16	13.77	1.77	0.30
Simulation III	1970	100.00	98.27	1.36	0.37	0.01
	1975	100.00	95.65	3.46	0.86	0.03
	1980	100.00	89.89	7.92	2.07	0.13
	1985	100.00	82.69	13.53	3.48	0.30
Simulation IV	1970	100.00	98.27	1.36	0.37	0.01
	1975	100.00	95.65	3.46	0.86	0.03
	1980	100.00	87.09	5.11	7.35	0.45
	1985	100.00	76.31	6.24	16.08	1.38

TABLE III-32
United States
Projection of Labor Force, by Occupation, Race, and Sex, 1970-1985

Chemical Engineering	Year	Total	White Male	White Female	Black Male	Black Female
Simulation I	1970	47,079	46,380	450	227	22
	1975	64,468	63,341	761	353	14
	1980	84,776	82,489	1,528	735	25
	1985	107,229	102,990	2,621	1,554.	64
Simulation II	1970	47,079	46,380	450	227	22
	1975	64,468	·63,341	761	353	14
	1980	85,028	82,489	1,880	636	25
	1985	108,305	102,990	4,173	1,079	64
Simulation III	1970	47,079	46,380	450	227	22
	1975	64,468	63,341	761	353	14
	1980	85,128	82,489	1,880	735	25
	1985	108,781	102,990.	4,173	1,554	64
Simulation IV	1970	·47,079	46,380	450	227	22
	1975	64,468	63,341	761	353	14
	1980	85,609	82,409	1,528	1,529	64
	1985	111,243	102,990	2,621	5,356	276

Percentage Distribution of Projection of Labor Force, by Occupation, Race, and Sex, 1970-1985

Chemical Engineering	Year	Total	White Male	White Female	Black Male	Black Female
Simulation I	1970	100.00	98.52	0.96	0.48	0.05
	1975	100.00	98.25	1.18	0.55	0.02
	1980	100.00	97.30	1.80	0.87	0.03
	1985	100.00	96.05	2.44	1.45	0.06
Simulation II	1970	100.00	98.52	0.96	0.48	0.05
	1975	100.00	98.25	1.18	0.55	0.02
	1980	100.00	97.01	2.21	0.75	0.03
	1985	100.00	95.09	3.85	1.00	0.06
Simulation III	1970	100.00	98.52	0.96	0.48	0.05
	1975	100.00	98.25	1.18	0.55	0.02
	1980	100.00	96.90	2.21	0.86	0.03
	1985	100.00	94.68	3.84	1.43	0.06
Simulation IV	1970	100.00	98.52	0.96	0.48	0.05
	1975	100.00	98.25	1.18	0.55	0.02
	1980	100.00	96.36	·1.78	1.79	0.07
	1985	100.00	92.58	2.36.	4.81	0.25

trical engineering is that, of all the engineering disciplines, it has the highest representation of blacks among its new entrants and in its labor force. The doubling of the numbers of black graduates called for in Simulation I produces a level of black representation in the new entrants pool at about 9.1 percent in 1985 (Table III-33). When compared to the base line projections in Table III-19, the 9.1 percent representation level is 10 times the level experienced in 1970 and 190 percent of the 1985 base line projection. Achieving the ME[3] goal of a 10-fold increase in black graduates (Simulation IV) would mean a 1985 new entrants pool that would be 33 percent black (Table III-33) and 9.6 percent participation in the electrical engineering labor force (Table III-34).

The base line projections for women showed a net decline in female representation in the associated labor force. Simulation II results indicate a doubling of the number of degrees awarded to women would produce a 1985 entrants pool with female representation at 5.5 percent (Table III-33) and female participation in the electrical engineering labor force at 1.6 percent in 1985 (Table III-34).

Mechanical Engineering. The effects of the 4 simulations on the composition of new entrants to the mechanical engineering labor force are shown in Table III-35, and the resultant labor force projections are provided in Table III-36. If the numbers of black and/or female degree recipients are doubled, as dictated by Simulation I and Simulation II, the proportion of new entrants claimed by blacks would be 7.7 percent in 1985, and the corresponding representation level achieved by women would be 4.3 percent. If these results were attained, black participation in the mechanical engineering labor force would reach 2.6 percent in 1985, an addition of 0.8 percentage points to the 1985 base line labor force projections enumerated in Table III-23 and 2.0 percentage points above the 1970 level of black penetration.

The base line projections for women in the labor force indicated no net gain in participation from the 1970 level of 0.8 percent. A doubling of women mechanical engineering graduates produces an increase in female participation of 0.4 percentage points or a 1985 female representation level of 1.2 percent.

If the numbers of black graduates were increased 10-fold by 1985, as required in Simulation IV, blacks would make up almost 30 percent of the new entrants pool in that year. Associated with the 10-fold increase in black graduates is a 1985 mechanical engineering labor force that would be 8.6 percent black.

TABLE III-33
United States
New Labor Force Entrants, by Occupation,
Race, and Sex, 1970-1985

Electrical Engineering	Year	Total	White		Black	
			Male	Female	Male.	Female
Simulation I	1970	14,383	14,170	82	130	1
	1975	12,078	11,659	163	252	3
	1980	14,407	13,381	289	722	15
	1985	14,743	13,025	380	1,301	36
Simulation II	1970	14,383	14,170	82	130	1
	1975	12,078	11,659	163	252	3
	1980	14,310	13,381	433	481	15
	1985	14,472	13,025	761	651	36
Simulation III	1970	14,383	14,170	82	130	1
	1975	12,078	11,659	163	252	3
	1980	14,551	13,381	433	722	15
	1985	15,123	13,025	761	1,301	36
Simulation IV	1970	14,383	14,170	82	130	1
	1975	12,078	11,659	163	252	3
	1980	16,372	13,381	289	2,648	54
	1985	20,091	13,025	380	6,505	180

Percentage Distribution of New Labor Force Entrants,
by Occupation, Race, and Sex, 1970-1985

Electrical Engineering	Year	Total	White		Black	
			Male	Female	Male	Female
Simulation I	1970	100.00	98.52	0.57	0.90	0.01
	1975	100.00	96.53	1.35	2.09	0.03
	1980	100.00	92.88	2.00	5.01	0.10
	1985	100.00	88.35	2.58	8.82	0.24
Simulation II	1970	100.00	98.52	0.57	0.90	0.01
	1975	100.00	96.53	1.35	2.09	0.03
	1980	100.00	93.51	3.03	3.36	0.10
	1985	100.00	90.00	5.26	4.49	0.25
Simulation III	1970	100.00	98.52	0.57	0.90	0.01
	1975	100.00	96.53	1.35	2.09	0.03
	1980	100.00	91.96	2.98	4.96	0.10
	1985	100.00	86.13	5.03	8.60	0.24
Simulation IV	1970	100.00	98.52	0.57	0.90	0.01
	1975	100.00	96.53	1.35	2.09	0.03
	1980	100.00	81.73	1.76	16.17	0.33
	1985	100.00	64.83	1.89	32.38	0.90

The Availability of Minorities and Women

TABLE III-34
United States
Projection of Labor Force, by Occupation,
Race, and Sex, 1970-1985

Electrical Engineering	Year	Total	White		Black	
			Male	Female	Male	Female
Simulation I	1970	175,820	171,300	2,280	2,219	21
	1975	231,946	226,383	2,316	3,219	28
	1980	285,286	276,760	2,783	5,675	68
	1985.	342,273	327,694	3,603	10,793	182
Simulation II	1970	175,820	171,300	2,280	2,219	21
	1975	231,946	226,383	2,316	3,219	28
	1980	285,015	276,760	3,141	·5,046	68
	1985	340,836	327,694	5,145	7,815	182
Simulation III	1970	175,820	171,300	2,280	2,219	21
	1975	231,946	226,383	2,316	3,219	28
	1980	285,644	276,760	3,141	5,675	68
	1985	343,814	327,694	5,145	10,793·	182
Simulation IV	1970	175,820	171,300	2,280	2,219	21
	1975	231,946	226,383	2,316	3,219	28
	1980	290,413	276,760	2,783	10,711	160
	1985	366,629	327,694	3,603	34,617	715

Percentage Distribution of Projection of Labor Force,
by Occupation, Race, and Sex, 1970-1985

Electrical Engineering	Year	Total	White		Black	
			Male	Female	Male	Female
Simulation I	1970	100.00	97.43	1.30	1.26	0.01
	1975	100.00	97.60	1.00	1.39	0.01
	1980	100.00	97.01	0.98	1.99	0.02
	1985	100.00	95.74	1.05	3.15	0.05
Simulation II	1970	100.00	97.43	1.30	1.26	0.01
	1975	100.00	97.60	1.00	1.39	0.01
	1980	100.00	97.10	1.10	1.77	0.02
	1985	100.00	96.14	1.51	2.29	0.05
Simulation III	1970	100.00	97.43	1.30	1.26	0.01
	1975	100.00	97.60	1.00	1.39	0.01
	1980	100.00	96.89	1.10	1.99	0.02
	1985	100.00	95.31	1.50	3.14	0.05
Simulation IV	1970	100.00	97.43	1.30	1.26	0.01
	1975	100.00	97.60	1.00	1.39	0.01
	1980	100.00	95.30	0.96	3.69	0.05
	1985	100.00	89.38	0.98	9.44	0.19

TABLE III-35
United States
*New Labor Force Entrants, by Occupation,
Race, and Sex, 1970-1985*

Mechanical Engineering	Year	Total	White		Black	
			Male	Female	Male	Female
Simulation I	1970	9,900	9,780	41	79	0
	1975	7,782	7,561	81	138	2
	1980	9,956	9,368	155	427	7
	1985	10,160	9,167	208	768·	17
Simulation II	1970	9,900	9,780	41.	79	0
	1975	7,782	7,561	81	138	2
	1980	9,892	9,368	232	284	7
	1985	9,983	9,167	416	384	17
Simulation III	1970	9,900	9,780	41	79	0
	1975	7,782	7,561	81	138	2
	1980·	10,034	9,368	232	427	7
	1985	10,367	9,167	416	768	17
Simulation IV	1970	9,900	9,780	41	79	0
	1975	7,782	7,561	81	138	2
	1980	11,112	9,368	155	1,564	25
	1985	13,300	9,167	208	3,841	85

*Percentage Distribution of New Labor Force Entrants,
by Occupation, Race, and Sex, 1970-1985*

Mechanical Engineering	Year	Total	White		Black	
			Male	Female	Male	Female
Simulation I	1970	100.00	98.79	0.41	0.80	0.00
	1975	100.00	97.16	1.05	1.78	0.02
	1980	100.00	94.09	1.55	4.28	0.07
	1985	100.00	90.23	2.05	7.56	0.17
Simulation II	1970	100.00	98.79	0.41	0.80	0.00
	1975	100.00	97.16	1.05	1.78	0.02
	1980	100.00	94.71	2.34	2.88	0.07
	1985	100.00	91.82	4.16	3.85	0.17
Simulation III	1970	100.00	98.79	0.41	0.80	0.00
	1975	100.00	97.16	1.05	1.78	0.02
	1980	100.00	93.37	2.31	4.25	0.07
	1985	100.00	88.42	4.01	7.41	0.16
Simulation IV	1970	100.00	98.79	0.41	0.80	0.00
	1975	100.00	97.16	1.05	1.78	0.02
	1980	100.00	84.31	1.39	14.08	0.23
	1985	100.00	68.92	1.56	28.88	0.64

TABLE III-36
United States
Projection of Labor Force, by Occupation,
Race, and Sex, 1970-1985

Mechanical Engineering	Year	Total	White Male	White Female	Black Male	Black Female
Simulation I	1970	107,413	105,910	852	651	0
	1975	142,035	139,927	913	1,191	4
	1980	176,688	172,856	1,223	2,587	22
	1985	213,973	206,679	1,726	5,498	70
Simulation II	1970	107,413	105,910	852	651	0
	1975	142,035	139,927	913	1,191	4
	1980	176,511	172,856	1,412	2,220	22
	1985	213,077	206,679	2,554	3,774	70
Simulation III	1970	107,413	105,910	852	651	0
	1975	142,035	139,927	913	1,191	4
	1980	176,878	172,856	1,412	2,587	22
	1985	214,807	206,679	2,554	5,498	70
Simulation IV	1970	107,413	105,910	852	651	0
	1975	142,035	139,927	913	1,191	4
	1980	179,665	172,856	1,223	5,523	63
	1985	227,995	206,679	1,726	19,292	298

Percentage Distribution of Projection of Labor Force,
by Occupation, Race, and Sex, 1970-1985

Mechanical Engineering	Year	Total	White Male	White Female	Black Male	Black Female
Simulation I	1970	100.00	98.60	0.79	0.61	0.00
	1975	100.00	98.52	0.64	0.84	0.00
	1980	100.00	97.83	0.69	1.46	0.01
	1985	100.00	96.59	0.81	2.57	0.03
Simulation II	1970	100.00	98.60	0.79	0.61	0.00
	1975	100.00	98.52	0.64	0.84	0.00
	1980	100.00	97.93	0.80	1.26	0.01
	1985	100.00	97.00	1.20	1.77	0.03
Simulation III	1970	100.00	98.60	0.79	0.61	0.00
	1975	100.00	98.52	0.64	0.84	0.00
	1980	100.00	97.73	0.80	1.46	0.01
	1985	100.00	96.22	1.19	2.56	0.03
Simulation IV	1970	100.00	98.60	0.79	0.61	0.00
	1975	100.00	98.52	0.64	0.84	0.00
	1980	100.00	96.21	0.68	3.07	0.03
	1985	100.00	90.65	0.76	8.46	0.13

Other Engineering. The projections of new entrants and the projections of the labor force resulting from the 4 simulations for the other engineering subfield are provided in Tables III-37 and III-38. When compared to the base line projections in Tables III-25 and III-26, the changes in the level of representation in the new entrants pool and in participation in the labor force are similar to the findings for the total engineering group.

A doubling of black and/or female degree earners by 1985 would yield a new entrants pool in that year of about 9.8 percent women and 6.3 percent blacks. The comparable figures in 1970 were 1.1 percent for women and 0.6 percent for blacks. The resultant change in the composition in the labor force is small. Women comprised 1.2 percent of the labor force in 1970 and would comprise 2.7 percent in 1985. The 1985 level of 2.7 percent is 0.9 percentage points above the 1985 base line projection. Black participation would increase from 1.0 percent in 1970 to 2.3 percent in 1985, which is a 0.6 percentage point addition to the base line projection for that year. A 10-fold increase in the number of black graduates results in 25.1 percent black representation among new labor force entrants and 7.1 percent level of black participation in the labor force.

TABLE III-37
United States
New Labor Force Entrants, by Occupation,
Race, and Sex, 1970-1985

Other Engineering	Year	Total	White Male	White Female	Black Male	Black Female
Simulation I	1970	19,353	19,027	206	119	1
	1975	22,189	21,307	557	317	8
	1980	25,015	23,212	918	858	32
	1985	26,198	23,280	1,272	1,563	83
Simulation II	1970	19,353	19,027	206	119	1
	1975	22,189	21,307	557	317	8
	1980	25,190	23,212	1,377	568	32
	1985	26,689	23,280	2,545	781	83
Simulation III	1970	19,353	19,027	206	119	1
	1975	22,189	21,307	557	317	8
	1980	25,474	23,212	1,377	852	32
	1985	27,470	23,280	2,545	1,563	83
Simulation IV	1970	19,353	19,026	206	119	1
	1975	22,189	21,307	557	317	8
	1980	27,373	23,212	918	3,123	119
	1985	32,780	23,280	1,272	7,815	413

Percentage Distribution of New Labor Force Entrants,
by Occupation, Race, and Sex, 1970-1985

Other Engineering	Year	Total	White Male	White Female	Black Male	Black Female
Simulation I	1970	100.00	98.31	1.07	0.62	0.01
	1975	100.00	96.02	2.51	1.43	0.04
	1980	100.00	92.80	3:67	3.40	0.13
	1985	100.00	88.86	4.86	5.97	0.32
Simulation II	1970	100.00	98.31	1.07	0.62	0.01
	1975	100.00	96.02	2.51	1.43	0.04
	1980	100.00	92.15	5.47	2.25	0.13
	1985	100.00	87.23	9.53	2.93	0.31
Simulation III	1970	100.00	98.31	1.07	0.62	0.01
	1975	100.00	96.02	2.51	1.43	0.04
	1980	100.00	91.12	5.41	3.34	0.13
	1985	100.00	84.75	9.26	5.69	0.30
Simulation IV	1970	100.00	98.31	1.07	0.62	0.01
	1975	100.00	96.02	2.51	1.42	0.04
	1980	100.00	84.80	3.35	11.41	0.43
	1985	100.00	71.02	3.88	23.84	1.26

TABLE III-38
United States
Projection of Labor Force, by Occupation,
Race, and Sex, 1970-1985

Other Engineering	Year	Total	White		Black	
			Male	Female	Male	Female
Simulation I	1970	311,689	304,971	3,681	2,922	115
	1975	391,686	383,118	4,487	3,974	107
	1980	476,934	463,239	6,700	6,820	175
	1985	.567,632	544,381	10,038	12,805	409
Simulation II .	.1970	311,689	304,971	.3,681	2,922	115
	1975	391,686	383,118	4,487	3,974	107
	1980	477,325	463,239	7,832	6;079	175
	1985	569,151	544,381	15,082	9,280	409
Simulation III	1970	311,689	304,971	3,681	2,922	115
	1975	391,686	383,118	4,487	3,974	107
	1980	478,066	463,239	7,832	6,820	175
	1985	572,676	544,381	15,082	12,805	409
Simulation IV	1970	311,689	304,971	3,681	2,922	115
	1975	391,686	383,118	4,487	3,974	107
	1980	483,059	463,239	6,700	12,749	371
	1985	.596,988	.544,381	10,038	41,005	1,564

Percentage Distribution of Projection of Labor Force,
by Occupation, Race, and Sex, 1970-1985

Other Engineering	Year	Total	White		Black	
			Male	Female	Male	Female
Simulation I	1970	100.00	97.84	1.18	0.94	0.04
	1975	100.00	97.81	1.15	1.01	0.03
	1980	100.00	97.13	1.40	1.43	0.04
	1985	100.00	95.90	1.77	2.26	0.07
Simulation II	1970	100.00	97.84	1.18	0.94	0.04
	1975	100.00	97.81	1.15	1.01	0.03
	1980	100.00	97.05	1.64	1.27	0.04
	1985	100.00	95.65	2.65	1.63	0.07
Simulation III	1970	100.00	97.84	1.18	0.94	0.04
	1975	100.00	97.81	1.15	1.01	0.03
	1980	100.00	96.90	1.64	1.43	0.04
	1985	100.00	95.06	2.63	2.24	0.07
Simulation IV	1970	100.00	97.84	1.18	0.94	0.04
	1975	100.00	97.81	1.15	1.01	0.03
	1980	100.00	95.90	1.39	2.64	0.08
	1985	100.00	91.19	1.68	6.87	0.26

Minorities and Women in Accountancy

The evolution of business organizations during the last century, with their attendant complexities, has led to the increased utilization of professionally trained and educated individuals in the functional areas of the firm and in administrative positions. A major source of such professional managers has been colleges of business administration.

The following two chapters will examine the status of minorities and women in accounting and other related business and managerial occupations by reviewing the relevant literature and implementing the labor supply process model to assess the trends in minority and female participation in the future. Accountants are treated in a separate chapter because of the longevity of their profession.

Background

Because of the increased use of accounting information in business management, the greater use of accounting services by small business organizations, the complex and changing tax systems, and the growth in the size and number of business corporations required to provide financial reports to their stockholders, the accounting profession has grown rapidly in recent years. Between 1945 and 1976 the membership of the American Institute of Certified Public Accountants (AICPA) increased from 9,000 to over 120,000.[1] Despite the recent growth in the accounting profession, however, the number of minorities and women in the field is still small. Although women represent 22 percent of all persons working as accountants, only 3 percent of the Certified Public Accountants (CPAs) in this country are women.[2]

---

[1] Gary John Previts, "The Accountant in our History: A Bicentennial Overview," *Journal of Accountancy*, Vol. 142 (July 1976), p. 50.

[2] *Occupational Outlook Handbook: 1974-75 Edition*, Bulletin 1785 (Washington, D.C.: Government Printing Office, 1974), p. 128.

Moreover, blacks currently make up only 0.3 percent of the total number of CPAs in the United States.[3]

In his 1968 inaugural address, Ralph Kent, President of AICPA, noted that the time had come to integrate the CPA profession in fact and not merely in ideal. The next year the Institute established a Committee for Recruitment from Disadvantaged Groups to achieve integration in the accounting profession. In the early 1970s the Committee was renamed and is now known as the Committee on Minority Recruitment & Equal Opportunity.

The Committee is currently involved with student seminars to expose students to the opportunities available in the accounting profession; CPA firm seminars to encourage the accounting employers in public accounting to recruit, to hire, and to promote minorities and women; and scholarship programs to provide financial assistance for minority accounting students. Through the Committee's internship program, firms are encouraged to give summer jobs to black college juniors who have completed twelve to fifteen hours of accounting courses. The Committee has also initiated fund-raising programs to expand libraries, to increase graduate fellowships, and to improve black accounting faculties.[4]

AICPA's Committee on Doctoral Fellows and Visiting Scholars is working with the American Accounting Association (AAA) to encourage black accounting faculty members from predominantly black colleges to return to school for a Ph.D. Through this program the black faculty member receives a fellowship to help finance his study, and another professor is brought to the college to assume the teaching obligations of the fellowship recipient during his absence.

Census Data

Census data on experienced accountants from 1940 to 1970 are shown in Table IV-1. Numbers from the 1940 Census are inflated because the figures include bookkeepers, cashiers, and ticket agents.

---

[3] Bert N. Mitchell, "The Status of the Black CPA—An Update," *Journal of Accountancy*, Vol. 141 (May 1976), p. 52.

[4] Marylin Bender, "Black C.P.A.'s a Rare Breed," *New York Times*, October 18, 1970, sec. 3, p. 3.

TABLE IV-1

Number of Experienced Civilian Accountants by Sex and Race,
1940-1970

Sex and Race	1940	1950	1960	1970
Accountants Total[a]	957,100	383,490	474,904	720,617
Male Accountants	478,480	326,520	396,106	536,900
White	476,580	325,230	390,596	519,911
Negro	—	960	2,417	9,064
Other Races	1,900[b]	330	3,093	7,925
Male Accountants with 4 or More Years of College	74,000	114,690	172,581	283,866
White	73,600	114,150	169,933	—
Nonwhite	400	540	2,648	4,148[c]
Female Accountants	478,620	56,970	78,798	183,717
White	475,700	56,460	76,931	173,071
Negro	2,920[b]	450	1,217	7,526
Other Races	—	60	650	3,120
Female Accountants with 4 or More Years of College	17,560	7,470	8,936	25,170
White	17,240	7,290	8,573	—
Nonwhite	320	180	363	1,159[c]

Sources: *Sixteenth Census of the United States: 1940 Population, The Labor Force, Occupational Characteristics* (Washington, D.C.: Government Printing Office, 1943), pp. 59-70 *passim*, Table 3.
United States Census of Population 1950, Occupational Characteristics, P-E No. 1B (Washington, D.C.: Government Printing Office, 1956), pp. 29, 107, 115, Tables 3, 10, 11.
United States Census of Population 1960, Occupational Characteristics, PC(2)-7A (Washington, D.C.: U.S. Department of Commerce, 1961), pp. 21, 116, 123, 130, 137, Tables 3, 9, 10.
1970 Census of Population Subject Report, Occupational Characteristics, PC(2)-7A (Washington, D.C.: U.S. Department of Commerce, 1973), pp. 12, 59, 73, 87, 101, Tables 2, 5, 6.

[a] Data for 1940 includes bookkeepers, cashiers, and ticket agents.
[b] Only nonwhite data available.
[c] Only Negro data available.

Since Census occupational data are self-reported by individuals or by members of their families, there is reason to question their accuracy. Furthermore, because occupational data reported in the 1970 Census are based on a 5 percent sample of the population, the sampling errors may be substantial.

BLACKS

Of the estimated 150,000 CPAs in the United States 450 are black, according to a 1976 survey of black CPAs. Although that number of black CPAs may look small in comparison to the total, it represents more than twice the number of black CPAs identified in 1969.[5]

Education, Recruitment, and Employment of Black Accountants

Predominantly black colleges in the South produce the majority of all black accounting graduates. Because so few blacks are majoring in accounting at colleges in other regions, many accounting firms are now concentrating their black recruiting efforts primarily at the southern colleges. The number of accounting graduates from Southern University, the largest of the traditionally black schools, increased from nine students in 1964 to seventy-seven students in 1972. In 1971 Southern's accounting graduates peaked at eighty-three, but then the accounting department decided to restrict the size of classes for fear quality would suffer if expansion continued at such a rapid rate.

It is not unusual for major accounting firms to lose some of their best black prospects after they have been recruited and have worked in the firm for a short time. Blacks most frequently leave because of exceptional outside offers they receive, their desire to return to school, or their interest in entering a different career.

The 1970 AICPA survey showed 13 black CPAs in the nation's major public accounting firms, but by 1972 that number had increased to 41. The total number of black professionals employed in major accounting firms increased from 197 in 1969 to 764 in 1972.[6] The 1975 survey of these firms showed 118 black CPAs and 1,026 black professionals employed by major accounting firms.[7]

---

[5] Mitchell, "The Status of the Black CPA—An Update," p. 52.

[6] William R. Gifford, "Black Accountants," *Price Waterhouse & Company Review*, Vol. 18 (1973), p. 44.

[7] Information supplied by the American Institute of Certified Public Accountants, New York.

Mitchell Surveys of Black CPAs: 1968 and 1976

The first survey to determine the representation of blacks in the CPA profession, sponsored by the Ford Foundation, was conducted from November 1968 through May 1969 by Bert N. Mitchell. The 1968 survey results showed that of the 100,000 CPAs in the United States, 150 CPAs were black. This means that in 1968 blacks represented 0.15 percent of the total number of CPAs.

Results of the survey questionnaire showed that the 52 accounting firms responding employed 3,139 partners, of whom 1 was black. Black CPAs were found to be concentrated in large urban centers with only Illinois, New York, and California having more than 10. During recent years the rate of growth in the number of black CPAs has been less than 20 per year. The reason most consistently mentioned by respondents to the questionnaire as a cause for the lack of blacks' participation in accounting was that black college students were unaware of opportunities in the profession.[8]

Mitchell's second survey of black CPAs was concluded in 1976. It showed that there are 450 black CPAs among the estimated 150,000 CPAs in the United States which means that black CPAs represented 0.3 percent of the total number of CPA professionals.

The data from this second survey showed that black CPAs have increased at a much more rapid rate over the last 7 years than in previous periods. Black women are entering the profession at a faster rate than black men. Black women represented 8.8 percent of the identified black CPAs in the 1968 survey and 11.5 percent of those identified in the 1976 survey.

Responses to Mitchell's questionnaire indicated that 60 percent of black CPAs are in public practice, 13 percent in teaching, 11 percent in government accounting, and 10 percent in commercial enterprises. Public accounting has shown the most significant gain in the employment of black CPAs: in 1968 only 30 percent of the black CPAs were working in public accounting, as compared to 60 percent in 1976. While in 1968 only 3 states had more than 10 black CPAs, now 13 states have more than 10. Illinois, New York, and California represented 55 percent of the black CPAs in 1968, and now they account for 45 percent of the total number of black CPAs.[9]

---

[8] Bert N. Mitchell, "The Black Minority in the CPA Profession," *Journal of Accountancy*, Vol. 128 (October 1969), pp. 41-45.

[9] Mitchell, "The Status of the Black CPA—An Update," pp. 53-55.

Even though the percentage increase of blacks in the CPA profession has been greater than most other professions because of the small base from which it is measured, the percentage representation of blacks in the CPA profession still falls behind black representation in other key occupations such as medicine and law.

OTHER MINORITIES

The 1975 report issued by AICPA on the number of professionals in major accounting firms showed 2,128 minority accounting professionals employed by United States public accounting firms. The total of 2,128 included 583 Orientals, 497 Spanish-surnamed Americans, 22 American Indians, and 1,026 black professionals who represented the largest single minority group of professionals working in the major accounting firms. Orientals with a total of 167 led as the minority group having the largest number of CPAs employed by firms.[10]

Minority groups and their percentage increases in CPA positions between 1969 and 1972 were: blacks, 288 percent; Orientals, 80 percent; American Indians, 80 percent; and Spanish-surnamed Americans, 165 percent.[11] The percentage increases for minority professionals in accounting are large because of the small base numbers from which they are computed. The absolute numbers of minority professionals in accounting and their representation in the accounting labor force are still very small.

American Assembly of Collegiate Schools of Business (AACSB) Survey

Between August 1974 and January 1975, the AACSB conducted a survey of its member schools to determine the participation of minority-group members in business study. The results for accounting are shown in Tables IV-2 and IV-3. The absolute numbers for enrollments and degrees awarded are not accurate totals since the survey did not include all business schools. Nevertheless, the proportion of minority-group members identified through the AACSB survey does give a good indication of the participation of minorities in accounting.

----

[10] Information supplied by the Institute of Certified Public Accountants, New York.

[11] "CPA Hiring of Minority Professionals up 264 Percent," *Journal of Accountancy*, Vol. 135 (February 1973), p. 23.

TABLE IV-2
Accounting Enrollment in AACSB Member Schools for 1973-74

Race	Undergraduate		Master		Doctoral	
	Number	Percent of Total	Number	Percent of Total	Number	Percent of Total
Total Accounting Enrollment	29,838	100.0	2,560	100.0	395	100.0
American Caucasians	26,202	87.8	2,228	87.0	327	82.8
American Indians	85	0.3	1	0.0	—	—
American Negroes	1,622	5.4	63	2.5	3	0.8
American Orientals	553	1.9	59	2.3	1	0.2
Spanish Americans	882	2.9	27	1.1	1	0.2
Foreign Students	494	1.7	182	7.1	63	16.0

Source: *1974 Minority Report: Student Enrollments and Faculty Distribution* (St. Louis, Missouri: American Assembly of Collegiate Schools of Business, n.d.), pp. iii, iv, v, Tables I, II, III.

TABLE IV-3

Accounting Degrees Awarded by AACSB Member Schools for 1973-74

Race	Undergraduate		Master		Doctoral	
	Number	Percent of Total	Number	Percent of Total	Number	Percent of Total
Total Accounting Degrees	8,724	100.0	1,252	100.0	157	100.0
American Caucasians	8,047	92.2	1,132	90.4	137	87.3
American Indians	28	0.3	1	0.1	—	—
American Negroes	257	2.9	36	2.9	1	0.6
American Orientals	82	0.9	13	1.0	—	—
Spanish Americans	178	2.0	8	0.6	1	0.6
Foreign Students	132	1.6	62	4.9	18	11.5

Source: *1974 Minority Report: Student Enrollments and Faculty Distribution.* (St. Louis, Missouri: American Assembly of Collegiate Schools of Business, n.d.), pp. vii, viii, ix, Tables IV, V, VI.

WOMEN

Very little information is available regarding the participation of women in the accounting profession. It is estimated in the *Occupational Outlook Handbook*, 1974-75 edition, that women represented 22 percent of all accountants and 3 percent of all CPAs.[12]

Data from the National Center for Educational Statistics (NCES) showed that between 1968-69 and 1974-75, the percentage of women receiving undergraduate degrees in accounting increased from 7.9 percent to 17.7 percent. Table IV-4 lists the number of degrees awarded to women in accounting by degree level between 1968-69 and 1974-75.

According to the American Woman's Society of Certified Public Accountants (AWSCPA), the first woman to receive a CPA certificate was Christine Ross Barker of New York State in 1899. As of May 1976 a total of 9,500 women had passed the CPA exam since its inception in December 1896. Not all of the total can be counted as CPAs, however, since most of these women have only recently passed the exam and are currently fulfilling the experience requirement necessary before receiving the CPA certificate.[13]

CURRENT PROGRAMS

The AICPA, various state accounting societies, and accounting firms have produced the leadership and opportunity for much of the growth that has occurred in the accounting profession recently. These groups have worked closely with many of the predominantly black colleges and their faculties in helping them upgrade the quality of their accounting curricula. AICPA's Committee on Recruitment & Equal Opportunity has raised over $1.2 million primarily from within the profession to provide financial aid for minority group students studying accounting in the United States.[14]

Accounting firms are involved in various activities relating to black education through student internship programs, participation of their staff members in professional accounting societies,

---

[12] *Occupational Outlook Handbook*, p. 128.

[13] Telephone interview with Barbara Rausch, American Woman's Society of Certified Public Accountants, December 17, 1976.

[14] Mitchell, "The Status of the Black CPA," p. 54.

TABLE IV-4

Degrees Awarded to Women in Accounting,
1968-69 through 1974-75

Year	Bachelor		Master		Doctoral	
	Number	Percent of Total	Number	Percent of Total	Number	Percent of Total
1968-69	1,572	7.9	79	5.9	2	5.0
1969-70	1,840	8.7	79	7.3	3	5.4
1970-71	2,063	9.3	103	9.4	3	4.9
1971-72	2,494	10.1	108	7.8	—	—
1972-73	3,237	11.6	141	8.7	1	1.2
1973-74	4,028	13.7	188	10.5	4	5.7
1974-75	5,515	17.7	279	12.5	4	6.7

Source: Information supplied by the National Center for Educational Statistics, Washington, D.C.

faculty fellowship programs, and loan of their staff members to black schools. The faculty fellowship programs that are sponsored by some accounting firms expose accounting faculty members to the profession and, as a result, help them expand and improve the curricula at their colleges when they return.[15]

PREDICTING THE NUMBERS OF MINORITIES AND WOMEN IN ACCOUNTING

The review of the minority and female experience in the accounting profession indicates a rather limited attachment of blacks to the profession while material numbers of women are identified as accountants, although not certified as public accountants. The labor supply model was implemented to examine the racial and sexual composition of the accountant labor force in the coming years. Four projections of new labor force entrants and the resulting accountant labor force were developed for the 1970 to 1985 period. The first projection is a base line forecast presented in Table IV-5, which represents the best available data. Three simulations were implemented in order to show the effect of altering the racial and sexual distributions of degree recipients on the labor supply. In summary, the analysis indicates that black representation will increase very slowly in the next several years while women are in a better position because of their relative status in the initial supply base and among degree earners.

Base Line Projections

The input data used to develop the projections for accountants is shown in Table IV-5 with the base line projections of new entrants and the labor force presented in Table IV-6 and Table IV-7. Information on the racial composition of accounting degree earners is limited to a survey conducted by the American Assembly of Collegiate Schools of Business (AACSB), which provides the data necessary for this exercise for only 2 years, 1973-74 and 1974-75.[16] Because of this data limitation, the alternative projections (simulations) take on more importance in

---

[15] Gifford, "Black Accountants," p. 52.

[16] *Minority Report: Student Enrollments and Faculty Distribution* (St. Louis: American Assembly of Collegiate Schools of Business, n.d.), pp. vii-ix, 117-140.

TABLE IV-5
Input Data for Simulation -/2
of Accountants in the Labor Force to 1985 2 0

	MALE	FEMALE
SEPARATION RATE	WHITE	
1970	0.0211	0.0590
1985	0.0192	0.0618
	BLACK	
1970	0.0091	0.0630
1985	0.0079	0.0650
ENTRY RATE		
BACHELOR	0.8000	0.8000
MASTER	0.9000	0.9000
DOCTOR	1.0000	1.0000
SUPPLY BASE − 1970		
TOTAL	283866	25170
BLACK	4148	1159

	DEGREES AWARDED	
	% FEMALE	% BLACK
BACHELOR		
1969	7.85	0.80
1970	8.69	0.90
1971	9.33	1.20
1972	10.06	1.70
1973	11.58	2.30
1974	13.73	2.97
1975	17.72	4.84
MASTER		
1969	5.93	1.40
1970	7.29	1.80
1971	9.39	2.20
1972	7.84	2.40
1973	8.70	2.60
1974	10.46	2.87
1975	12.53	2.97
DOCTOR		
1969	5.00	0.07
1970	5.36	0.10
1971	4.92	0.10
1972	0.00	0.30
1973	1.21	0.45
1974	5.71	0.64
1975	6.67	1.75

TABLE IV-6
United States
New Labor Force Entrants, by Occupation,
Race, and Sex, 1970 to 1985

ACCOUNTANCY

YEAR	TOTAL	WHITE		BLACK	
		MALE	FEMALE	MALE	FEMALE
1970	17977	16317	1494	153	14
1971	18727	16713	1756	234	25
1972	21131	18540	2184	364	43
1973	23898	20502	2795	528	73
1974	25162	21016	3358	679	109
1975	27892	22315	4378	1001	199
1976	30155	23957	4848	1121	229
1977	31448	24427	5431	1298	291
1978	32625	24776	6012	1475	362
1979	33966	25226	6635	1662	442
1980	34598	25125	7133	1817	523
1981	35124	24940	7611	1965	608
1982	35889	24915	8143	2126	705
1983	36309	24646	8596	2264	802
1984	36318	24106	8945	2373	895
1985	36235	23514	9261	2471	990

Percentage Distribution of
New Labor Force Entrants, by Occupation,
Race, and Sex, 1970-1985

ACCOUNTANCY

YEAR	TOTAL	WHITE		BLACK	
		MALE	FEMALE	MALE	FEMALE
1970	100.00	90.76	8.31	0.85	0.08
1971	100.00	89.24	9.38	1.25	0.13
1972	100.00	87.74	10.34	1.72	0.20
1973	100.00	85.79	11.70	2.21	0.30
1974	100.00	83.52	13.34	2.70	0.43
1975	100.00	80.00	15.69	3.59	0.71
1976	100.00	79.45	16.08	3.72	0.76
1977	100.00	77.67	17.27	4.13	0.93
1978	100.00	75.94	18.43	4.52	1.11
1979	100.00	74.27	19.54	4.89	1.30
1980	100.00	72.62	20.62	5.25	1.51
1981	100.00	71.01	21.67	5.60	1.73
1982	100.00	69.42	22.69	5.92	1.96
1983	100.00	67.88	23.68	6.24	2.21
1984	100.00	66.37	24.63	6.53	2.46
1985	100.00	64.89	25.56	6.82	2.73

TABLE IV-7
United States
Projection of Labor Force, by Occupation,
Race, and Sex, 1970 to 1985

ACCOUNTANCY

YEAR	TOTAL	WHITE		BLACK	
		MALE	FEMALE	MALE	FEMALE
1970	309036	279718	24011	4148	1159
1971	320365	290564	24346	4345	1110
1972	333885	303046	25085	4670	1083
1973	349900	317269	26386	5157	1087
1974	366837	331752	28167	5791	1127
1975	386129	347276	30856	6742	1255
1976	407228	364170	33850	7805	1403
1977	429117	381236	37240	9037	1605
1978	451653	398354	40999	10436	1864
1979	474973	415629	45146	12011	2187
1980	498340	432510	49531	13729	2569
1981	521638	448927	54118	15582	3011
1982	545102	465052	58947	17581	3522
1983	568374	480652	63922	19704	4096
1984	591042	495468	68928	21920	4725
1985	613024	509469	73929	24218	5408

Percentage Distribution of
Projection of Labor Force, by Occupation,
Race, and Sex, 1970 to 1985

ACCOUNTANCY

YEAR	TOTAL	WHITE		BLACK	
		MALE	FEMALE	MALE	FEMALE
1970	100.00	90.51	7.77	1.34	0.38
1971	100.00	90.70	7.60	1.36	0.35
1972	100.00	90.76	7.51	1.40	0.32
1973	100.00	90.67	7.54	1.47	0.31
1974	100.00	90.44	7.68	1.58	0.31
1975	100.00	89.94	7.99	1.75	0.32
1976	100.00	89.43	8.31	1.92	0.34
1977	100.00	88.84	8.68	2.11	0.37
1978	100.00	88.20	9.08	2.31	0.41
1979	100.00	87.51	9.50	2.53	0.46
1980	100.00	86.79	9.94	2.76	0.52
1981	100.00	86.06	10.37	2.99	0.58
1982	100.00	85.31	10.81	3.23	0.65
1983	100.00	84.57	11.25	3.47	0.72
1984	100.00	83.83	11.66	3.71	0.80
1985	100.00	83.11	12.06	3.95	0.88

this occupation than the others included in this study. The data set was completed by a simple linear extrapolation.

New labor force entrants in accountancy are expected to double from 1970 to 1985 with substantial changes in the racial and sexual composition of the new entrants. The female proportion of new accountants is estimated to increase from 8.4 percent in 1970 to 28.3 percent in 1985. New black accountants, who comprised slightly less than 1 percent of the total in 1970, will increase their representation approximately 10-fold by 1985 at 9.6 percent of new entrants.

The projections of the labor force, provided in Table IV-7, show how the large changes in new entrants are scaled down because of the large proportion of white males in the initial supply base. Female accountants will gain less than 5 percentage points in their participation in the labor force, increasing from 8.2 percent in 1970 to 13 percent in 1985. The 10-fold increase in black entrants translates into less than a 3-fold increase in labor force penetration, which represents a change from 1.7 percent black accountants in 1970 to 4.8 percent in 1985.

Sensitivity Analysis

Three alternative projections were developed by simulating the effects of changes in the racial and sexual composition of degree earners and calculating the resultant labor force. For the first simulation the number of black degree recipients was doubled by 1985, while the base line projection of degrees awarded to whites was maintained. The second simulation repeated the same procedure for female recipients. The third exercise doubled the number of degrees awarded to blacks and women by 1985, while the base number of white male awarded degrees was maintained.

Table IV-8 and Table IV-9 show the results of the first simulation. Doubling the number of degrees awarded to blacks yielded an increase of 5.3 percentage points in the proportion of black accountants, from 1970 to 1985, or an additional 2.2 percentage points over the base line projection for 1985. The impact on the Female Labor Force through black female degree recipients was minimal.

The results of the second simulation, which entailed a 100 percent increase in the number of female degree earners, are shown in Table IV-10 and Table IV-11. If these results were achieved, the percentage of females in the accountancy labor force would increase to 18.4 percent in 1985 from 8.2 percent

TABLE IV-8
United States
New Labor Force Entrants, by Occupation, Race, and Sex, 1970 to 1985

ACCOUNTANCY

YEAR	TOTAL	WHITE MALE	WHITE FEMALE	BLACK MALE	BLACK FEMALE
1970	17977	16317	1494	153	14
1971	18727	16713	1756	234	25
1972	21131	18540	2184	364	43
1973	23898	20502	2795	528	73
1974	25162	21016	3358	679	109
1975	27892	22315	4378	1001	199
1976	30290	23957	4848	1233	252
1977	31766	24427	5431	1558	350
1978	33176	24776	6012	1918	470
1979	34808	25226	6635	2327	.619
1980	35768	25125	7133	2726	784
1981	36668	24940	7611	3144	973
1982	37871	24915	8143	3614	1199
1983	38762	24646	8596	4076	1444
1984	39259	24106	8945	4508	1700
1985	39695	23514	9261	4942	1979

Percentage Distribution of
New Labor Force Entrants, by Occupation, Race, and Sex, 1970 to 1985

ACCOUNTANCY

YEAR	TOTAL	WHITE MALE	WHITE FEMALE	BLACK MALE	BLACK FEMALE
1970	100.00	90.76	8.31	0.85	0.08
1971	100.00	89.24	9.38	1.25	0.13
1972	100.00	87.74	10.34	1.72	0.20
1973	100.00	85.79	11.70	2.21	0.30
1974	100.00	83.52	13.34	2.70	0.43
1975	100.00	80.00	15.69	3.59	0.71
1976	100.00	79.09	16.01	4.07	0.83
1977	100.00	76.90	17.10	4.90	1.10
1978	100.00	74.68	18.12	5.78	1.42
1979	100.00	72.47	19.06	6.69	1.78
1980	100.00	70.24	19.94	7.62	2.19
1981	100.00	68.02	20.76	8.58	2.65
1982	100.00	65.79	21.50	9.54	3.16
1983	100.00	63.58	22.18	10.51	3.72
1984	100.00	61.40	22.78	11.48	4.33
1985	100.00	59.24	23.33	12.45	4.99

TABLE IV-9
United States
Projection of Labor Force, by Occupation,
Race, and Sex, 1970 to 1985

ACCOUNTANCY

YEAR	TOTAL	WHITE		BLACK	
		MALE	FEMALE	MALE	FEMALE
1970	309036	279718	24011	4148	1159
1971	320365	290564	24346	4345	1110
1972	333885	303046	25085	4670	1083
1973	349900	317269	26386	5157	1087
1974	366837	331752	28167	5791	1127
1975	386129	347276	30856	6742	1255
1976	407363	364170	33850	7917	1426
1977	429568	381236	37240	9408	1685
1978	452646	398354	40999	11246	2047
1979	476790	415629	45146	13480	2535
1980	501292	432510	49531	16094	3156
1981	526077	448927	54118	19107	3925
1982	551435	465052	58947	22566	4870
1983	577032	480652	63922	26460	5999
1984	602464	495468	68928	30758	7310
1985	627669	509469	73929	35457	8814

Percentage Distribution of
Projection of Labor Force, by Occupation,
Race, and Sex, 1970 to 1985

ACCOUNTANCY

YEAR	TOTAL	WHITE		BLACK	
		MALE	FEMALE	MALE	FEMALE
1970	100.00	90.51	7.77	1.34	0.38
1971	100.00	90.70	7.60	1.36	0.35
1972	100.00	90.76	7.51	1.40	0.32
1973	100.00	90.67	7.54	1.47	0.31
1974	100.00	90.44	7.68	1.58	0.31
1975	100.00	89.94	7.99	1.75	0.32
1976	100.00	89.40	8.31	1.94	0.35
1977	100.00	88.75	8.67	2.19	0.39
1978	100.00	88.01	9.06	2.48	0.45
1979	100.00	87.17	9.47	2.83	0.53
1980	100.00	86.28	9.88	3.21	0.63
1981	100.00	85.33	10.29	3.63	0.75
1982	100.00	84.33	10.69	4.09	0.88
1983	100.00	83.30	11.08	4.59	1.04
1984	100.00	82.24	11.44	5.11	1.21
1985	100.00	81.17	11.78	5.65	1.40

TABLE IV-10
United States
New Labor Force Entrants, by Occupation,
Race, and Sex, 1970 to 1985

ACCOUNTANCY

		WHITE		BLACK	
YEAR	TOTAL	MALE	FEMALE	MALE	FEMALE
1970	17977	16317	1494	153	14
1971	18727	16713	1756	234	25
1972	21131	18540	2184	364	43
1973	23898	20502	2795	528	73
1974	25162	21016	3358	679	109
1975	27892	22315	4378	1001	199
1976	30663	23957	5333	1121	252
1977	32592	24427	6517	1298	350
1978	34537	24776	7815	1475	470
1979	36797	25226	9289	1662	619
1980	38426	25125	10700	1817	784
1981	40055	24940	12177	1965	973
1982	42083	24915	13843	2126	1199
1983	43828	24646	15473	2264	1444
1984	45174	24106	16995	2373	1700
1985	46485	23514	18521	2471	1979

Percentage Distribution of
New Labor Force Entrants, by Occupation,
Race, and Sex, 1970 to 1985

ACCOUNTANCY

		WHITE		BLACK	
YEAR	TOTAL	MALE	FEMALE	MALE	FEMALE
1970	100.00	90.76	8.31	0.85	0.08
1971	100.00	89.24	9.38	1.25	0.13
1972	100.00	87.74	10.34	1.72	0.20
1973	100.00	85.79	11.70	2.21	0.30
1974	100.00	83.52	13.34	2.70	0.43
1975	100.00	80.00	15.69	3.59	0.71
1976	100.00	78.13	17.39	3.66	0.82
1977	100.00	74.95	20.00	3.98	1.07
1978	100.00	71.74	22.63	4.27	1.36
1979	100.00	68.55	25.24	4.52	1.68
1980	100.00	65.38	27.85	4.73	2.04
1981	100.00	62.26	30.40	4.91	2.43
1982	100.00	59.21	32.90	5.05	2.85
1983	100.00	56.23	35.31	5.17	3.29
1984	100.00	53.36	37.62	5.25	3.76
1985	100.00	50.58	39.84	5.32	4.26

TABLE IV-11
United States
Projection of Labor Force, by Occupation, Race, and Sex, 1970 to 1985

ACCOUNTANCY

YEAR	TOTAL	WHITE MALE	WHITE FEMALE	BLACK MALE	BLACK FEMALE
1970	309036	279718	24011	4148	1159
1971	320365	290564	24346	4345	1110
1972	333885	303046	25085	4670	1083
1973	349900	317269	26380	5157	1087
1974	366837	331752	28167	5791	1127
1975	386129	347276	30856	6742	1255
1976	407735	364170	34335	7805	1426
1977	430739	381236	38781	9037	1685
1978	455088	398354	44251	10436	2047
1979	481030	415629	50855	12011	2535
1980	507855	432510	58459	13729	3156
1981	535501	448927	67067	15582	3925
1982	564307	465052	76803	17581	4870
1983	593913	480652	87559	19704	5999
1984	623857	495468	99159	21920	7310
1985	654053	509469	111552	24218	8814

Percentage Distribution of
Projection of Labor Force, by Occupation, Race, and Sex, 1970 to 1985

ACCOUNTANCY.

YEAR	TOTAL	WHITE MALE	WHITE FEMALE	BLACK MALE	BLACK FEMALE
1970	100.00	90.51	7.77	1.34	0.38
1971	100.00	90.70	7.60	1.36	0.35
1972	100.00	90.76	7.51	1.40	0.32
1973	100.00	90.67	7.54	1.47	0.31
1974	100.00	90.44	7.68	1.58	0.31
1975	100.00	89.94	7.99	1.75	0.32
1976	100.00	89.32	8.42	1.91	0.35
1977	100.00	88.51	9.00	2.10	0.39
1978	100.00	87.53	9.72	2.29	0.45
1979	100.00	86.40	10.57	2.50	0.53
1980	100.00	85.16	11.51	2.70	0.62
1981	100.00	83.83	12.52	2.91	0.73
1982	100.00	82.41	13.61	3.12	0.86
1983	100.00	80.93	14.74	3.32	1.01
1984	100.00	79.42	15.89	3.51	1.17
1985	100.00	77.89	17.06	3.70	1.35

in 1970. This would represent an increase of 5.5 percentage points over the base line projection for 1985. The change in the projection of labor force that would be black, attributable to changes for black females, was not material.

In the third simulation when the number of degrees awarded to both blacks and women are doubled, new entrants would be almost 42 percent female and more than 14 percent black in 1985, as the figures in Table IV-12 indicate. Blacks would comprise 6.7 percent of the labor force, and women would make up 18.1 percent of all accountants in 1985 (Table IV-13). These projections of the labor force would represent an increase of 5.2 percentage points for women and only a 1.9 percentage point increase for blacks in 1985 over the initial base line projections for that year.

These simulations indicate that women can make some substantial gains in their participation in the labor force for accountants by virtue of their representation in the profession in 1970 and the increasing number of accounting degrees granted to women. The outlook for black accountants is promising, but because of their meager initial position and their small representation among new accountants, progress can be expected to be steady but slow.

TABLE IV-12
United States
New Labor Force Entrants, by Occupation,
Race, and Sex, 1970 to 1985

ACCOUNTANCY

| YEAR | TOTAL | WHITE | | BLACK | |
		MALE	FEMALE	MALE	FEMALE
1970	17977..	16317	1494	153	14
1971	18727	16713	1756	234	25
1972	21131	18540	2184	364	43
1973	23898	20502	2795	528	73
1974	25162	21016	3358	679	109
1975	27892	22315	4378	1001	199
1976	30775	23957	5333	1233.	252
1977	32852	24427	6517	1558	350
1978	34980	24776	7815	1918	470
1979	37462	25226	9289	2327	619
1980	39335	25125	10700	2726	784
1981	41234	24940	12177	3144	973
1982	43571	24915	13843	3614	1199
1983	45639	24646	15473	4076	1444
1984	47309	24106	16995	4508	1700
1985	48956	23514	18521	4942	1979

Percentage Distribution of
New Labor Force Entrants, by Occupation,
Race, and Sex, 1970 to 1985

ACCOUNTANCY

| YEAR | TOTAL | WHITE | | BLACK | |
		MALE	FEMALE	MALE	FEMALE
1970	100.00	90.76	8.31	0.85	0.08
1971	100.00	89.24	9.38	1.25	0.13
1972	100.00	87.74	10.34	1.72	0.20
1973	100.00	85.79	11.70	2.21	0.30
1974	100.00	83.52	13.34	2.70	0.43
1975	100.00	80.00	15.69	3.59	0.71
1976	100.00	77.85	17.33	4.01	0.82
1977	100.00	74.35	19.84	4.74	1.06
1978	100.00	70.83	22.34	5.48	1.34
1979	100.00	67.34	24.80	6.21	1.65
1980	100.00	63.87	27.20	6.93	1.99
1981	100.00	60.48	29.53	7.63	2.36
1982	100.00	57.18	31.77	8.29	2.75
1983	100.00	54.00	33.90	8.93	3.16
1984	100.00	50.95	35.92	9.53	3.59
1985	100.00	48.03	37.83	10.09	4.04

TABLE IV-13
United States
Projection of Labor Force, by Occupation,
Race, and Sex, 1970 to 1985

ACCOUNTANCY

YEAR	.TOTAL	WHITE		BLACK	
		MALE	FEMALE	MALE	FEMALE
1970	309036	279718	24011	4148	1159
1971	320365	290564	24346	4345	1110
1972	333885	303046	25085	4670	1083
1973	349900	317269	26386	5157	·1087.
1974	366837	331752	28167	5791	1127
1975	386129	347276	30856	6742	1255
1976	407848	364170	34335	7917	1426
1977	431109	381236	38781	9408	1685
1978	455898	398354	44251	11246	2047
1979	482498	415629	50855	13480	2535
1980	510220	432510	58459	16094	3156
1981	539026	448927	67067	19107	3925
1982	569291	465052	76803	22566	4870
1983	600669	480652	87559	26460	5999
1984	632694	495468	99159	30758	7310
1985	665291	509469	111552	35457	8814

Percentage Distribution of
Projection of Labor Force, by Occupation,
Race, and Sex, 1970 to 1985

ACCOUNTANCY

YEAR	TOTAL·	WHITE		BLACK	
		MALE	FEMALE	MALE	FEMALE
1970	100.00	90.51	7.77	1.34	0.38
1971	100.00	90.70	7.60	1.36	0.35
1972	100.00	90.76	7.51	1.40	0.32
1973	100.00	90.67	7.54	1.47	0.31
1974	100.00	90.44	7.68	1.58	0.31
1975	100.00	89.94	7.99	1.75	0.32
1976	100.00	89.29	8.42	1.94	0.35
1977	100.00	88.43	·9.00	2.18	0.39
1978	100.00	87.38	9.71	2.47	0.45
1979	100.00	86.14	10.54	2.79	0.53
1980	100.00	84.77	11.46	3.15	0.62
1981	100.00	83.28	12.44	3.54	0.73
1982	100.00	81.69	13.49	3.96	0.86
1983	100.00	80.02	14.58	4.41	1.00
1984	100.00	78.31	15.67	4.86	1.16
1985	100.00	76.58	16.77	5.33	1.32

Minorities and Women in
Other Business and Management

Labor economists at the Labor Department's Bureau of Labor Statistics predict that jobs for managers and administrators will grow more rapidly in the next ten years than they did between 1960 and 1972. Managerial and administrative jobs, which numbered 8 million in 1972, will increase to 10.5 million in 1985.[1]

Colleges report that the number of seniors planning business careers has doubled in the last 3 or 4 years. At Harvard 14 percent of the 1975 graduates said they planned careers in business, which is up from 5.5 percent 3 years earlier. Stanford University's Graduate School of Business reported applications for its 300 first-year places jumped to 3,300 in 1975. This represented an increase in applications of 60 percent in 2 years. The University of Pennsylvania's Wharton School received 3,300 applications for its graduate business program in 1975-76, which was up from 1,400 four years before. Applications to Harvard's Graduate School of Business Administration also showed an increase by rising from 2,900 in 1973 to nearly 4,300 in 1976. The overcrowding of other professions and the availability of jobs in business are the prime reasons students are planning business careers. Moreover, minorities and women see improved opportunities in business.[2]

Background

Recruiters for university MBA programs report that their job of attracting top students to the study of business is much

---

[1] "More Technically Trained Managers Are Seen Needed in Future for Automated Data Systems," *Daily Labor Report*, No. 22 (January 31, 1975), p. A-6.

[2] Roger Ricklefs, "Glutted Professions Put Students in Job Market at Corporations Again," *Wall Street Journal*, January 14, 1976, pp. 1, 22.

easier now than it was ten years ago. The student rebellions of the 1960s produced an antibusiness bias that made recruitment of students to business careers difficult. This campus antibusiness bias, however, goes back much further than the 1960s. In the 1930s there was also a widely held opposition to business by students on college campuses.

In the late sixties and early seventies the student revolutionaries became the student reformers, and the study of law became popular among graduate students. Law was further enhanced by the work of Ralph Nader who became the role model for many aspiring law students of the period. During the early seventies, its popularity began to fade as many law school graduates had difficulty finding employment. As the seventies have progressed, advanced degree opportunities in university teaching and the sciences have also declined. The MBA degree now appeals to holders of advanced degrees in other fields.[3] According to Richard J. Thain of the University of Chicago's graduate business school, "the result of this all is a business school populace that is much more broadly drawn, more varied, more eclectic than it was ten years ago." [4]

Census Data

Census data on experienced managers, excluding farmers and farm managers, are shown in Table V-1. Since Census occupational data are self-reported by individuals or by members of their families and based on a sample of the population, there is reason to question its accuracy.

According to the Census numbers given to Table V-1, the representation of females in the experienced management labor force has increased from 11.3 percent in 1940 to 16.7 percent in 1970. The proportion of nonwhites in management has risen from 1.7 percent to 3.5 percent during the same period; however, white males who made up 87.4 percent of all managers in 1940 still hold the largest portion of the management labor force with 80.7 percent in 1970.

BLACKS

Even though proportionally more black graduates are going into business, there is a continuing scarcity of qualified blacks for

---

[3] Richard J. Thain, "The Flowering of the MBA—Ten Years of Change," *MBA*, Vol. 9 (January 1975), pp. 28-32.

[4] *Ibid.*, p. 31.

TABLE V-1

Number of Experienced Civilian Managers (except farm)
by Sex and Race, 1940-1970

Sex and Race	1940	1950	1960	1970
Managers Total	3,839,920	4,953,270	5,488,933	6,478,186
Male Managers	3,406,020	4,272,510	4,694,541	5,394,585
White	3,354,220	4,185,480	4,600,502	5,227,635
Negro	—	71,130	65,346	121,949
Other Races	51,800 [a]	15,900	28,693	45,001
Male Managers with 4 or More Years of College	318,180	505,770	787,244	1,349,883
White	315,800	500,370	776,927	—
Nonwhite	2,380	5,400	10,317	24,393 [b]
Female Managers	433,900	680,760	794,392	1,083,601
White	421,760	653,130	763,137	1,023,190
Negro	—	25,950	25,867	48,007
Other Races	12,140 [a]	1,680	5,388	12,404
Female Managers with 4 or More Years of College	26,960	50,100	62,605	152,127
White	26,520	49,080	60,201	—
Nonwhite	440	1,020	2,404	8,891 [b]

Sources: *Sixteenth Census of the United States: 1940 Population, The Labor Force, Occupational Characteristics* (Washington, D.C.: Government Printing Office, 1943), pp. 59-70 *passim*, Table 3.
United States Census of Population 1950, Occupational Characteristics, P-E No. 1B (Washington, D.C.: Government Printing Office, 1956), pp. 30, 108, 116, Tables 3, 10, 11.
United States Census of Population 1960, Occupational Characteristics, PC(2)-7A (Washington, D.C.: U.S. Department of Commerce, 1961), pp. 22, 117, 124, 131, 138, Tables 3, 9, 10.
1970 Census of Population Subject Report, Occupational Characteristics, PC(2)-7A (Washington, D.C.: U.S. Department of Commerce, 1973), pp. 15, 61, 75, 89, 103, Tables 2, 5, 6.

[a] Only nonwhite data available.
[b] Only Negro data available.

managerial positions: blacks are particularly underrepresented in middle and top management.

Participation of Blacks in Business

In the early 1700s most of the colonies had slave codes restricting the economic activity of black slaves. The New York Colonial Council enacted a statute in 1707 making all bargains or contracts with slaves null and void and preventing all trading with any slave without the owner's consent. Even after the Emancipation Proclamation the freed black man still found his business activity limited. The business opportunities for blacks in the South were limited to those in which whites did not want to engage or those whites did not want to perform for blacks. The major limitations on black business in the North were competition from white businessmen, racial oppression, the success of immigrants displacing blacks, and the greatly dispersed black population in the North.[5]

Within the business world the majority of blacks have traditionally worked as proprietors of small businesses that were dependent on the segregated Negro community for their market. It is estimated that in 1930 there were about 70,000 business enterprises owned by Negroes, most of which were small service businesses.[6] Barbers, beauticians, and undertakers represented the most flourishing Negro businesses primarily because segregation provided a monopoly for blacks offering these services. Particularly important is the fact that Negro business generally has not been of the size and efficiency to offer many positions that would give good training to Negro youths wanting to prepare themselves for a business career.[7] Moreover, the lack of successful black managers as role models has further retarded the exposure of black students to the career opportunities available in business.

With regard to capital invested, banking and insurance companies were the Negro's most important types of business in the 1930s. A detailed explanation of Negro banks of that period

---

[5] Flournoy A. Coles, Jr., *Black Economic Development* (Chicago: Nelson Hall, 1975), pp. 102-104.

[6] Abram L. Harris, *The Negro As Capitalist* (Philadelphia: The American Academy of Political and Social Sciences, 1936), p. xi.

[7] Gunnar Myrdal, *An American Dilemma*, Vol. 1 (New York: Harper & Row, 1962), pp. 309-310.

is provided in *The Negro As Capitalist,* and *An Economic Detour* relates a history of the Negro life insurance business.[8]

Recent Surveys of Black Managers

In 1966 the Equal Employment Opportunity Commission surveyed 100 major companies based in New York City that contributed nearly 16 percent of our gross national product. The study showed that blacks then made up only 2.6 percent of the white-collar headquarters staffs of these companies. This figure was below New York City's average of 5.2 percent blacks in white-collar job categories. The commission also obtained the 1967 figures from 70 of the corporations: these showed that the number of Negro white-collar workers had increased from 2.5 percent in 1966 to 3.2 percent in 1967.[9]

In 1969 a Labor Department analysis showed a "sharp acceleration" in the movement of black workers into "higher status" jobs. In fact, approximately two-thirds of the net increase in black employment from 1962 to 1967 was in professional, technical, managerial, clerical, and sales positions. During the 5-year upgrading, salaried managerial jobs held by blacks went up 49 percent to 115,000. These were, in part, a result of more black people going to college and of corporations recruiting at predominantly black colleges, which are attended by about 40 percent of all black undergraduates.[10]

It is estimated that the nation's 1,000 largest corporations have 14,000 directors serving on their boards. In 1973 there were 72 blacks serving on the boards of directors of more than 100 major United States companies (some serve on more than 1 board).[11]

The past decade has shown a growing concern for the lack of participation by blacks in management. The problem involves not only developing blacks with the requisite qualifications and education, but also integrating these people into managerial positions. In the early 1970s a black manager's article in the *Harvard Business Review* listed what he considered the necessary

[8] Harris, *The Negro As Capitalist,* and M.S. Stuart, *An Economic Detour* (College Park, Maryland: McGrath Publishing Company, 1940).

[9] John S. Morgan and Richard L. Van Dyke, *White-Collar Blacks* (n.p.: American Management Association, Inc., 1970), p. 11.

[10] *Ibid.,* pp. 16-17.

[11] Lester Carson, "The Black Director—Mostly Black, or Mostly Director?," *Management Review,* Vol. 62 (December 1973), p. 50.

elements for the acceptance and success of blacks entering management. These include: unquestionable involvement and commitment of top management; direct two-way channels of communication between top management and black trainees; appraisal of managers on their contributions to the company's equal opportunity objectives; avoidance of the temptations to create special showcase black jobs; and assignments for the new black managers, which are challenging, yet do not in themselves increase his chances of failure.[12]

Participation of Blacks in Business Study

Colleges have recently been recruiting more black graduate students. The University of Pennsylvania's Wharton School increased its black enrollment to 32 from only 4 in 1966-67 by sending recruiters to predominantly black colleges. At Harvard's Graduate School of Business Administration, a special recruiting drive increased the number of black students from 30 in 1968-69 to 105 the following year. Similarly, increased junior college recruiting helped UCLA double the number of blacks in its graduate business school between 1968 and 1970.[13]

American Assembly of Collegiate Schools of Business (AACSB) Survey

The data on business school enrollments and degrees awarded are the result of a survey done by the AACSB between August 1974 and January 1975. Questionnaires were sent to 525 schools, and 206 schools returned responses. Because this survey did not include data from all business schools, the absolute numbers for enrollments and degrees awarded are not accurate totals. The proportion of blacks identified through the AACSB survey does, however, give a good indication of the participation of blacks in business study. Since accounting was examined separately, these numbers include enrollments and degrees earned in business fields other than accounting.

This survey showed that in 1973-74 blacks represented 7.0 percent of the total nonaccounting undergraduate business enrollment of 89,579; 3.5 percent of the masters level enrollment

---

[12] Edward W. Jones, Jr., "What It's Like to Be a Black Manager," *Harvard Business Review*, Vol. 51 (July 1973), p. 115.

[13] Morgan and Van Dyke, *White-Collar Blacks*, p. 17.

of 28,730; and 6.3 percent of the doctoral level enrollment of
2,918. That same year blacks accounted for 4.8 percent of the
total 25,959 nonaccounting undergraduate business degrees
awarded; 3.9 percent of the total 12,903 masters degrees awarded;
and 1.4 percent of the total 1,169 doctoral degrees awarded.[14]

OTHER MINORITIES

In 1974 minority group members, including blacks, held slightly
over 3 percent of the managerial positions in this country, which
is up from the 2.5 percent they represented in 1960. This up-
ward trend has not been strong enough, however, to change the
fact that the majority of minorities do not work as managers:
they are instead overrepresented in lower level occupations.[15]

Employment of Minorities in Business

Like blacks, other minorities in the United States have traditionally been underrepresented among white-collar workers, business
managers, and industrial enterpreneurs, but well represented in
retail business. In 1930 one out of every three wholesale and retail
dealers in the United States was a foreign-born person.[16] The
Chinese and Japanese have been particularly successful as re-
tailers:

> In 1929 they [Chinese and Japanese] owned one-and-a-half times
> as many stores, restaurants, and eating places per 1,000 popula-
> tion as other residents of the United States. Negroes, on the other
> hand, operated but one-sixth of the number of such establishments
> as would correspond to their proportion in the population. Nor is
> this all. The stores and restaurants operated by the Orientals were
> larger and gave employment to an average of four persons per store
> (proprietors and employees), whereas the corresponding ratio for
> Negro establishments was but 1.6. The net sales of the Oriental-
> operated stores ($89,000,000) were not much lower than those of
> the Negro-owned stores ($101,000.000), in spite of the fact that
> the Negro population was about fifty times larger than the Oriental
> population of the country.[17]

---

[14] *1974 Minority Report: Student Enrollments and Faculty Distribution*
(St. Louis, Missouri: American Assembly of Collegiate Schools of Business,
n.d.), pp. ii-ix, Tables I, II, III, IV, V, VI.

[15] John B. Miner, *The Human Constraint* (Washington, D.C.: The Bureau
of National Affairs, Inc., 1974), p. 151.

[16] Myrdal, *An American Dilemma*, p. 310.

[17] *Ibid.*

Chinese

When Chinese immigration to the United States began in 1848, Chinese laborers were unpopular with white laborers who complained of their inexpensive dietary habits and pernicious effect on the wage rate for unskilled labor. Even following passage of the Chinese Exclusion Act in 1882 limiting Chinese immigration, whites took action to exclude Chinese labor from employment while also pressing Chinese-owned firms to cease competition with white businesses. For a livelihood, Chinese had to turn to domestic service, laundry work, restaurants, and small retail stores catering primarily to other Chinese. Whites did not interfere with Chinese development in domestic service since these occupations were ones in which white males did not care to work. By 1920 more than 50 percent of the Chinese in the United States were employed or self-employed in restaurants or laundries with the majority of others working as domestic servants.[18]

Japanese

The Japanese who began immigrating to the United States around 1900 were much more rural than were the Chinese who preceded them. Japanese were principally employed as agricultural laborers in California, although others were employed as railroad and construction workers, lumber mill and logging laborers, cannery hands, and domestic servants. As early as 1910, Japanese laborers became unpopular with California ranchers as they began to demand higher wages. Moreover, many Japanese began to lease and buy land for their own farming. This activity had the 2-fold effect of increasing agricultural competition while also decreasing the number of Japanese laborers available to work as farmhands. By 1921 the Alien Land Laws had been passed, which halted the development of Japanese agriculture. Forced to seek a living from the urban areas, Japanese were denied by the action of the Asiatic Exclusion League. The League succeeded in forcing the curtailment of Japanese immigration and the exclusion of Japanese in the general labor market. In response to the discriminatory opportunity structure that denied nonmenial wage or salary employment, the Japanese turned to commercial self-employment. By 1919, 47 percent of hotels and

[18] Ivan H. Light, *Ethnic Enterprise in America: Business and Welfare Among Chinese, Japanese, and Blacks* (Berkeley: University of California Press, 1972), pp. 6-8.

25 percent of grocery stores in Seattle were Japanese owned. Furthermore, the 1940 Census reported that 40 percent of the Japanese men in Los Angeles were self-employed.[19]

An advantage that the early ethnic retailer had over the black retailer was the special demands of ethnic consumers. These special demands created protected markets for ethnic tradesmen who were familiar with the products their customers wanted. The lack of special demands by black consumers and the resulting white competition for the black consumer market is a contributing factor to the underrepresentation of blacks in retail trade. According to a survey of Japanese retail businesses in 1909, 63 percent of their retail trade in California was with other Japanese.[20]

Other Minorities as Managers

There remains a slow increase of nonwhites as managers. Between 1950 and 1960 the number of self-employed managers, proprietors, and officials of all races declined by more than half a million. This represented a large decrease in the area of business where minorities had been most active. Moreover, no large number of nonwhites have reached the managerial levels of the large corporation or government bureaucracies.[21]

The results of a survey conducted in 1971 by the Bureau of National Affairs show that minorities are more likely to be in management in larger companies, but at lower levels of management. Of the companies studied, 45 percent had no minorities in middle management, and 67 percent had none in top management. It was found that small nonprofit organizations such as hospitals, government, and educational institutions provide the best management opportunities for minorities who want to get ahead in business. The manufacturing sector showed the smallest usage of minority group members in management. The survey indicates that between 1967 and 1971 the largest increases in the proportion of minorities in management occurred in larger firms. The major problem reported as limiting the use of minorities in management was their lack of qualifica-

---

[19] *Ibid.*, pp. 8-10.

[20] *Ibid.*, pp. 11-15.

[21] Norval D. Glenn, "Some Changes in the Relative Status of American Nonwhites, 1940 to 1960," *Phylon*, Vol. XXIV (Summer 1963), p. 111.

tions. Nevertheless, discrimintion, stereotyping, and prejudice were listed as factors slowing promotion in some companies.[22]

Minorities' Participation in Business Study

In 1973 the College Placement Council Foundation of Bethlehem, Pennsylvania, released the findings of a survey concerning changes in the career plans of graduates between 1965 and 1970. These results show that nonwhite students are more interested in business and engineering careers than they are in natural and social sciences. The proportion of all nonwhite male graduates choosing business careers rose from 6 percent in 1965 to 19 percent in 1970, and the proportion of nonwhite female graduates interested in business careers increased from 1 percent in 1965 to 5 percent in 1970.[23] Despite the increase in minority students' interest in business, though, a recent survey by the Alfred P. Sloan Foundation showed that less than 2.5 percent of the students in 15 major graduate business schools are from minority groups.[24]

American Assembly of Collegiate Schools of Business (AACSB) Survey

The data in Tables V-2 and V-3 are taken from the AACSB survey described earlier in this chapter. It is important to realize that these numbers do not include data from all business schools; consequently, the absolute numbers do not represent the total number of students enrolled and the total number of degrees awarded in 1973-74. The percentages do, however, show the trend of minority-group representation in business school enrollments and degrees awarded.

WOMEN

Even though women represent over 35 percent of the national labor force, they make up only 16 percent of the country's managerial positions, and they most frequently hold the lowest management jobs. This is, however, an increase from the 12 percent of management jobs women held in 1940.[25]

---

[22] Miner, *The Human Constraint*, p. 151.

[23] "More Nonwhite Grads Plan Business Careers," *Industry Week*, Vol. 179 (December 3, 1973), pp. 17-18.

[24] Morgan, *White-Collar Blacks*, pp. 17-18.

[25] Miner, *The Human Constraint*, p. 143.

TABLE V-2

Student Enrollment in AACSB Member Schools for 1973-74 [a]

Race	Undergraduate		Master		Doctoral	
	Number	Percent of Total	Number	Percent of Total	Number	Percent of Total
Total Enrollment	89,579	100.0	28,730	100.0	2,918	100.0
American Caucasians	78,191	87.3	25,027	87.1	2,075	71.1
American Indians	354	0.4	81	0.3	1	0.0
American Negroes	6,307	7.0	1,014	3.5	185	6.3
American Orientals	999	1.1	286	1.0	18	0.6
Spanish Americans	2,107	2.4	313	1.1	5	0.2
Foreign Students	1,621	1.8	2,009	7.0	634	21.7

Source: *1974 Minority Report: Student Enrollments and Faculty Distribution* (St. Louis, Missouri: American Assembly of Collegiate Schools of Business, n.d.), pp. iii, iv, v, Tables I, II, III.
[a] Data in this table do not include enrollments in accounting.

TABLE V-3
Degrees Awarded by AACSB Member Schools in 1973-74 [a]

Race	Undergraduate		Master		Doctoral	
	Number	Percent of Total	Number	Percent of Total	Number	Percent of Total
Total Degrees	25,959	100.0	12,903	100.0	1,169	100.0
American Caucasians	23,695	91.3	11,034	85.5	866	74.1
American Indians	96	0.4	52	0.4	5	0.4
American Negroes	1,254	4.8	497	3.9	16	1.4
American Orientals	184	0.7	88	0.7	2	0.2
Spanish Americans	328	1.3	203	1.6	9	0.8
Foreign Students	402	1.5	1,029	8.0	271	23.2

Source: *1974 Minority Report: Student Enrollments and Faculty Distribution* (St. Louis, Missouri: American Assembly of Collegiate Schools of Business, n.d.), pp. vii, viii, ix, Tables IV, V, VI.
[a] Data in this table do not include degrees awarded in accounting.

Employment of Women in Business

Newspaper advertisements from the colonial period reveal that women were actively involved in varied business enterprises. It was not unusual for a woman to act as her husband's partner in business as a tanner, silversmith, printer, gunsmith, or tailor and to continue as proprietor of the business after her husband's death. Other women operated bakeries, taverns, inns, and dry goods stores on their own during the colonial period.[26]

By 1940 almost 27,000 women were proprietors, managers, and officials in industry: this is over 100 times as many as were reported in the 1870 Census. World War I provided an opportunity for women to replace men in various business fields. This was particularly evident in banking and finance institutions where there was an exceptional rate of increase of women proprietors, managers, officials, and salesmen between 1910 and 1920.[27]

As might be expected from the past role of women in business, banks, insurance companies, and merchandising firms currently employ the most female managers, but they are employed most frequently as first-line supervisors. Women in top management are almost nonexistent. Moreover, a third of all companies have practically no women in management at all.[28] It is estimated that women directors of major corporations total 400 today, which represents 2.7 percent of the 15,000 directorships of those corporations.[29]

The companies' experience with women in managerial positions is good overall. Women succeed in management for the same reasons men do: they have the intelligence to make decisions, a desire to manage, and the required knowledge. Women, however, have not been attracted to the study of business. The proportion of women studying business is far below their representation in the total college student populace. For some women, management is still considered a male occupation. As a

---

[26] Janet M. Hooks, *Women's Occupations through Seven Decades* (Washington, D.C.: Government Printing Office, 1947), p. 180.

[27] *Ibid.*, pp. 185, 188.

[28] Miner, *The Human Constraint*, p. 143.

[29] "A Big Jump in the Ranks of Female Directors," *Business Week*, No. 2465 (January 10, 1977), p. 50.

result of these factors, the supply of qualified female managers is small, and women remain underrepresented in management.[30]

Women's Participation in Business Study

The College Placement Council survey previously noted indicates an increase in the interest of female graduates in business careers. The survey shows that between 1965 and 1970 the proportion of white female graduates interested in business remained constant at 5 percent; yet, the proportion of nonwhite female graduates increased from 1 percent in 1965 to 5 percent in 1970.[31]

National Center for Educational Statistics (NCES) Data

Table V-4 shows the number of degrees, reported by NCES, awarded to women in other business and management from 1968-69 through 1974-75. During the past few years, women have steadily increased their numbers in graduate business schools; thus, women now make up 15 to 30 percent of incoming classes.[32]

CURRENT PROGRAMS

The programs described in this section are representative of those designed during the past decade when the participation of minority group members and women in management became an area of concern.

Consortium Program for Graduate Study in Management

In 1966 the Consortium was begun by Indiana University, Washington University (St. Louis), and the University of Wisconsin with a grant from the Ford Foundation to "hasten the entry of Negroes into managerial positions in business." [33] Since then, the University of Southern California, the University of Rochester, and the University of North Carolina at Chapel Hill have joined the Consortium; and, in addition to blacks, recipients

---

[30] Miner, *The Human Constraint*, pp. 143-150.

[31] "More Nonwhite Grads Plan Business Careers," pp. 17-18.

[32] Thain, "The Flowering of the MBA," p. 32.

[33] Mary E. Stronk, "Modest Growth in the Number of Blacks in Business Schools," *MBA*, Vol. 6 (January 1972), p. 42.

TABLE V-4

Degrees Awarded to Women in Other Business and Management,
1968-69 through 1974-75

Year	Bachelor		Master		Doctoral	
	Number	Percent of Total	Number	Percent of Total	Number	Percent of Total
1968-69	6,764	9.1	598	3.3	12	2.4
1969-70	7,399	8.7	690	3.4	7	1.2
1970-71	8,404	9.0	935	3.7	20	2.7
1971-72	9,098	9.4	1,093	3.8	20	2.4
1972-73	10,148	10.3	1,387	4.7	52	6.1
1973-74	12,918	12.5	1,965	6.3	46	5.0
1974-75	16,149	15.7	2,784	8.2	37	3.9

Source: Information supplied by National Center for Educational Statistics, Washington, D.C.

now include Chicanos, Cubans, Indian Americans, and Puerto Ricans.

Now funded by three foundations and many corporate contributors, students who qualify for admission to the Consortium receive a fellowship to pursue MBAs at one of the six Consortium universities. In addition, the Consortium provides a summer preparatory program for students before their first year of study and a summer business internship program for students after their first year of study.

Council for Opportunity in Graduate Management Education (COGME)

The ten business schools represented by COGME, which was formed in 1970, are the University of California at Berkeley, Carnegie-Mellon University, the University of Chicago, Columbia University, Cornell University, Amos Tuck (Dartmouth), Harvard University, Alfred P. Sloan School of Management (MIT), Wharton (University of Pennsylvania), and Stanford University. COGME is an independent nonprofit organization with the objective of increasing the number of minority members in positions of managerial responsibility.

A student must have already been accepted to one of the participating schools to win a COGME fellowship. Federal funding for this program is currently being administered under Title III of the Comprehensive Employment and Training Act.[34]

Association for the Integration of Management, Inc. (AIM)

A group of black executives and managers formed the Council of Concerned Black Executives (CCBE) out of a concern for the underutilization of blacks in the corporate structure. In 1971 CCBE was replaced by AIM with the objective of "developing a systematic approach to the elimination of racism in the management structure of American business corporations."[35] AIM's programs include self-development projects and services for black managers, direct assistance projects and services for corporations, educational projects for black students at the graduate and undergraduate levels, and educational projects

[34] *Ibid.,* pp. 41-42.

[35] Flournoy A. Coles, "The Vanderbilt Program, A Long-term Solution?," *MBA,* Vol. 6 (January 1972), p. 88.

for administrative faculties and staff at both predominantly white and predominantly black universities.[36]

PREDICTING THE NUMBERS OF MINORITIES AND WOMEN IN OTHER BUSINESS AND MANAGEMENT FIELDS

The review of the experiences of minorities and women in business-related occupations documents the reasons for their present status as managers and administrators. The evidence indicates that the black and female portions of the labor force have been active in business, but in small owner-operated enterprises and in lower level supervisory positions for women.

The model of the labor supply process was implemented to examine the future course of minorities and women in this area. In contrast to the other occupations included in this study, two base line projections were produced because of problems of definition related to the initial supply base. Three simulations were implemented in order to show the effects on the labor supply of varying the racial and sexual distributions of potential new labor force entrants. In summary, the analysis suggests very limited improvement in the representation of women in these occupations, but substantial improvement in black penetration of the labor force from 1970 to 1985.

Base Line Projections

The basic input data necessary to exercise the model for the business and management category appears in Table V-5. Data on the racial characteristics of degree earners were available for only 2 years from the 1974 AACSB survey, the source of data for accountants.[37] This data component was completed by a simple extrapolation of the AACSB data. New entrants to the labor force with college degrees in business administration should grow from 87,000 in 1970 to 122,000 in 1985, and the proportions of female and black entrants should increase from 7.5 percent and 1.9 percent in 1970 to 20.8 percent and 12.3 percent, respectively, in 1985. These figures are presented in Table V-6.

---

[36] "AIM—A New Approach for Black Managers," *MBA*, Vol. 6 (January 1972), p. 44.

[37] *Minority Report: Student Enrollments and Faculty Distribution* (St. Louis: American Assembly of Collegiate Schools of Business, n.d.), pp. vi-ix and 117-40.

TABLE V-5
Input Data for Simulation
of Other Business and Management Labor Force to 1985

	MALE	FEMALE
SEPARATION RATE	**WHITE**	
1970	0.0245	0.0517
1965	0.0224	0.0568
	BLACK	
1970	0.0204	0.0513
1985	0.0186	0.0527
ENTRY RATE		
BACHELOR	0.8000	0.8000
MASTER	0.9000	0.9000
DOCTOR	1.0000	1.0000
SUPPLY BASE — 1970		
TOTAL	674941	76063
BLACK	12196	4445

		DEGREES AWARDED	
		% FEMALE	% BLACK
BACHELOR			
	1969	9.08	1.50
	1970	8.72	2.00
	1971	9.00	3.00
	1972	9.36	3.50
	1973	10.26	4.00
	1974	12.54	4.83
	1975	15.72	6.37
MASTER			
	1969	8.27	1.50
	1970	8.36	1.50
	1971	0.67	2.00
	1972	3.76	2.50
	1973	4.69	3.00
	1974	6.35	3.85
	1975	8.15	5.41
DOCTOR			
	1969	2.87	1.00
	1970	1.24	0.80
	1971	2.67	1.00
	1972	2.35	1.10
	1973	6.13	1.30
	1974	5.04	1.37
	1975	6.89	1.45

A labor supply base consistent with the other occupations examined in this study requires the use of the Census classification of managers and administrators, except farm, with 4 or more years of college. This supply base definition, by which Table V-5 was figured, was used to produce the base line estimates of the labor force to 1985 shown in Table V-7. The model output indicates that the labor force which was 10.1 percent female and 2.2 percent black in 1970, will be 10.4 percent female and 5.7 percent black by 1985. The small change in female participation is a result of the size of the white female separation rate and their relative standing in the initial supply base. Although an increasing proportion of new entrants are white women, their representation in the 1970 labor force exceeds their percentage of accessions, and the number of white female entrants just manages to offset their separations, so the net result is a small increase in the proportion of this group in the labor force.

The 1970 supply base used to generate the estimates shown in Table V-7 may be inappropriate because of the nature of the detailed occupations aggregated into this classification. In order to compensate for this problem of definition, the decision was made to reduce the initial base by 50 percent across racial and sexual categories. The resultant labor force projections are provided in Table V-8. The adjustment of the initial base yields 1985 estimates of the labor force that are 11.4 percent female and 6.6 percent black. Although the increase in female participation is more than the increase in the full supply base, the differences in black and female participation between the 100 percent and 50 percent supply bases are just about 1 percent. The results of the analysis, therefore, are not sensitive to the size of the initial supply base.

Sensitivity Analysis

Founded on the full 1970 labor supply base, 3 simulations were implemented to examine the impact of increasing the representation of minority and female degree recipients on the labor force. The first alteration involved increasing the number of degrees awarded to blacks by 100 percent by 1985 and maintaining the same number of white degree earners in the base line projection. The second simulation repeated this process on the basis of sex, increasing female degree earners and maintaining

TABLE V-6
United States
New Labor Force Entrants, by Occupation,
Race, and Sex, 1970 to 1985

OTHER BUSINESS AND MANAGEMENT

| YEAR | TOTAL | WHITE | | BLACK | |
		MALE	FEMALE	MALE	FEMALE
1970	86927	78892	6362	1544	129
1971	98394	88073	7645	2452	222
1972	104768	92664	8632	3164	308
1973	106428	92569	9684	3765	409
1974	111232	94365	11647	4630	590
1975	111358	91464	13434	5609	851
1976	109470	89547	13133	5896	893
1977	110966	89204	14120	6568	1074
1978	115413	91067	15590	7442	1314
1979	118162	91566	16823	8216	1557
1980	119846	91220	17900	8921	1804
1981	121072	90514	18908	9586	2063
1982	122852	90186	20019	10294	2353
1983	123630	89135	20946	10909	2640
1984	122931	87057	21596	11373	2905
1985	121842	84724	22165	11780	3173

Percentage Distribution of
New Labor Force Entrants, by Occupation,
Race, and Sex, 1970 to 1985

OTHER BUSINESS AND MANAGEMENT

| YEAR | TOTAL | WHITE | | BLACK | |
		MALE	FEMALE	MALE	FEMALE
1970	100.00	90.76	7.32	1.78	0.15
1971	100.00	89.51	7.77	2.49	0.23
1972	100.00	88.45	8.24	3.02	0.29
1973	100.00	86.98	9.10	3.54	0.38
1974	100.00	84.84	10.47	4.16	0.53
1975	100.00	82.14	12.06	5.04	0.76
1976	100.00	81.80	12.00	5.39	0.82
1977	100.00	80.39	12.72	5.92	0.97
1978	100.00	78.90	13.51	6.45	1.14
1979	100.00	77.49	14.24	6.95	1.32
1980	100.00	76.11	14.94	7.44	1.51
1981	100.00	74.76	15.62	7.92	1.70
1982	100.00	73.41	16.30	8.38	1.92
1983	100.00	72.10	16.94	8.82	2.14
1984	100.00	70.82	17.57	9.25	2.36
1985	100.00	69.54	18.19	9.67	2.60

Table V-7
United States
Projection of Labor Force, by Occupation,
Race, and Sex, 1970 to 1985

OTHER BUSINESS AND MANAGEMENT

YEAR	TOTAL	WHITE MALE	WHITE FEMALE	BLACK MALE	BLACK FEMALE
1970	1502009	1325491	143236	24392	8890
1971	1559705	1381275	143427	26349	8656
1972	1622526	1440483	144546	28981	8518
1973	1685626	1498365	146609	32164	8488
1974	1752126	1556858	150477	36153	8639
1975	1817230	1611268	155876	41044	9043
1976	1878923	1662691	160632	46132	9468
1977	1940699	1712787	166065	51797	10050
1978	2005497	1763808	172618	58232	10841
1979	2071524	1814382	179988	65323	11833
1980	2137667	1863689	187971	72990	13019
1981	2203453	1911412	196458	81183	14401
1982	2269433	1957978	205518	89938	16000
1983	2334587	2002705	214931	99154	17799
1984	2397450	2044620	224392	108672	19768
1985	2457685	2083543	233811	118433	21900

Percentage Distribution of
Projection of Labor Force, by Occupation,
Race, and Sex, 1970 to 1985

OTHER BUSINESS AND MANAGEMENT

YEAR	TOTAL	WHITE MALE	WHITE FEMALE	BLACK MALE	BLACK FEMALE
1970	100.00	88.25	9.54	1.62	0.59
1971	100.00	88.56	9.20	1.69	0.55
1972	100.00	88.78	8.91	1.79	0.52
1973	100.00	88.89	8.70	1.91	0.50
1974	100.00	88.86	8.59	2.06	0.49
1975	100.00	88.67	8.58	2.26	0.50
1976	100.00	88.49	8.55	2.46	0.50
1977	100.00	88.26	8.56	2.67	0.52
1978	100.00	87.95	8.61	2.90	0.54
1979	100.00	87.59	8.69	3.15	0.57
1980	100.00	87.18	8.79	3.41	0.61
1981	100.00	86.75	8.92	3.68	0.65
1982	100.00	86.28	9.06	3.96	0.71
1983	100.00	85.78	9.21	4.25	0.76
1984	100.00	85.28	9.36	4.53	0.82
1985	100.00	84.78	9.51	4.82	0.89

TABLE V-8
United States
Projection of Labor Force, by Occupation, Race, and Sex, 1970 to 1985

OTHER BUSINESS AND MANAGEMENT

YEAR	TOTAL	WHITE MALE	WHITE FEMALE	BLACK MALE	BLACK FEMALE
1970	751004	662745	71618	12196	4445
1971	829050	734674	75536	14401	4439
1972	911548	809544	80211	17274	4518
1973	993673	882619	85666	20692	4695
1974	1078573	955854	92768	24910	5042
1975	1161474	1024569	101248	30024	5632
1976	1240377	1089875	108940	35329	6234
1977	1318801	1153444	117168	41206	6984
1978	1399704	1217542	126382	47847	7935
1979	1481310	1280811	136285	55138	9078
1980	1562526	1342444	146675	63001	10408
1981	1642897	1402135	157451	71385	11927
1982	1722989	1460323	166688	80326	13655
1983	1801801	1516336	180167	89722	15578
1984	1877882	1569213	191591	99417	17663
1985	1950912	1618785	202873	109349	19906

Percentage Distribution of
Projection of Labor Force, by Occupation, Race, and Sex, 1970 to 1985

OTHER BUSINESS AND MANAGEMENT

YEAR	TOTAL	WHITE MALE	WHITE FEMALE	BLACK MALE	BLACK FEMALE
1970	100.00	88.25	9.54	1.62	0.59
1971	100.00	88.62	9.11	1.74	0.54
1972	100.00	88.81	8.80	1.90	0.50
1973	100.00	88.82	8.62	2.08	0.47
1974	100.00	88.62	8.60	2.31	0.47
1975	100.00	88.21	8.72	2.59	0.48
1976	100.00	87.87	8.78	2.85	0.50
1977	100.00	87.46	8.88	3.12	0.53
1978	100.00	86.99	9.03	3.42	0.57
1979	100.00	86.46	9.20	3.72	0.61
1980	100.00	85.91	9.39	4.03	0.67
1981	100.00	85.35	9.58	4.35	0.73
1982	100.00	84.76	9.79	4.66	0.79
1983	100.00	84.16	10.00	4.98	0.86
1984	100.00	83.56	10.20	5.29	0.94
1985	100.00	82.98	10.40	5.61	1.02

the number of male graduates. The numbers of female and black graduates were doubled by 1985 for the third exercise, while the number of degrees awarded to white men was maintained at the base line level.

Tables V-9 and V-10 record the results of the black degree recipient manipulation. In 1985, blacks would comprise 21.9 percent of new labor force entrants as shown in Table V-9. This represents an increase of 20 percentage points over their 1970 share and an increase of 9.6 percentage points from the base line projection for 1985. Incorporating these results into the supply calculations yields a labor force that is 8.1 percent black in 1985, a gain of 5.9 percentage points from 1970 and a difference of 2.4 percentage points from the base line projection previously discussed. The gain for females as a result of the increased proportion of degrees granted to black females is not material.

The output of the second simulation, which doubled the number of degrees claimed by women, is presented in Tables V-11 and V-12. Increasing the number of female degree recipients in this manner translates into an improvement of 26.9 percentage points for female new entrants by 1985 over their 1970 level of 7.5 percent. The presence of women in the relevant labor force would be 14.1 percent in 1985, an improvement of only 4.0 percentage points from the 1970 situation. The gain for blacks by way of the increased number of degrees claimed by black women would not be substantial.

The third and final simulation involved increasing the numbers of black and female degree earners by 100 percent from their base line levels while maintaining the number of degrees awarded to white males. This manipulation produces a stock of new labor force entrants in 1985 that would be 31.9 percent female and 18.8 percent black, as shown in Table V-13. This represents increases of 24.4 percentage points for women and 16.9 percentage points for blacks over their participation in this pool in 1970. If these changes were achieved, women and blacks would comprise 13.8 percent and 7.8 percent, respectively, of the 1985 labor force, as the figures in Table V-14 reveal. These results represent improvements of 3.7 percentage points for women and 5.6 percentage points for blacks from their levels of participation in 1970 and increases of 3.4 percentage points and 2.1 percentage points for women and blacks from their base line projections (Table V-7).

TABLE V-9
United States
New Labor Force Entrants, by Occupation,
Race, and Sex, 1970 to 1985

OTHER BUSINESS AND MANAGEMENT

YEAR	TOTAL	WHITE		BLACK	
		MALE	FEMALE	MALE	FEMALE
1970	86927	78892	6362	1544	129
1971	98394	88073	7645	2452	222
1972	104768	92664	8632	3164	308
1973	106428	92569	9684	3765	409
1974	111232	94365	11647	4630	590
1975	111358	91464	13434	5609	851
1976	110149	89547	13133	6486	983
1977	112494	89204	14120	7882	1289
1978	118040	91067	15590	9675	1709
1979	122071	91566	16823	11503	2179
1980	125209	91220	17900	13382	2706
1981	128061	90514	18908	15338	3301
1982	131705	90186	20019	17499	4001
1983	134469	89135	20946	19636	4752
1984	135781	87057	21596	21609	5520
1985	136795	84724	22165	23560	6346

Percentage Distribution of
New Labor Force Entrants, by Occupation,
Race, and Sex, 1970 to 1985

OTHER BUSINESS AND MANAGEMENT

YEAR	TOTAL	WHITE		BLACK	
		MALE	FEMALE	MALE	FEMALE
1970	100.00	90.76	7.32	1.78	0.15
1971	100.00	89.51	7.77	2.49	0.23
1972	100.00	88.45	8.24	3.02	0.29
1973	100.00	86.98	9.10	3.54	0.38
1974	100.00	84.84	10.47	4.16	0.53
1975	100.00	82.14	12.06	5.04	0.76
1976	100.00	81.30	11.92	5.89	0.89
1977	100.00	79.30	12.55	7.01	1.15
1978	100.00	77.15	13.2?	8.20	1.45
1979	100.00	75.01	13.78	9.42	1.79
1980	100.00	72.85	14.30	10.69	2.16
1981	100.00	70.68	14.76	11.98	2.58
1982	100.00	68.48	15.20	13.29	3.04
1983	100.00	66.29	15.58	14.60	3.53
1984	100.00	64.12	15.90	15.91	4.07
1985	100.00	61.93	16.20	17.22	4.64

TABLE V-10
United States
Projection of Labor Force, by Occupation,
Race, and Sex, 1970 to 1985

OTHER BUSINESS AND MANAGEMENT

		WHITE		BLACK	
YEAR	TOTAL	MALE	FEMALE	MALE	FEMALE
1970	1502009	1325491	143236	24392	8890
1971	1559705	1381275	143427	26349	8656
1972	1622526	1440483	144546	28981	8518
1973	1685626	1498365	146609	32164	8488
1974	1752126	1556858	150477	36153	8639
1975	1817230	1611268	155876	41044	9043
1976	1879601	1662691	160632	46722	9557
1977	1942890	1712787	166065	53689	10350
1978	2010263	1763808	172618	62319	11520
1979	2080035	1814382	179988	72618	13098
1980	2151384	1863689	187971	84605	15121
1981	2223828	1911412	196458	98329	17631
1982	2298167	1957978	205518	113965	20708
1983	2373460	2002705	214931	131455	24372
1984	2448224	2044620	224392	150605	28610
1985	2522168	2083543	233811	171366	33448

Percentage Distribution of
Projection of Labor Force, by Occupation,
Race, and Sex, 1970 to 1985

OTHER BUSINESS AND MANAGEMENT

		WHITE		BLACK	
YEAR	TOTAL	MALE	FEMALE	MALE	FEMALE
1970	100.00	88.25	9.54	1.62	0.59
1971	100.00	88.56	9.20	1.69	0.55
1972	100.00	88.78	8.91	1.79	0.52
1973	100.00	88.89	8.70	1.91	0.50
1974	100.00	88.86	8.59	2.06	0.49
1975	100.00	88.67	8.58	2.26	0.50
1976	100.00	88.46	8.55	2.49	0.51
1977	100.00	88.16	8.55	2.76	0.53
1978	100.00	87.74	8.59	3.10	0.57
1979	100.00	87.23	8.65	3.49	0.63
1980	100.00	86.63	8.74	3.93	0.70
1981	100.00	85.95	8.83	4.42	0.79
1982	100.00	85.20	8.94	4.96	0.90
1983	100.00	84.38	9.06	5.54	1.03
1984	100.00	83.51	9.17	6.15	1.17
1985	100.00	82.61	9.27	6.79	1.33

TABLE V-11
United States
New Labor Force Entrants, by Occupation,
Race, and Sex, 1970 to 1985

OTHER BUSINESS AND MANAGEMENT

		WHITE		BLACK	
YEAR	TOTAL	MALE	FEMALE	MALE	FEMALE
1970	86927	78892	6362	1544	129
1971	98394	88073	7645	2452	222
1972	104768	92664	8632	3164	308
1973	106428	92569	9684	3765	409
1974	111232	94365	11647	4630	590
1975	111358	91464	13434	5609	851
1976	110873	89547	14447	5896	983
1977	114005	89204	16944	6568	1289
1978	120484	91067	20267	7442	1709
1979	125514	91566	23552	8216	2179
1980	129698	91220	26850	8921	2706
1981	133655	90514	30253	9586	3301
1982	138512	90186	34032	10294	4001
1983	142499	89135	37704	10909	4752
1984	144982	87057	41032	11373	5520
1985	147180	84724	44330	11780	6346

Percentage Distribution of
New Labor Force Entrants, by Occupation,
Race, and Sex, 1970 to 1985

OTHER BUSINESS AND MANAGEMENT

		WHITE		BLACK	
YEAR	TOTAL	MALE	FEMALE	MALE	FEMALE
1970	100.00	90.76	7.32	1.78	0.15
1971	100.00	89.51	7.77	2.49	0.23
1972	100.00	88.45	8.24	3.02	0.29
1973	100.00	86.98	9.10	3.54	0.38
1974	100.00	84.84	10.47	4.16	0.53
1975	100.00	82.14	12.06	5.04	0.76
1976	100.00	80.77	13.03	5.32	0.89
1977	100.00	78.25	14.86	5.76	1.13
1978	100.00	75.58	16.82	6.18	1.42
1979	100.00	72.95	18.76	6.55	1.74
1980	100.00	70.33	20.70	6.88	2.09
1981	100.00	67.72	22.64	7.17	2.47
1982	100.00	65.11	24.57	7.43	2.89
1983	100.00	62.55	26.46	7.66	3.33
1984	100.00	60.05	28.30	7.84	3.81
1985	100.00	57.56	30.12	8.00	4.31

TABLE V-12
United States
Projection of Labor Force, by Occupation,
Race, and Sex, 1970 to 1985

OTHER BUSINESS AND MANAGEMENT

YEAR	TOTAL	WHITE		BLACK	
		MALE	FEMALE	MALE	FEMALE
1970	1502009	1325491	143236	24392	8890
1971	1559705	1381275	143427	26349	8656
1972	1622526	1440483	144546	28981	8518
1973	1685626	1498365	146609	32164	8488
1974	1752126	1556858	150477	36153	8639
1975	1817230	1611268	155876	41044	9043
1976	1880914	1662691	161946	46722	9557
1977	1946956	1712787	170131	53689	10350
1978	2018785	1763808	181140	62319	11520
1979	2094869	1814382	194773	72618	13098
1980	2174304	1863689	210891	84605	15121
1981	2256822	1911412	229452	98329	17631
1982	2343333	1957978	250685	113965	20708
1983	2432849	2002705	274320	131455	24372
1984	2523696	2044620	299864	150605	28610
1985	2615518	2083543	327162	171366	33448

Percentage Distribution of
Projection of Labor Force, by Occupation,
Race, and Sex, 1970 to 1985

OTHER BUSINESS AND MANAGEMENT

YEAR	TOTAL	WHITE		BLACK	
		MALE	FEMALE	MALE	FEMALE
1970	100.00	88.25	9.54	1.62	0.59
1971	100.00	88.56	9.20	1.69	0.55
1972	100.00	88.78	8.91	1.79	0.52
1973	100.00	88.89	8.70	1.91	0.50
1974	100.00	88.86	8.59	2.06	0.49
1975	100.00	88.67	8.58	2.26	0.50
1976	100.00	88.40	8.61	2.48	0.51
1977	100.00	87.97	8.74	2.76	0.53
1978	100.00	87.37	8.97	3.09	0.57
1979	100.00	86.61	9.30	3.47	0.63
1980	100.00	85.71	9.70	3.89	0.70
1981	100.00	84.69	10.17	4.36	0.78
1982	100.00	83.56	10.70	4.86	0.88
1983	100.00	82.32	11.28	5.40	1.00
1984	100.00	81.02	11.88	5.97	1.13
1985	100.00	79.66	12.51	6.55	1.28

TABLE V-13
United States
New Labor Force Entrants, by Occupation,
Race, and Sex, 1970 to 1985

OTHER BUSINESS AND MANAGEMENT

YEAR	TOTAL	WHITE		BLACK	
		MALE	FEMALE	MALE	FEMALE
1970	86927	78892	6362	1544	129
1971	98394	88073	7645	2452	222
1972	104768	92664	8632	3164	308
1973	106428	92569	9684	3765	409
1974	111232	94365	11647	4630	590
1975	111356	91464	13434	5609	851
1976	111462	89547	14447	6486	983
1977	115318	89204	16944	7882	1289
1978	122717	91067	20267	9675	1709
1979	128800	91566	23552	11503	2179
1980	134159	91220	26850	13382	2706
1981	139406	90514	30253	15338	3301
1982	145718	90186	34032	17499	4001
1983	151226	89135	37704	19636	4752
1984	155218	87057	41032	21609	5520
1985	158960	84724	44330	23560	6346

Percentage Distribution of
New Labor Force Entrants, by Occupation,
Race, and Sex, 1970 to 1985

THER BUSINESS AND MANAGEMENT

YEAR	TOTAL	WHITE		BLACK	
		MALE	FEMALE	MALE	FEMALE
1970	100.00	90.76	7.32	1.78	0.15
1971	100.00	89.51	7.77	2.49	0.23
1972	100.00	88.45	8.24	3.02	0.29
1973	100.00	86.98	9.10	3.54	0.38
1974	100.00	84.84	10.47	4.16	0.53
1975	100.00	82.14	12.06	5.04	0.76
1976	100.00	80.34	12.96	5.82	0.88
1977	100.00	77.35	14.69	6.84	1.12
1978	100.00	74.21	16.52	7.88	1.39
1979	100.00	71.09	18.29	8.93	1.69
1980	100.00	67.99	20.01	9.97	2.02
1981	100.00	64.93	21.70	11.00	2.37
1982	100.00	61.89	23.35	12.01	2.75
1983	100.00	58.94	24.93	12.98	3.14
1984	100.00	56.09	26.44	13.92	3.56
1985	100.00	53.30	27.89	14.82	3.99

TABLE V-14
United States
Projection of Labor Force, by Occupation,
Race, and Sex, 1970 to 1985

OTHER BUSINESS AND MANAGEMENT

YEAR	TOTAL	WHITE		BLACK	
		MALE	FEMALE	MALE	FEMALE
1970	1502009	1325491	143236	24392	8890
1971	1559705	1381275	143427	26349	8656
1972	1622526	1440483	144546	28981	8518
1973	1685626	1498365	146609	32164	8488
1974	1752126	1556858	150477	36153	8639
1975	1811230	1611268	155876	41044	9043
1976	1880325	1662691	161946	46132	9557
1977	1945064	1712787	170131	51797	10350
1978	2014697	1763808	181140	58232	11520
1979	2087574	1814382	194773	65323	13098
1980	2162688	1863689	210891	72990	15121
1981	2239676	1911412	229452	81183	17631
1982	2319307	1957978	250685	89938	20708
1983	2400548	2002705	274320	99154	24372
1984	2481763	2044620	299864	108672	28610
1985	2562584	2083543	327162	118433	33448

Percentage Distribution of
Projection of Labor Force, by Occupation,
Race, and Sex, 1970 to 1985

OTHER BUSINESS AND MANAGEMENT

YEAR	TOTAL	WHITE		BLACK	
		MALE	FEMALE	MALE	FEMALE
1970	100.00	88.25	9.54	1.62	0.59
1971	100.00	88.56	9.20	1.69	0.55
1972	100.00	88.78	8.91	1.79	0.52
1973	100.00	88.89	8.70	1.91	0.50
1974	100.00	88.86	8.59	2.06	0.49
1975	100.00	88.67	8.58	2.26	0.50
1976	100.00	88.43	8.61	2.45	0.51
1977	100.00	88.06	8.75	2.66	0.53
1978	100.00	87.55	8.99	2.89	0.57
1979	100.00	86.91	9.33	3.13	0.63
1980	100.00	86.17	9.75	3.37	0.70
1981	100.00	85.34	10.24	3.62	0.79
1982	100.00	84.42	10.81	3.88	0.89
1983	100.00	83.43	11.43	4.13	1.02
1984	100.00	82.39	12.08	4.38	1.15
1985	100.00	81.31	12.77	4.62	1.31

The base line projections and the three simulations indicate an interesting set of circumstances for the future course of women in business professions. Although women will be increasingly represented among degree earners and new labor force entrants, their proportional representation in the labor force will increase minimally, the possibility of any substantial improvement in penetration being doubtful. Despite the existence of several areas of uncertainty in the analysis (specifically, the size of the initial supply base and the separation rates), the relative participation of men and women in the initial labor force creates a relationship that is insensitive to large changes in the female-related variable values, such as female representation among annual degree recipients. Any progress in the representation of women in the labor force, therefore, would take a long time to become apparent.

The prognosis for black participation in these business and management areas, based on this analysis, is positive but not overwhelming. If these results were achieved, black penetration in the labor force in 1985 would be two and one-half to three and one-half times the 1970 black participation rate. Although this is a favorable change, the proportion of blacks in these occupations will probably not exceed their representation in the population.

CHAPTER VI

Minorities and Women in Law

It was not until 1964 that the Association of American Law Schools (AALS) was able to publish as a matter of firm belief, but not as a matter of fact, that none of its member-schools were denying admission to any applicants on the basis of race, religion, color, or national or ethnic origin. The mere declaration of a nondiscrimination policy without further action did little, however, to change the traditional profile of law school classes in the United States. During the academic years 1964-65 and 1965-66, minority students made up less than 2 percent of the students enrolled in this country's law schools. It was not until the 1967-68 academic year that AALS was able to gather reliable statistics, which are listed in Table VI-1. Minority students comprised 1,616 of the total 1967-68 law school enrollment of 64,406, or 2.5 percent of the total enrollment.[1] Women law students numbered 2,906 that same year, or 4.5 percent of the total law school enrollment.[2]

In 1975-76 the total law student enrollment was 116,991, which included 8,703 minority students and 26,737 women, or 7.4 percent minority students and 22.9 percent women students.[3] The distribution of women and nonwhites in the United States labor force is 38 percent and 11 percent, respectively, according to the 1970 Census data. Comparison of their representation in the labor force with their representation in the 1975-76 law school en-

---

[1] Walter J. Leonard, "Report of the Section on Minority Groups," *Association of American Law Schools 1974 Annual Meeting Proceedings* (Washington, D.C.: Association of American Law Schools, 1974), p. 113.

[2] Millard H. Ruud and James P. White, "Legal Education and Profession Statistics 1973-74," *Journal of Legal Education*, Vol. 26 (1974), p. 343, Table 1.

[3] *Law Schools & Bar Admission Requirements: A Review of Legal Education in the United States—Fall 1975* (Chicago: American Bar Association, 1976), pp. 42, 45.

TABLE VI-1
Minority Status of Law School Enrollments,
1967-68 Academic Year

Group	Enrollment
Black	1,254
American Indian	32
Puerto Rican	69
Chicano	180
Other Latin American	81

Source: Walter J. Leonard, "Report of the Section on Minority Groups," *Association of American Law Schools 1974 Annual Meeting Proceedings* (Washington, D.C.: Association of American Law Schools, 1974), p. 113.

rollments shows both minorities and women to be underrepresented in legal education.

Background

The development of programs to assist minorities in studying law began during the mid-1960s. As explained in the proceedings of the 1970 AALS Annual Meeting:

> By the mid-1960's individual law schools and their collective conscience, the AALS, had recognized that it was not enough merely to remove restrictions, at least where the real objective was to increase the number of minority group lawyers in the profession. Belatedly, the American legal community, the law schools, the bar associations, and the law firms developed programs to attract minority group members to the study and practice of law in larger numbers.[4]

AALS organized an Advisory Committee for the Minority Groups Study, and in the *AALS 1967 Annual Meeting Proceedings,* the committee reported a need for more minority lawyers and recommended ways to increase the entry of minority students into legal study. The committee report emphasized the need to improve prelegal education, to identify new resources for finan-

---

[4] Robert B. McKay, "The Law Schools and the Minority Group Law Students: A Survey for the AALS Committee on Minority Groups," *Association of American Law Schools 1970 Annual Meeting Proceedings* (Washington, D.C.: Association of American Law Schools, 1970), p. 10.

cial aid to needy students, and to reconsider evaluation standards for admission to law school.

Ensuing discussions brought about development of the Council on Legal Education Opportunity (CLEO) in the late 1960s. CLEO is jointly sponsored by the AALS, the American Bar Association (ABA), the National Bar Association, and the Law School Admission Test Council, with additional funding from the Office of Economic Opportunity (OEO) and private foundations. The objective of CLEO is to make certain that law schools in this country recognize the potential of nontraditional students.

Committee on Minority Groups

The Committee on Minority Groups was made a standing AALS committee in 1969 when it became more obvious that increasing the number of minority law school graduates involved more than just attracting a larger number of minority group students to legal education and finding financial assistance for their needs. Problems within the law schools regarding these students included the need for special academic assistance for some students, students' complaints about the relevance of the first years of law study, and students' uneasiness about the conflicting demands of their ethnic background and the profession.

The 1970 incoming members of the Committee on Minority Groups accepted a proposal to evaluate and report on law school programs for minority group students. In January 1970 a subcommittee agreed to analyze through interview sessions at selected law schools current programs designed to maximize the prospects for successful completion of legal education by minority group students.

Interviewers followed a common set of instructions and evaluated programs related to the following: curriculum changes; academic assistance programs before or during law school, including remedial programs; financial aid programs, including any noteworthy efforts of a local or regional character that might be replicated elsewhere; and a study of attitudes and responses to these efforts on the part of minority students, other students, faculty, and alumni.

The subcommittee decided to interview at law schools that had either a substantial number of minority group students enrolled during the survey period, spring 1970, or a conscious program of assistance for its minority group students. Just over 50 schools were selected by this process; those schools, however, enrolled more than 80 percent of all minority group students in American law schools during the academic year 1969-70.

The aim of the committee was accomplished by providing useful information to schools for evaluating existing programs or initiating new ones. The results of the interviews are published in the *Association of American Law Schools 1970 Annual Meeting Proceedings*.[5]

During 1971 the AALS Committee on Minority Groups began publishing a *Newsletter* to report current developments affecting minority groups in legal education. Moreover, on April 23 and 24 of that year the committee sponsored a program in New Orleans on minority students in legal education. Discussion topics at the conference ranged from minority recruitment and admission to special programs in law school, graduation, placement, and the bar examination.[6]

History

In 1970 the American Bar Foundation reported that there were approximately 300,000 lawyers in the country, or 1 lawyer for every 650 persons in the population. This includes those who identify themselves as lawyers, although many lawyers are also engaged in gainful activity other than the practice of law. Furthermore, there are many persons with legal education who are employed in some other occupation and who do not identify themselves as lawyers. Consequently, the estimate of the American Bar Foundation and data compiled by the Bureau of Census on the number of lawyers in the United States include a considerable number of persons who are only partially active as lawyers and excludes some who have been trained as lawyers, but are not active as such.[7]

Census data on experienced lawyers from 1940-1970, which are shown in Table VI-2, illustrate the dominance of white males in law. Data from Table VI-2 show that in 1940 white males

---

[5] *Ibid.*, pp. 5-63.

[6] Robert B. McKay, "Report of the Committee on Minority Groups," *Association of American Law Schools 1971 Annual Meeting Proceedings* (Washington, D.C.: Association of American Law Schools, 1971), pp. 82-83.

[7] *The Legal Profession in the United States* (Chicago: The American Bar Foundation, 1970), p. 32.

TABLE VI-2

Number of Experienced Civilian Lawyers and Judges
by Sex and Race, 1940-1970

Sex and Race	1940	1950	1960	1970
Lawyers and Judges Total	183,080	172,290	209,684	277,695
Male Lawyers and Judges	178,080	165,300	202,341	264,378
White	177,140	163,830	199,613	259,711
Negro	940 a	1,410	2,218	3,309
Other Races		60	510	1,358
Male Lawyers and Judges with 5 or more Years of College c	142,840	144,900	156,455	228,859
White	142,080	143,550	154,180	
Nonwhite	760	1,350	2,275	2,387 b
Female Lawyers and Judges	5,000	6,990	7,343	13,317
White	4,940	6,900	7,101	12,723
Negro	60 a	90	222	394
Other Races	—		20	200

Female Lawyers and Judges with 5 or more Years of College [c]	3,620	5,190	3,721	8,396
White	3,580	5,100	3,519	
Nonwhite	40	90	202	150 [b]

Sources: *Sixteenth Census of the United States: 1940 Population, The Labor Force, Occupational Characteristics* (Washington, D.C.: Government Printing Office, 1943), pp. 59-70 passim, Table 3.
United States Census of Population 1950, Occupational Characteristics, P-E No. 1B (Washington, D.C.: Government Printing Office, 1956), pp. 29, 107, 115, Tables 3, 10, 11.
United States Census of Population 1960, Occupational Characteristics, PC(2)-7A (Washington, D.C.: U.S. Department of Commerce, 1961), pp. 21, 116, 123, 130, 137, Tables 3, 9, 10.
1970 Census of Population Subject Report, Occupational Characteristics, PC(2)-7A (Washington, D.C.: U.S. Department of Commerce, 1973), pp. 12, 59, 73, 87, 101, Tables 2, 5, 6.

[a] Only nonwhite data available.
[b] Only Negro data available.
[c] For 1940 and 1950 data are only available for 4 or more years of college completed.

represented 97 percent of all those reporting their occupation to the Bureau of Census as lawyer or judge; furthermore, in 1970 the white male proportion remained high at 93 percent.

BLACKS

Statistics gathered of New York City's 26 major industry groups by the Equal Employment Opportunity Commission in January 1968 show that law firms ranked next to last in the employment of blacks and twentieth in the employment of Puerto Ricans. Even though 6.7 percent of the white-collar workers in banking firms were black, the Negro white-collar workforce in law firms comprised just 1.4 percent of the total employment of law firms.[8]

Prior to 1950

Before 1950 the black lawyer in private practice in the North was usually a general practitioner working as a neighborhood attorney in black communities of the city. With an office located in the black neighborhood, he handled cases restricted to negligence, probate, real estate, matrimonial matters, and criminal law. Cases involving corporate-business matters were nonexistent for him.

Since his clients were poor, the black lawyer could not demand high fees for his services; consequently, he relied on volume to make a living. There were a number of partnerships with two to four partners, but there were relatively few black firms with five members or more prior to 1950. The majority of black attorneys were sole practitioners.

Black attorneys lost black clients to white lawyers for several reasons during this period. Some blacks believed that white lawyers were better qualified than black lawyers; some black clients thought white lawyers had more political influence than blacks; and some blacks felt that because of prejudice against them, they had a better chance with the judge and jury if represented by a white lawyer.

It was common for young black lawyers to enter public service to obtain good legal training after graduation from law school. Working on the legal staff of district attorneys, public defenders,

---

[8] William H. Brown III, "Racial Discrimination in the Legal Profession," *Judicature*, Vol. 53 (April-May 1970), p. 385.

state attorneys general, and United States attorneys provided good professional training, experience, and higher incomes. In most cases, being hired depended on connections and political affiliations. In the pre-1950 period black judges were scarce. There were no blacks in the highest appellate state courts, and the only black federal district court judge was in the Virgin Islands where the population is predominantly black. The University of Chicago was the only predominantly white law school in the United States that had a black member on its faculty. During the period prior to 1950, approximately 1 percent or less of the lawyers in this country were black. Medicine, social work, and religion were economically more secure and attracted more black students during the years before 1950.[9]

During the pre-1950 period, many bar associations in the United States discriminated against black lawyers. It was not until 1943 that black attorneys were admitted to the American Bar Association.[10]

Since 1950

During the 1950s, white law firms and large companies began hiring black attorneys; however, it is still exceptional for black lawyers to practice in an integrated setting. Black lawyers are now losing fewer black clients to white lawyers. This is partially attributable to the growing racial pride in the black population of America. Since 1950 black attorneys have earned better livings as the black people have gained more affluence over the past two decades.

Although the trend is changing for black attorneys under thirty-four years of age, most black lawyers prefer to operate alone. More blacks are specializing in the corporate-business area of law, in fields such as taxation, labor law, corporate financing, and reorganization.

Many black attorneys are moving their offices from the black neighborhoods to prestigious downtown locations. Today a substantial amount of the practice of a number of black lawyers is composed of white clients. Even though bar associations are

---

[9] Samuel R. Pierce, Jr., "Black Advocate in the North," *Minority Opportunities in Law for Blacks, Puerto Ricans and Chicanos*, ed. Christine Philpot Clark (New York: Law Journal Press, 1974), pp. 45-46.

[10] Christine Philpot Clark and LeRoy Clark, "The Black Lawyer—A New Day, But Slow Dawning," *Minority Opportunities in Law*, p. 255.

open to blacks now, and many are working hard to get more black attorneys to join their organizations, these efforts have not met with much success. Many black lawyers feel that the predominantly white bar associations are not relevant to their needs; consequently, the blacks maintain their separate bar associations. The black attorneys who tend to be active in predominantly white bar associations are interested in the practice of corporate-business law, have a substantial white clientele, are associated with a white law firm, or are employed in the legal department of a business concern.

The number of black judges has increased significantly at all levels since 1950: one black was appointed to the Supreme Court in 1967. Black judges have also served in United States Circuit Courts of Appeals and the appellate courts of several states. Since 1954 several black attorneys have been appointed to sub-cabinet positions in the federal government, and since 1964 several black attorneys have been elected to the boards of large national and international corporations. Black lawyers have also progressed in the academic world. Many predominantly white law schools now have black faculty members, and one has a black dean.[11]

As a result of the accomplishments of black lawyers, the increased economic security of the profession, and the active recruitment of black students, the field of law is much more attractive to young blacks today than it was prior to 1950. Howard University estimates that blacks comprised 2 percent of the 1972 lawyer workforce in the United States and 4 percent of the 1971-72 total law school enrollment.[12] In 1974 there were 325,000 lawyers in this country; 3,250, or 1 percent, were black.[13] Table VI-3 shows the enrollment of black students from 1969 through 1975 in ABA-approved law schools.

The Future

Looking ahead twenty to thirty years, the data indicate that the practice of law will slowly integrate. The number of white clients whom black lawyers service will grow; the percentage

---

[11] Pierce, "Black Advocate in the North," pp. 49-50.

[12] Betty M. Vetter and Eleanor L. Babco, *Professional Women and Minorities: A Manpower Resource Service* (Washington, D.C.: Scientific Manpower Commission, 1975), p. 86, Tables G-Pro-7 and G-Pro-8.

[13] Christine Philpot Clark, ed., *Minority Opportunities in Law*, p. 4.

TABLE VI-3

Black Students Enrolled in ABA-Approved Law Schools,
1969-70 through 1975-76 [a]

Academic Year	Black Student Enrollment	Total Enrollment	Black Enrollment as a Percent of Total Enrollment
1969-70	2,128	68,386	3.11
1971-72	3,744	93,118	4.02
1972-73	4,423	101,664	4.35
1973-74	4,817	106,102	4.54
1974-75	4,995	110,713	4.51
1975-76	5,127	116,991	4.38

Source: *Law Schools & Bar Admission Requirements; A Review of Legal Education in the United States, Fall 1975* (Chicago: American Bar Association, 1976), pp. 42, 44.
[a] Data for 1970-71 are not available.

of black lawyers who practice as sole practitioners in black neighborhoods will decrease; the number of black partnerships will
increase; more black lawyers will move their offices to downtown
locations; and there will be many more black lawyers practicing
in the suburbs than there are today. Moreover, many more black
lawyers will head legal departments of large corporations, serve
on boards of directors of corporations, act as presidents of predominantly white bar associations, and hold high public office.[14]

OTHER MINORITY GROUPS

It was not until the late 1960s that the AALS was able to
gather reliable statistics on the number of minority students
enrolled in law schools; consequently, data on the ethnic and
racial composition of the legal profession are scarce. As a result, only the current status of Puerto Rican and Chicano minority groups in the legal profession will be discussed. Enrollments
in ABA-approved law schools for these groups and American
Indians and Asian Americans are shown in Table VI-4.

Spanish-surnamed Americans

The second largest minority group according to the Bureau
of Census data is the Spanish-surnamed, or perhaps better described, the Spanish-descended group, which represents 5 percent
of the United States population. The Spanish-descended group includes Chicanos (Mexican-Americans), Puerto Ricians, Cubans,
South Americans, and all other Spanish-related Americans. Even
though the number of Spanish-descended law students is increasing, there is still a tremendous shortage of Spanish-speaking
lawyers to serve the Spanish-speaking population in this country.
While the ratio of Anglo attorneys to Anglo citizens is about 1
to 500, the ratio of Spanish-descended is 1 to 9,000.[15]

Chicanos

In 1975-76 minorities represented 7 percent of the total law
school enrollment; however, Chicanos numbered only 1,297, or
1 percent of the total. Recently Chicanos have demonstrated
their interest in law by applying for financial support through

---

14 Pierce, "Black Advocate in the North," pp. 50-51.

15 Law Students Civil Rights Research Council, "Chicano and Other Spanish-
Descended Groups," *Minority Opportunities in Law*, p. 23.

TABLE VI-4

Minority Enrollments in ABA-Approved Law Schools,
1969-70 through 1975-76 [a]

Group	Year	Enrollment	Group Enrollment as Percent of Total
Chicano	1969-70	412	.60
	1971-72	883	.95
	1972-73	1,072	1.05
	1973-74	1,259	1.19
	1974-75	1,357	1.23
	1975-76	1,297	1.11
Puerto Rican	1969-70	61	.09
	1971-72	94	.10
	1972-73	143	.14
	1973-74	180	.17
	1974-75	263	.24
	1975-76	333	.28
American Indian	1969-70	72	.11
	1971-72	140	.15
	1972-73	173	.17
	1973-74	222	.21
	1974-75	265	.24
	1975-76	295	.25
Asian American	1969-70	185	.27
	1971-72	480	.52
	1972-73	681	.67
	1973-74	850	.80
	1974-75	1,063	.96
	1975-76	1,099	.94

Source: *Law School & Bar Admission Requirements: A Review of Legal Education in the United States—Fall 1975* (Chicago: American Bar Association, 1976), pp. 42, 44.

[a] Data for 1970-71 are not available.

CLEO. In 1973 the national offices of CLEO received 2,097 applications for 232 available positions: 373, or 17.8 percent, of the applications were from Chicanos.

The high schools attended by Chicanos are typically inferior academically, underfinanced, and often ethnically segregated. Chicano students often lose interest in school and do poorly because teachers, textbooks, and curricula are not attuned to the Chicano culture. Those students who do graduate from high school and decide to attend college usually enroll in local institutions. Their majors are most likely to be social work or education. Consequently, those applying for law school often present credentials, which include LSAT scores and GPAs, that cannot compete favorably with credentials of top Anglo students. Chicano students have no lawyer-heroes to attract them to the law profession as the blacks have. Moreover, a Chicano's perception of law influences his idea of the lawyer. Anglo attorneys are often associated with policemen and with remembrances of evictions, repossessions, and other personal misfortune.[16]

Puerto Ricans

Between 1950 and 1970 the United States mainland Puerto Rican population tripled to nearly 1.4 million; about 1 out of every 3 Puerto Ricans lives on the mainland United States. Even though its proportion of the mainland Puerto Rican population declined from 82 percent in 1950 to 59 percent in 1970, New York City continues to have a larger concentration of Puerto Ricans than any other city in the world. In 1970 the Puerto Rican population in New York City was 812,000, and they represented 6 percent of the city's working population. The best source of detailed data is the 1970 Census, which shows that Puerto Ricans are concentrated in blue-collar, low-skilled occupations and in the declining sectors of New York City's economy. Moreover, they suffer higher levels of unemployment and seasonal work than other residents. In 1970 only 33 percent of New York City's Puerto Ricans held white-collar jobs, and less than 5 percent of these were in professional and technical occupations. Those in the professional and technical occupations were primarily technicians. In law, medicine, education, and engineering,

---

[16] Leo M. Romero, Richard Delgado, and Cruz Reynoso, "Legal Education of Chicano Students: A Study in Mutual Accommodation and Cultural Conflict," *New Mexico Law Review*, Vol. 5 (May 1975), pp. 191-95.

Puerto Ricans represented less than 1 percent of the city's total employment in those occupations.[17]

The economic profile of the Puerto Ricans who were counted by the Bureau of the Census indicates that the Puerto Ricans are by far the most severely deprived major ethnic group in the cities of America. Among adults over 25 years of age, only 1 Puerto Rican in 100 had a college degree in 1970. Puerto Rican professional groups estimate that New York State, which has a Puerto Rican population of more than one million, has less than 70 Puerto Rican lawyers. Furthermore, New Jersey's Spanish-speaking population of more than 300,000 is served by 3 Puerto Rican lawyers.[18]

WOMEN

In 1954-55 women earned 3.5 percent of the LL.B. and J.D. degrees conferred in law;[19] however, by 1974-75 that percentage had increased to 15 percent.[20] Although only 2.8 percent of this country's attorneys were women in 1972, the ABA reported in 1975 that women constituted 5 to 7 percent of the 400,000 practicing lawyers in the United States.[21]

Past Participation of Women in Law

In 1869 Belle A. Mansfield was admitted to the state bar of Iowa; she is reputed to be the first female admitted to practice in the United States.[22] In the 1873 case *Bradwell* v. *Illinois*, however, the Supreme Court sustained denial of Bradwell's application to practice law in Illinois. In his concurring opinion, Mr. Justice Bradly dismissed the contention that the Fourteenth amendment gave women the right to pursue any legitimate employment. He stated:

---

[17] Lois S. Gray, "The Jobs Puerto Ricans Hold in New York City," *Monthly Labor Review*, Vol. 98 (October 1975), p. 12.

[18] José A. Cabranes, "A Puerto Rican Perspective," *Minority Opportunities in Law*, pp. 11-12.

[19] Vetter and Babco, *Professional Women and Minorities*, p. 82, Table G-Pro-2-A.

[20] *Law Schools & Bar Admission Requirements*, p. 43.

[21] "Women: Still Number Two But Trying Harder," *Time*, May 26, 1975, pp. 40-41.

[22] James J. White, "Women in the Law," *Michigan Law Review*, Vol. 65 (March 1967), p. 1051.

> The paramount destiny and mission of woman are to fulfill the noble and benign affairs of wife and mother. This is the law of the Creator.[23]

By 1920 all states had admitted women to practice before the bar, and the ABA opened its membership to women. Yet, it was not until 1950 that Harvard Law School admitted its first woman.[24]

Although the trend is changing, in previous years women lawyers have not enjoyed equality in financial remuneration and in the types of jobs available to them. The *American Bar News* reported in October 1970 that nine out of ten law firms refused to interview women lawyers. Consequently, in the past female attorneys have been concentrated in the government sector.[25]

Participation of women in the legal profession is shown in Table VI-5 for past years. Table VI-6 shows the representations of women in ABA-approved law schools from 1963 to 1975.

Present Trends

As of October 1975 women represented 23 percent of the 116,991 students enrolled in ABA-approved law schools in the United States; during academic year 1974-75, women received 15 percent of the LL.B. and J.D. degrees conferred;[26] and the ABA reported in 1975 that women comprised 5 to 7 percent of the 400,000 practicing lawyers in this country.[27] These statistics demonstrate the rapid increase of women entering law education.

Women attorneys are no longer limited to finding good jobs in the government sector. Table VI-7 shows the 1970 distribution of lawyers in the various practice situations.

Some law schools are responding to the increased number of women law students by including special courses on women's legal rights. Furthermore, two Harvard professors have written a "desexified" casebook, which presents an equal number of men and women in prominent roles.[28]

---

[23] James F. Gilsinan, Lynn Obernyer, and Christine A. Gilsinan, "Women Attorneys and the Judiciary," *Denver Law Review*, Vol. 52 (1975), p. 883.

[24] Janette Barnes, "Women and Entrance to the Legal Profession," *Journal of Legal Education*, Vol. 23 (1970-71), p. 276.

[25] Gilsinan, Obernyer, and Gilsinan, "Women Attorneys and the Judiciary," p. 887.

[26] *Law Schools & Bar Admission Requirements*, pp. 43, 45.

[27] "Women: Still Number Two But Trying Harder," p. 41.

[28] *Ibid.*, p. 41.

TABLE VI-5
Participation of Women in the Legal Profession,
Selected Years 1948-1963

Year	Total Lawyers	Female Lawyers	Female Lawyers as a Percent of Total Lawyers
1948	171,110	2,997	1.8
1951	204,111	5,059	2.5
1954	221,600	5,036	2.3
1957	235,783	6,350	2.7
1960	252,385	6,488	2.6
1963	268,782	7,143	2.7

Source: Faye A. Hankin and Duane W. Krohnke, *The 1964 Lawyer Statistical Report* (Chicago: American Bar Foundation, 1965), pp. 25, 29, Tables 1 and 4.

TABLE VI-6

Women Enrolled in ABA-Approved Law Schools, 1963-1975

Year [a]	Enrollment of Women	Total Enrollment	Enrollment of Women as a Percent of Total Enrollment
1963	1,883	49,552	3.80
1964	2,183	54,265	4.02
1965	2,537	59,744	4.25
1966	2,678	62,556	4.28
1967	2,906	64,406	4.51
1968	3,704	62,779	5.90
1969	4,715	68,386	6.89
1970	7,031	82,499	8.52
1971	8,914	94,468	9.43
1972	12,173	101,707	11.97
1973	16,760	106,102	15.80
1974	21,788	110,713	19.68
1975	26,737	116,991	22.85

Source: *Law Schools & Bar Admission Requirements: A Review of Legal Education in the United States—Fall 1975* (Chicago: American Bar Association, 1976), p. 45.

[a] Enrollment as of October 1 of each year.

TABLE VI-7

National Distribution of Lawyers in Each Practice Situation by Sex, 1970

	Total in All Practice Situations		Men in All Practice Situations			Women in All Practice Situations		
	No.	% of Total	No.	% of Total	% of Men	No.	% of Total	% of Women
ALL PRACTICE SITUATIONS	339,535	100.00	330,087	97.22	100.00	9,448	2.78	100.00
Government Sector (total)	46,152	13.59	44,654	96.75	13.53	1,498	3.25	15.86
Executive & Legislative (total)	35,803	10.54	34,488	96.33	10.45	1,315	3.67	13.92
City or County	7,800	2.30	7,598	97.41	2.30	202	2.59	2.14
State	9,293	2.74	8,893	95.70	2.69	400	4.30	4.23
Federal	18,710	5.51	17,997	96.19	5.45	713	3.81	7.55
Judicial (total)	10,349	3.05	10,166	98.23	3.08	183	1.77	1.94
City	1,923	0.57	1,890	98.28	0.57	33	1.72	0.35
County or State	7,548	2.22	7,417	98.26	2.25	131	1.74	1.39
Federal	878	0.26	859	97.84	0.26	19	2.16	0.20
Private Sector (total)	276,571	81.46	269,868	97.58	81.76	6,703	2.42	70.95
Private Practice (total)	236,085	69.54	230,359	97.57	69.79	5,726	2.43	60.61
Individuals	118,963	35.04	115,120	96.77	34.88	3,843	3.23	40.68
Partners	92,442	27.23	91,215	98.67	27.63	1,227	1.33	12.99
Associates	24,680	7.27	24,024	97.34	7.28	656	2.66	6.94
Private Employment (total)	40,486	11.92	39,509	97.59	11.97	977	2.41	10.34
Private Industry	33,593	9.89	33,051	98.39	10.01	542	1.61	5.74
Educational Institutions	3,732	1.10	3,573	95.74	1.08	159	4.26	1.68
Other	3,161	0.93	2,885	91.27	0.87	276	8.73	2.92
Inactive or Retired	16,812	4.95	15,565	92.58	4.72	1,247	7.42	13.20

Source: Martha Grossblat and Bette H. Silas, eds., *Women Lawyers: Supplementary Data to the 1971 Lawyer Statistical Report* (Chicago: American Bar Foundation, 1973), p. 8.

The Future

The increasing number of women entering law schools shows women's awareness of the career opportunities available in law. Even though continuation of the current female entry rate into law schools will raise the percentage of women attorneys significantly, the current entry rate is not strong enough to bring female attorneys to a parity level in the national labor force during the next decade.

The absence of minorities in law firms and courts has tainted the legal profession with an image of insensitivity and insincerity toward the nation's ills and minority groups. As a result, a large number of law school graduates are not entering traditional legal work, but instead they are working for social action agencies of the government. A survey done in the early 1970s showed that nineteen of twenty-five members of the *Harvard*

Law Review wanted to work where they could make a contribution to solving the nation's social problems. This is evidence of the increasing number of young lawyers entering social action law.[29]

The growing number of lawyers is another force pushing law school graduates out of traditional law careers. This factor is explained in a 1973 issue of the *Journal of Legal Education*:

> The demand for lawyers is growing, but it hardly seems possible that it can expand at a rapid enough rate in the next few years to absorb the already incipient supply. To absorb the rising tide, there would have to be a re-structuring of the profession to meet the needs of those who are not now adequately served. In the near future, it seems unlikely that society will so change its priorities that lawyers will be adequately compensated for meeting these needs. Hence up to half of the graduates in the near future may have to seek employment in fields where traditionally legal training is not a prerequisite.[30]

In June 1975, 31,000 students were graduated from law schools in the United States, which is more than 3 times the number graduated in 1963. School administrators estimate that 10 to 20 percent of these graduates were still looking for jobs in February 1976. Since enrollments have stabilized at the high level of 100,000 students, the number of lawyers in the country is expected to double to 700,000 between now and 1985.[31]

Continuing expansion of business activity and of the population, as well as the increased use of legal services by low- and middle-income groups, will provide growth in the number of legal positions available. Community Action Programs authorized under the Economic Opportunity Act of 1964 provide for the expansion of legal services for low-income groups. Furthermore, the growing complexity of business and government regulatory laws dealing with environmental protection, occupational health and safety, and truth-in-lending and pension regulation are expected to create a steadily expanding demand for lawyers who have extensive experience in corporation, patent, administrative, labor, and international law. Nevertheless, continuing a recent

---

[29] Brown, "Racial Discrimination in the Legal Profession," pp. 386-87.

[30] John C. York and Rosemary D. Hale, "Too Many Lawyers? The Legal Services Industry: Its Structure and Outlook," *Journal of Legal Education*, Vol. 26 (1974), p. 31.

[31] Tom Goldstein, "Law Students Find Shortage of Jobs," *New York Times*, February 11, 1976, p. 39.

trend, the number of lawyers in independent practice will remain stable or decline somewhat.[32]

CURRENT PROGRAMS

Responses to a minority law student recruitment program survey conducted by the Law Student Division of the ABA during the 1970-71 academic year indicate that an active and aggressive campaign to recruit students from minority groups for the study of law requires five basic activities: recruiting trips to undergraduate schools with significant minority enrollments; recruiting by mail with a larger number of undergraduate schools having significant minority enrollments; minority recruiting weekends at the law school; summer programs for minority students; and financial assistance. Summer programs for minority students were particularly stressed as a means of providing law schools with an opportunity to assess applicants on a basis other than the traditional grade point average and Law School Aptitude Test and, also, of assisting the minority student to bridge the gap between his earlier educational experience and the significantly different experience he will encounter in law school. Financial assistance can be made available in the form of grants, obtaining employment for spouses, part-time student employment, low-cost housing, and summer employment.[33]

Council of Legal Education Opportunity (CLEO)

The Council of Legal Education Opportunity (CLEO), which was founded in the late 1960s, is a federally funded program seeking to enable "economically disadvantaged" students with "marginal" or less than conventional admissions credentials to have an opportunity to attend an accredited law school. To achieve this, CLEO inspires and co-sponsors recruiting programs to inform and encourage students to choose law as a career; operates with the cooperation of several accredited law schools six-week summer institutes to provide selected students a vehicle to identify their capacity to become adjusted to the process of law study; and provides an annual living stipend to those sum-

---

[32] *Occupational Outlook Handbook: 1972-73 Edition*, Bulletin 1700 (Washington, D.C.: Government Printing Office, n.d.), p. 248.

[33] Law Student Division of the American Bar Association, *Equal Rights Report* (Chicago: American Bar Association, 1972), pp. 55-58.

mer institute students who continue on in law school. CLEO is sponsored jointly by the ABA, AALS, the National Bar Association, and the Law School Admission Council.

The summer institutes provide students with exposure to three substantive law school courses and a legal writing course, each taught by experienced law school faculty. Moreover, these institutes are staffed by minority student assistants who are already attending law school.

The conditions of the CLEO grant are that: the student must enter an accredited law school; the student must continue in good standing as a regular full-time student for three consecutive years; and the law school in which the student enrolls must provide for the student's tuition in the form of a grant, loan, or a combination of the two.

CLEO enrolled its first class numbering 93 in September 1968. By June 1971, over 70 of the students had graduated. These students received an annual living stipend provided by a grant from the Ford Foundation. The 1970 class was the first to receive its stipends from federal funds. That year Office of Economic Opportunity (OEO) Legal Services provided for the costs of administering CLEO and also granted funds sufficient to provide stipends at an average annual amount of $1,000 each for a class of 200.[34]

Earl Warren Legal Training Program

The Earl Warren Legal Training Program, which was formed in 1971, was established to increase the number of black lawyers and to assure the quality and location of legal talent trained in civil rights law. This program awards both law school scholarships and postgraduate fellowships. During the 1975-76 academic year, the Warren Program awarded 243 scholarships to students attending 53 law schoools. Most of these students are attending Southern law schools, and 1/3 of them are women.[35]

The four-year postgraduate fellowship program includes a first year of internship in either the Legal Defense Fund's (LDF) national office or in the offices of LDF's cooperating attorneys. Following the year of internship, the fellows are helped to begin

---

[34] Clark, *Minority Opportunities in Law*, pp. 207-09.

[35] *Annual Report of the NAACP Legal Defense and Educational Fund, Inc.* (New York: The NAACP Legal Defense and Educational Fund, Inc., 1975-76), p. 26.

law practice in a mutually agreed upon location where there are few or no black lawyers to serve the black population. During the last three years of the fellowship, the fellows receive a beginning law library, assistance with office furniture and moving expenses, and support on a diminishing basis.[36]

As of April 1974 the Earl Warren Legal Training Program had received a total of $3.8 million from 21 foundations. Major donations have come from the Carnegie Foundation, the Rockefeller Foundation, the Field Foundation, the Alfred P. Sloan Foundation, and the Fleischmann Foundation.[37]

American Indian Law Center

OEO, HEW, and the Bureau of Indian Affairs provide funds for a program for forty American Indians interested in attending law school. The program offers summer training, assistance in gaining admission to law school, and financial assistance during law school. Any American Indian who has completed at least three years of college may apply.

Mexican American Legal Defense Fund

The Mexican American Legal Defense Fund (MALDEF), which is funded by foundations such as Ford, Fleischmann, and New World, provides grants for 190 to 200 Chicano students. No grant exceeds $1,000. About 25 law schools, mostly in the Southwest, cooperate with MALDEF. The school must provide resources to meet tuition cost.

Opportunity Fellowship Program

This program is open to blacks, Spanish Americans, Mexican-Americans, American Indians, and residents of United States territories. Awards range from $1,000 to $5,000 and are based on the nature of study undertaken and on the applicant's need.

Regional Programs

The Consortium of Metropolitan Law Schools provides scholarships to needy minority law students attending five law schools

---

[36] *Ibid.*

[37] Paul Delaney, "Blacks Given Aid in Law Studies," *New York Times*, April 18, 1974, p. 13.

in or near New York City: Brooklyn, Fordham, New York, St. John's, and Seton Hall.

The Legal Opportunities Scholarship Program provides funds to minority group students entering five Chicago area law schools: Chicago-Kent, DePaul, Loyola, Northwestern, and University of Chicago.

The Ohio Law Opportunity Fund aims to provide financial assistance averaging $2,000 a year for 3 years to 90 new law students who are members of groups economically disadvantaged as a result of racial, ethnic, or geographic factors. The law schools involved in this program are Case-Western Reserve, Cleveland-Marshall, Franklin, Ohio Northern, Ohio State, Salmon P. Chase College of Law, University of Akron, University of Cincinnati, and University of Toledo. A more complete listing of financial aid and loan funds available to minorities in law school appears in Appendix A of *Minority Opportunities in Law for Blacks, Puerto Ricans & Chicanos*.[38]

PREDICTING THE NUMBERS OF MINORITIES AND WOMEN IN LAW

The review of the past and present status of minorities and women in law explains the current experience and the ongoing efforts to improve the participation of these groups in the legal profession. The labor supply model was implemented in order to generate some estimates of the participation of minorities and women in the future. Four sets of projections were produced and are presented in this section. The first, a base line projection, represents the continuation of current trends in the composition of law school graduates. The last three are alternative projections which display the effect which alterations in the racial and sexual composition of law school graduates would have on the composition of the legal labor force.

The projections indicate that substantial progress can be expected in the representation of women and minorities in the legal profession in spite of the domination of the field by white men as documented by the 1970 Census.

---

[38] Christine Philpot Clark, *Minority Opportunities in Law for Blacks, Puerto Ricans & Chicanos* (New York: Law Journal Press, 1974), pp. 195-209.

Base Line Projections

The base line projections of new entrants to the legal labor force and of the labor force are based on the continuation of current trends in the racial and sexual composition of law school graduates. Table VI-8 summarizes the input data used to generate all four projection sets. Since data on the racial breakdown of annual graduates are not available, black representation among third-year enrollments, derived from a report by the Section of Legal Education and Admissions to the Bar of the American Bar Association, was used as a proxy measure.[39]

The labor force separation rates for men in law are higher than they are for men in other professional occupations, especially engineering and the sciences; the same holds true for men in medicine and dentistry. The reason behind this situation is the age distribution of the labor force, which is characterized by a greater number of older age groups. The relative size of male and female separation rates in this case should be a benefit in improving the representation of women in the legal profession.

The new entrants pool to the legal labor force, shown in Table VI-9, was almost 5.2 percent female and 2.7 percent black in 1970. These statistics coincide with the proportion of degrees awarded to these groups in 1970 because the model assumes that 100 percent of all graduates enter the labor force. The number of new entrants is projected to increase from almost 15,500 in 1970 to approximately 33,000 in 1983 and then remain at that level for several years. Current trends indicate that by 1985 women will occupy 27.6 percent of the positions in the pool of new entrants, and that blacks will increase their representation to 8.0 percent in that year.

In 1970, women and blacks comprised 3.5 percent and 1.1 percent, respectively, of lawyers in the labor force (Table VI-10). Given the trends in the new entrants pool, female participation should increase to 12.5 percent, which is an improvement of 9.0 percentage points over the 1970 level. Black penetration should increase to 4.5 percent in 1985, a level that is more than 4 times 1970 black participation.

These projections indicate that women will make substantial progress in increasing their participation in the legal profession as a result of continuing and increasing representation among new graduates and in spite of a large male contingent. The

---

[39] *Law School & Bar Admission Requirements*, pp. 42, 44.

TABLE VI-8
Input Data for Simulation
of Lawyers in the Labor Force to 1985

	MALE	FEMALE
SEPARATION RATE	WHITE	
1970	0.0315	0.0632
1985	0.0291	0.0641
	BLACK	
1970	0.0254	0.0407
1985	0.0232	0.0411
ENTRY RATE		
FIRST PROFESSIONAL	1.0000	1.0000
SUPPLY BASE – 1970		
TOTAL	228859	8396
BLACK	2387	150

	DEGREES AWARDED	
	% FEMALE	% BLACK
FIRST PROFESSIONAL		
1969	3.99	2.31
1970	5.37	2.66
1971	7.12	2.99
1972	6.88	3.40
1973	7.97	3.91
1974	11.39	4.05
1975	15.07	4.46

future for blacks is favorable, but limited when compared to women, because black representation among new graduates is increasing at a slower rate than female representation.

Sensitivity Analysis

Three alternative projections were produced in order to assess the sensitivity of the racial and sexual composition of the lawyer labor force to changes in black and female representation among new law school graduates. The first simulation altered the stream of black graduates from 1975 to 1985 in order to achieve a 100 percent increase in their number above the base line projection in 1985. The number of white degree recipients was maintained at the base line level. The second simulation incorporated the same specification, but altered the stream of women coming out of law schools, while the base line projections for men were maintained. The third and final simulation achieved a doubling of black and female graduates by 1985, while the number of degrees awarded to white men was maintained.

The first simulation produces a new entrants pool that is 14.8 percent black in 1985, almost 7.0 percentage points above the base line projection for that year (Table VI-11). The proportion of female new entrants is essentially the same as the base line figures with a small shift in representation from white to black women. Table VI-12 shows the resultant labor force after incorporating the new entrant streams. Black penetration would reach 6.8 percent in 1985, which is 6 times their 1970 level of participation. As a result of the greater number of incoming black women, female participation in the legal labor force would increase only 0.3 percentage points above base line projections.

The doubling of the number of women graduates, as dictated by the second simulation, produces a 1985 new entrants pool that is 43.3 percent female, which is approximately 8.5 times the 1970 proportion. These figures are shown in Table VI-13. The proportion of blacks in the new entrants pool would remain the same as the base line projection. If these changes occurred, the lawyer labor force, outlined in Table VI-14, would become 18.3 percent female, which is a 5.8 percentage point increase in female participation above 1985 base line projections. Black participation in the labor force would increase to 4.9 percent by 1985, which represents a 0.2 percentage point change from the base line projection for that year.

TABLE VI-9
United States
New Labor Force Entrants, by Occupation,
Race, and Sex, 1970 to 1985

LAWYERS

YEAR	TOTAL	WHITE		BLACK	
		MALE	FEMALE	MALE	FEMALE
1970	15445	14259	774	391	21
1971	17421	15733	1163	489	36
1972	21764	19426	1599	683	56
1973	27200	23810	2347	949	93
1974	29300	24873	3230	1059	138
1975	29296	24033	3954	1124	185
1976	29910	24265	4198	1233	213
1977	30710	24375	4741	1335	260
1978	31410	24390	5278	1432	310
1979	31710	24089	5750	1510	361
1980	32090	23850	6234	1590	416
1981	32420	23573	6707	1666	474
1982	32720	23275	7170	1739	536
1983	33010	22973	7628	1809	601
1984	33010	22475	8011	1861	663
1985	33010	21988	8384	1910	728

Percentage Distribution of
New Labor Force Entrants, by Occupation,
Race, and Sex, 1970 to 1985

LAWYERS

YEAR	TOTAL	WHITE		BLACK	
		MALE	FEMALE	MALE	FEMALE
1970	100.00	92.32	5.01	2.53	0.14
1971	100.00	90.31	6.67	2.81	0.21
1972	100.00	89.26	7.34	3.14	0.26
1973	100.00	87.54	8.63	3.49	0.34
1974	100.00	84.89	11.02	3.62	0.47
1975	100.00	82.03	13.50	3.84	0.63
1976	100.00	81.13	14.04	4.12	0.71
1977	100.00	79.37	15.44	4.35	0.85
1978	100.00	77.65	16.80	4.56	0.99
1979	100.00	75.97	18.13	4.76	1.14
1980	100.00	74.32	19.43	4.96	1.30
1981	100.00	72.71	20.69	5.14	1.46
1982	100.00	71.13	21.91	5.31	1.64
1983	100.00	69.59	23.11	5.48	1.82
1984	100.00	68.08	24.27	5.64	2.01
1985	100.00	66.61	25.40	5.79	2.21

TABLE VI-10
United States
Projection of Labor Force, by Occupation,
Race, and Sex, 1970 to 1985

LAWYERS

YEAR	TOTAL	WHITE		BLACK	
		MALE	FEMALE	MALE	FEMALE
1970	237255	226472	8246	2387	150
1971	246990	235108	8887	2816	180
1972	260783	247203	9923	3429	229
1973	279591	263345	11641	4293	313
1974	299907	280091	14132	5246	438
1975	319559	295525	17188	6241	605
1976	339174	310765	20294	7322	793
1977	358941	325698	23744	8479	1021
1978	378750	340246	27509	9706	1289
1979	398192	354107	31506	10983	1597
1980	417357	367369	35730	12311	1947
1981	436197	380016	40155	13685	2341
1982	454691	392050	44759	15101	2781
1983	472834	403488	49523	16556	3267
1984	490347	414157	54363	18031	3796
1985	507247	424092	59263	19523	4368

Percentage Distribution of
Projection of Labor Force, by Occupation,
Race, and Sex, 1970 to 1985

LAWYERS

YEAR	TOTAL	WHITE		BLACK	
		MALE	FEMALE	MALE	FEMALE
1970	100.00	95.46	3.48	1.01	0.06
1971	100.00	95.19	3.60	1.14	0.07
1972	100.00	94.79	3.80	1.31	0.09
1973	100.00	94.19	4.16	1.54	0.11
1974	100.00	93.39	4.71	1.75	0.15
1975	100.00	92.48	5.38	1.95	0.19
1976	100.00	91.62	5.98	2.16	0.23
1977	100.00	90.74	6.61	2.36	0.28
1978	100.00	89.83	7.26	2.56	0.34
1979	100.00	88.93	7.91	2.76	0.40
1980	100.00	88.02	8.56	2.95	0.47
1981	100.00	87.12	9.21	3.14	0.54
1982	100.00	86.22	9.84	3.32	0.61
1983	100.00	85.33	10.47	3.50	0.69
1984	100.00	84.46	11.09	3.68	0.77
1985	100.00	83.61	11.68	3.85	0.86

TABLE VI-11
United States
New Labor Force Entrants, by Occupation,
Race, and Sex, 1970 to 1985

LAWYERS

YEAR	TOTAL	WHITE		BLACK	
		MALE	FEMALE	MALE	FEMALE
1970	15445	14259	774	391	21
1971	17421	15733	1163	489	36
1972	21764	19426	1599	683	56
1973	27200	23810	2347	949	93
1974	29300	24873	3230	1059	138
1975	29296	24033	3954	1124	185
1976	30055	24265	4198	1357	235
1977	31029	24375	4741	1602	312
1978	31933	24390	5278	1862	403
1979	32458	24089	5750	2114	505
1980	33093	23850	6234	2386	624
1981	33704	23573	6707	2666	759
1982	34312	23275	7170	2956	911
1983	34938	22973	7628	3256	1081
1984	35282	22475	8011	3535	1260
1985	35648	21988	8384	3819	1457

Percentage Distribution of
New Labor Force Entrants, by Occupation,
Race, and Sex, 1970 to 1985

LAWYERS

YEAR	TOTAL	WHITE		BLACK	
		MALE	FEMALE	MALE	FEMALE
1970	100.00	92.32	5.01	2.53	0.14
1971	100.00	90.31	6.67	2.81	0.21
1972	100.00	89.26	7.34	3.14	0.26
1973	100.00	87.54	8.63	3.49	0.34
1974	100.00	84.89	11.02	3.62	0.47
1975	100.00	82.03	13.50	3.84	0.63
1976	100.00	80.74	13.97	4.51	0.78
1977	100.00	78.55	15.28	5.16	1.00
1978	100.00	76.38	16.53	5.83	1.26
1979	100.00	74.22	17.71	6.51	1.56
1980	100.00	72.07	18.84	7.21	1.88
1981	100.00	69.94	19.90	7.91	2.25
1982	100.00	67.83	20.90	8.61	2.65
1983	100.00	65.75	21.83	9.32	3.09
1984	100.00	63.70	22.71	10.02	3.57
1985	100.00	61.68	23.52	10.71	4.09

TABLE VI-12
United States
Projection of Labor Force, by Occupation,
Race, and Sex, 1970 to 1985

LAWYERS

		WHITE		BLACK	
YEAR	TOTAL	MALE	FEMALE	MALE	FEMALE
1970	237255	226472	8246	2387	150
1971	246990	235108	8887	2816	180
1972	260783	247203	9923	3429	229
1973	279591	263345	11641	4293	313
1974	299907	280091	14132	5246	438
1975	319559	295525	17188	6241	605
1976	339319	310765	20294	7445	815
1977	359401	325698	23744	8866	1093
1978	379720	340246	27509	10514	1451
1979	399885	354107	31506	12375	1897
1980	420007	367369	35730	14465	2443
1981	440060	380016	40155	16788	3101
1982	460041	392050	44759	19348	3884
1983	479960	403408	49523	22150	4806
1984	499558	414157	54363	25170	5869
1985	518845	424092	59263	28406	7084

Percentage Distribution of
Projection of Labor Force, by Occupation,
Race, and Sex, 1970 to 1985

LAWYERS

		WHITE		BLACK	
YEAR	TOTAL	MALE	FEMALE	MALE	FEMALE
1970	100.00	95.46	3.48	1.01	0.06
1971	100.00	95.19	3.60	1.14	0.07
1972	100.00	94.79	3.80	1.31	0.09
1973	100.00	94.19	4.16	1.54	0.11
1974	100.00	93.39	4.71	1.75	0.15
1975	100.00	92.48	5.38	1.95	0.19
1976	100.00	91.58	5.98	2.19	0.24
1977	100.00	90.62	6.61	2.47	0.30
1978	100.00	89.60	7.24	2.77	0.38
1979	100.00	88.55	7.88	3.09	0.47
1980	100.00	87.47	8.51	3.44	0.58
1981	100.00	86.36	9.12	3.81	0.70
1982	100.00	85.22	9.73	4.21	0.84
1983	100.00	84.07	10.32	4.61	1.00
1984	100.00	82.90	10.88	5.04	1.17
1985	100.00	81.74	11.42	5.47	1.37

TABLE VI-13
United States
New Labor Force Entrants, by Occupation,
Race, and Sex, 1970 to 1985

LAWYERS

YEAR	TOTAL	WHITE		BLACK	
		MALE	FEMALE	MALE	FEMALE
1970	15445	14259	774	391	21
1971	17421	15733	1163	489	36
1972	21764	19426	1599	683	56
1973	27200	23810	2347	949	93
1974	29300	24873	3230	1059	138
1975	29296	24033	3954	1124	185
1976	30351	24265	4618	1233	235
1977	31710	24375	5689	1335	312
1978	33086	24390	6861	1432	403
1979	34154	24089	8050	1510	505
1980	35415	23850	9351	1590	624
1981	36729	23573	10731	1666	759
1982	38114	23275	12190	1739	911
1983	39593	22973	13730	1809	1081
1984	40817	22475	15222	1861	1260
1985	42123	21988	16769	1910	1457

Percentage Distribution of
New Labor Force Entrants, by Occupation,
Race, and Sex, 1970 to 1985

LAWYERS

YEAR	TOTAL	WHITE		BLACK	
		MALE	FEMALE	MALE	FEMALE
1970	100.00	92.32	5.01	2.53	0.14
1971	100.00	90.31	6.67	2.81	0.21
1972	100.00	89.26	7.34	3.14	0.26
1973	100.00	87.54	8.63	3.49	0.34
1974	100.00	84.89	11.02	3.62	0.47
1975	100.00	82.03	13.50	3.84	0.63
1976	100.00	79.95	15.21	4.06	0.77
1977	100.00	76.87	17.94	4.21	0.98
1978	100.00	73.72	20.74	4.33	1.22
1979	100.00	70.53	23.57	4.42	1.48
1980	100.00	67.34	26.41	4.49	1.76
1981	100.00	64.18	29.22	4.54	2.07
1982	100.00	61.07	31.98	4.56	2.39
1983	100.00	58.02	34.68	4.57	2.73
1984	100.00	55.06	37.29	4.56	3.09
1985	100.00	52.20	39.81	4.53	3.46

TABLE VI-14
United States
Projection of Labor Force, by Occupation,
Race, and Sex, 1970 to 1985

LAWYERS

YEAR	TOTAL	WHITE		BLACK	
		MALE	FEMALE	MALE	FEMALE
1970	237255	226472	8246	2387	150
1971	246990	235108	8887	2816	180
1972	260783	247203	9923	3429	229
1973	279591	263345	11641	4293	313
1974	299907	280091	14132	5246	438
1975	319559	295525	17188	6241	605
1976	339615	310765	20714	7322	815
1977	360355	325698	25085	8479	1093
1978	381751	340246	30349	9706	1451
1979	403451	354107	36464	10983	1897
1980	425611	367369	43489	12311	2443
1981	448245	380016	51443	13685	3101
1982	471380	392050	60344	15101	3884
1983	495064	403488	70214	16556	4806
1984	518995	414157	80939	18031	5869
1985	543219	424092	92519	19523	7084

Percentage Distribution of
Projection of Labor Force, by Occupation,
Race, and Sex, 1970 to 1985

LAWYERS

YEAR	TOTAL	WHITE		BLACK	
		MALE	FEMALE	MALE	FEMALE
1970	100.00	95.46	3.48	1.01	0.06
1971	100.00	95.19	3.60	1.14	0.07
1972	100.00	94.79	3.80	1.31	0.09
1973	100.00	94.19	4.16	1.54	0.11
1974	100.00	93.39	4.71	1.75	0.15
1975	100.00	92.48	5.38	1.95	0.19
1976	100.00	91.51	6.10	2.16	0.24
1977	100.00	90.38	6.96	2.35	0.30
1978	100.00	89.13	7.95	2.54	0.38
1979	100.00	87.77	9.04	2.72	0.47
1980	100.00	86.32	10.22	2.89	0.57
1981	100.00	84.78	11.48	3.05	0.69
1982	100.00	83.17	12.80	3.20	0.82
1983	100.00	81.50	14.18	3.34	0.97
1984	100.00	79.80	15.60	3.47	1.13
1985	100.00	78.07	17.03	3.59	1.30

Achieving a 100 percent increase in both black and female law school graduates, shown in the third simulation, would increase black representation to 12.0 percent of the new entrants pool in 1985 with women occupying 41.4 percent of the pool in that year (Table VI-15). These levels of representation are substantial increases over and above 1970 levels and 1985 base line projections. The result of these changes in the new entrants pool is a 1985 legal labor force that is 18.0 percent female and 6.4 percent black, as shown in Table VI-16. This represents a 5.5 percentage point increase in the participation of women and a 1.7 percentage point increase in black participation above the representation levels for the groups determined by the continuation of current trends to 1985.

These three simulations indicate that the labor supply mechanism is quite sensitive to changes in the racial and sexual composition of new law degree recipients. This sensitivity is a function of several factors: the relatively high separation rate of men compared to women, and the obviously effective programs in operation designed to enroll more women and blacks in law schools.

TABLE VI-15
United States
New Labor Force Entrants, by Occupation,
Race, and Sex, 1970 to 1985

LAWYERS

YEAR	TOTAL	WHITE		BLACK	
		MALE	FEMALE	MALE	FEMALE
1970	15445	14259	774	391	21
1971	17421	15733	1163	489	36
1972	21764	19426	1599	683	56
1973	27200	23810	2347	949	93
1974	29300	24873	3230	1059	138
1975	29296	24033	3954	1124	185
1976	30474	24265	4618	1357	235
1977	31977	24375	5689	1602	312
1978	33516	24390	6861	1862	403
1979	34758	24089	8050	2114	505
1980	36210	23850	9351	2386	624
1981	37728	23573	10731	2666	759
1982	39331	23275	12190	2956	911
1983	41040	22973	13730	3256	1081
1984	42492	22475	15222	3535	1260
1985	44032	21988	16769	3819	1457

Percentage Distribution of
New Labor Force Entrants, by Occupation,
Race, and Sex, 1970 to 1985

LAWYERS

YEAR	TOTAL	WHITE		BLACK	
		MALE	FEMALE	MALE	FEMALE
1970	100.00	92.32	5.01	2.53	0.14
1971	100.00	90.31	6.67	2.81	0.21
1972	100.00	89.26	7.34	3.14	0.26
1973	100.00	87.54	8.63	3.49	0.34
1974	100.00	84.89	11.02	3.62	0.47
1975	100.00	82.03	13.50	3.84	0.63
1976	100.00	79.63	15.15	4.45	0.77
1977	100.00	76.23	17.79	5.01	0.97
1978	100.00	72.77	20.47	5.56	1.20
1979	100.00	69.30	23.16	6.08	1.45
1980	100.00	65.86	25.83	6.59	1.72
1981	100.00	62.48	28.44	7.07	2.01
1982	100.00	59.18	30.99	7.52	2.32
1983	100.00	55.98	33.46	7.93	2.63
1984	100.00	52.89	35.82	8.32	2.97
1985	100.00	49.94	38.08	8.67	3.31

TABLE VI-16
United States
Projection of Labor Force, by Occupation,
Race, and Sex, 1970 to 1985

LAWYERS

YEAR	TOTAL	WHITE MALE	WHITE FEMALE	BLACK MALE	BLACK FEMALE
1970	237255	226472	8246	2387	150
1971	246990	235108	8887	2816	180
1972	260783	247203	9923	3429	229
1973	279591	263345	11641	4293	313
1974	299907	280091	14132	5246	438
1975	319559	295525	17188	6241	605
1976	339738	310765	20714	7445	815
1977	360742	325698	25085	8866	1093
1978	382559	340246	30349	10514	1451
1979	404843	354107	36464	12375	1897
1980	427766	367369	43489	14465	2443
1981	451348	380016	51443	16788	3101
1982	475627	392050	60344	19348	3884
1983	500658	403488	70214	22150	4806
1984	526134	414157	80939	25170	5869
1985	552102	424092	92519	28406	7084

Percentage Distribution of
Projection of Labor Force, by Occupation,
Race, and Sex, 1970 to 1985

LAWYERS

YEAR	TOTAL	WHITE MALE	WHITE FEMALE	BLACK MALE	BLACK FEMALE
1970	100.00	95.46	3.48	1.01	0.06
1971	100.00	95.19	3.60	1.14	0.07
1972	100.00	94.79	3.80	1.31	0.09
1973	100.00	94.19	4.16	1.54	0.11
1974	100.00	93.39	4.71	1.75	0.15
1975	100.00	92.48	5.38	1.95	0.19
1976	100.00	91.47	6.10	2.19	0.24
1977	100.00	90.29	6.95	2.46	0.30
1978	100.00	88.94	7.93	2.75	0.38
1979	100.00	87.47	9.01	3.06	0.47
1980	100.00	85.88	10.17	3.38	0.57
1981	100.00	84.20	11.40	3.72	0.69
1982	100.00	82.43	12.69	4.07	0.82
1983	100.00	80.59	14.02	4.42	0.96
1984	100.00	78.72	15.38	4.78	1.12
1985	100.00	76.81	16.76	5.15	1.28

CHAPTER VII

Minorities and Women in Science

Although a very small portion of the total workforce, the scientific population of the United States is one of the country's most valuable manpower assets. The condition and development of our national well-being depends to a large extent, on the work of the scientific community. This chapter focuses on the participation of minorities and women in chemistry and physics by first assessing the information available in the literature and then using the model to determine the supply of physicists and chemists in future years.

MINORITIES AND WOMEN IN PHYSICS

The reduction of federal financial support for physics research, which began in the late 1960s, has had three effects on the physics community. The reduction reversed the trend of faculty expansion at American colleges and universities; as students became discouraged about the job market, it decreased first-year graduate physics enrollments at universities and colleges where most physicists are employed; moreover, it increased the teaching-loads of existing physics faculty members to accommodate increasing undergraduate enrollments at the introductory level.

Since 1967 there has been a change in the attitude of physicists toward applied research. The slowdown of industrial research and the economic recession around 1970 has forced physicists to become more receptive to the concept of adapting their physics training not only to interdisciplinary work, but also to many new areas of study such as biophysics, energy research, and geophysics.

The American Institute of Physics (AIP) surveys show that although job opportunities for new physics degree recipients are now improving over that of the early 1970s, 34 percent of the new Ph.D.s are still entering temporary postdoctoral positions, and physics enrollments and degrees awarded continue to decline on all levels, the largest drop being at the doctoral level.[1]

Background

During the 1860s and 1870s when science was just coming into vogue in the United States, there were probably fifty to seventy-five physicists in the country. Only the newly founded Massachusetts Institute of Technology (MIT) made lab work in physics a required part of the curriculum. Before MIT's innovation, the style of physics instruction did not lend itself to application in practice. Physics was learned from textbooks by rote, with almost no laboratory practice. The United States had only seventeen technical schools in 1870, and none were very well attended.[2]

The number of United States engineering schools rose from 17 in 1870 to 72 in 1872, and by then laboratory study in science was a cornerstone of educational policy. Harvard College was offering degrees in chemistry, physics, mathematics, astronomy, and natural history by the mid-1870s. At the time, chemistry was more popular than physics. A survey taken in 1880 showed that laboratory work in physics was offered in 35 technical schools, universities, and colleges, while 148 institutions offered similar work in chemistry. At Harvard the best attended physics elective drew 12 students, and the sophomore chemistry course registered 108 students.[3]

By the late 1880s there were 150 professional physicists in the United States. Most of those with advanced degrees had studied in Europe. Between 1873 and 1890 only 22 physics doctorates were awarded in the United States.[4]

Although most physicists of the early 1900s worked in academia, members of the profession were also establishing themselves in industry and government. Early in the twentieth century, American industry began to offer patronage to basic scientific investigation; for example, DuPont, Eastman Kodak, Standard Oil of Indiana, American Telephone and Telegraph, and Gen-

---

[1] Betty Vetter, ed., *Scientific, Engineering, Technical Manpower Comments*, Vol. 13 (September 1976), p. 12.

[2] Daniel J. Kevles, "The Study of Physics in America, 1865-1916" (Ph.D. dissertation, Princeton University, 1964), pp. 4, 5, 19.

[3] *Ibid.*, pp. 66, 68, 71, 72.

[4] *Ibid.*, pp. 121, 143.

eral Electric created research organizations. Physicists were also employed in the federal government's National Bureau of Standards. In 1914, of the Bureau's 230 employees, 144 were scientists.[5]

The American Physical Society was founded May 20, 1899 with a membership of 59, but that steadily increased until it reached 1,296 in 1920.[6] Today the society is a member of the American Institute of Physics (AIP), which was founded in 1931 as a federation of leading societies in the field of physics. Currently AIP is made up of 9 societies and thus represents 50,000 physicists. In addition, 4,500 students in 450 colleges and universities are members of the institute's Society of Physics Students.[7]

Census Data

Census data for experienced civilian physicists are presented in Table VII-1. The data are not comparable, however, because the occupational classification for physicists varies so much for each Census report. Data for 1940 are omitted in the table because that census report does not list physicists or a related occupational category. The numbers given for 1950 are for all natural scientists, which include agricultural scientists, biological scientists, chemists, geologists and geophysicists, mathematicians, physicists, and miscellaneous natural scientists. The 1960 data are for physicists only, but the 1970 data include astronomers as well as physicists.

According to the 1960 data, minorities represented 2.9 percent and women 3.4 percent of all people reporting their occupation as physicist. In 1970, minorities were 4.1 percent and women were 4.3 percent of those reporting their occupation as astronomer or physicist.

National Science Foundation (NSF) Estimate of Professional Physicists

Table VII-2 presents the number of physicists/astronomers in the United States by sexual and by racial composition as estimated by the National Science Foundation (NSF). The estimates were

---

[5] *Ibid.*, pp. 249, 284.

[6] *Ibid.*, pp. 211, 301, Appendix IV.

[7] *Physics Manpower, 1973* (New York: American Institute of Physics, 1973), inside front cover.

TABLE VII-1

Number of Experienced Civilian Physicists by Sex and Race, 1950-1970

Sex and Race	1950 [a]	1960	1970 [b]
Physicists Total	38,700	14,154	22,971
Male Physicists	33,120	13,672	21,992
White	32,550	13,322	21,171
Negro	420	142	237
Other Races	150	208	584
Male Physicists with 4 or More Years of College	23,280	11,880	19,850
White	23,100	11,530	
Nonwhite	180	350	189 [c]
Female Physicists	5,580	482	979
White	5,340	422	869
Negro	210	60	91
Other Races	30	—	19

Female Physicists with 4 or More Years
of College

	3,810	279	818
White	3,750	239	
Nonwhite	60	40	70 [c]

Sources: *Sixteenth Census of the United States; 1940 Population, The Labor Force, Occupational Characteristics* (Washington, D.C.: Government Printing Office, 1943), pp. 59-70 *passim*, Table 3.
United States Census of Population 1950, Occupational Characteristics, P-E No. 1B (Washington, D.C.: Government Printing Office, 1956), pp. 29, 107, 115, Tables 3, 10, 11.
United States Census of Population 1960, Occupational Characteristics, PC(2)-7A (Washington, D.C.: U.S. Department of Commerce, 1961), pp. 21, 116, 123, 130, 137, Tables 3, 9, 10.
1970 Census of Population Subject Report, Occupational Characteristics, PC(2)-7A (Washington, D.C.: U.S. Department of Commerce, 1973), pp. 12, 59, 73, 87, 101, Tables 2, 5, 6.

[a] Data for 1950 is for natural scientists.
[b] Data for 1970 includes astronomers.
[c] Only Negro data available.

TABLE VII-2

National Science Foundation Estimate, Physicists/Astronomers in the United States by Sex and Race, 1974[a]

	Total	White	Black	Indian	Asian	Other
Total	42,400	40,300	300	b	1,400	400
Male	39,900	37,800	300	b	1,400	400
Female	2,500	2,400	100	b	b	b

Source: *U.S. Scientists and Engineers: 1974*, NSF 76-329 (Washington, D.C.: Government Printing Office, 1976), p. 29, Table B-8.

[a] Detail may not add to total because of rounding.
[b] Too few cases to estimate.

made based on inputs from 5 NSF surveys: the 1974 National Survey of Scientists and Engineers, the Survey of College-Educated Men and Women—Class of 1971, 1972, and 1973, and the 1973 Survey of Doctoral Scientists and Engineers.[8] Based on this information, NSF estimates that there are 42,400 physicists/astronomers in the United States.

BLACKS

In 1876, Edward A. Bouchet became the first American Negro to receive a science doctorate when Yale University conferred the Ph.D. in physics upon him. Despite the fact that Bouchet was elected to Phi Beta Kappa during his senior year and ranked sixth in his graduating class, he spent nearly all of his post-doctoral years teaching in high schools.[9]

Education of Black Physicists

Between 1876 and 1969, thirty-four physics doctorates were awarded to blacks in the United States.[10] In 1974-75, sixteen physics doctorates were awarded to black students. Table VII-3 shows the physics degrees awarded to blacks between 1972-73 and 1974-75. Even though there was a drop in the actual number and percentage of blacks receiving physics degrees between 1972-73 and 1973-74, the latest data for 1974-75 show an increase in number and percentage of blacks receiving physics degrees.

OTHER MINORITIES

AIP first began collecting racial and ethnic data on physics students in 1972, but even today little more than impressions and opinions exist concerning the involvement of racial and ethnic groups in the physics community because they comprise such a small segment of the profession and the data are so scarce.

Education of Minority Physicists

Table VII-4 presents the number of physics degree awarded to minority students in 1974 and 1975. Included in this classifi-

---

[8] *U.S. Scientists and Engineers: 1974*, NSF 76-329 (Washington, D.C.: Government Printing Office, 1976), p. 12.

[9] James M. Jay, *Negroes in Science: Natural Science Doctorates, 1876-1969* (Detroit, Michigan: Balamp Publishing, 1971), pp. 52-53.

[10] *Ibid.*, p. 50.

TABLE VII-3

Number of Physics Degrees Awarded to Blacks by Degree Level,
1972-73 through 1974-75

Year	Bachelor		Master		Doctoral	
	Number	Percent of Total	Number	Percent of Total	Number	Percent of Total
1972-73	123	2.5	34	1.7	14	1.0
1973-74	71	1.5	27	1.5	7	0.6
1974-75	105	2.3	30	1.8	16	1.4

Sources: *Physics Manpower Report, Enrollments and Degrees,* No. R-151.11 (New York: American Institute of Physics, 1974), pp. 2, 6, Tables I, VIII. *Physics Manpower Report, Enrollments and Degrees,* No. R-151.12 (New York: American Institute of Physics, 1975), p. 8, Table VIII. *Physics Manpower Report, Enrollments and Degrees,* No. R-151.13 (New York: American Institute of Physics, 1976), p. 7, Table IX.

TABLE VII-4

Number of Physics Degrees Awarded to Other Minorities [a]
by Degree Level, 1973-74 and 1974-75

Year	Bachelor		Master		Doctoral	
	Number	Percent of Total	Number	Percent of Total	Number	Percent of Total
1973-74	117	2.5	189	10.7	174	14.1
1974-75	102	2.2	125	7.6	136	11.7

Sources: *Physics Manpower Report, Enrollments and Degrees*, No. R-151.12 (New York: American Institute of Physics, 1975), p. 8, Table VIII.
Physics Manpower Report, Enrollments and Degrees, No. R-151.13 (New York: American Institute of Physics, 1975), p. 8, Table IX.
[a]Other minorities includes American Indian, Mexican-American, Puerto Rican, Asian Indian, and Oriental Students.

cation of minorities are American Indian, Mexican-American, Puerto Rican, Asian Indian, and Oriental students. According to these AIP data, both the absolute number and percentage of minorities receiving physics degrees fell between 1973-74 and 1974-75.

WOMEN

Until perhaps as late as 1950, James Cattell's *American Men of Science* was a favorite source of data on both men and women of science. In his third edition of the directory, which was published in 1921, Cattell listed twenty-one women physicists.[11]

Since 1920 women have earned only 2.3 percent of the doctorates awarded in physics, but the percentage is rising. In 1975, 62 doctoral physics degrees were awarded to women; this represents 5.3 percent.[12]

Education of Women Physicists

Among physics students, women have always constituted a very small minority. Yet the past decade has witnessed a small but steady increase in the number and percentage of women who receive bachelor and graduate degrees. Table VII-5 provides data on the number of physics degrees awarded to women in recent years.

Participation of Women in the Physics Profession

Of the 1,354 women reporting themselves as physicists to the National Register in 1970, 57.7 percent worked in educational institutions, where they made up 4.3 percent of the total. The 9.0 percent who worked in industry or business represented only 1.2 percent of the physics workforce for that type of employment. According to work activity, 37.7 percent of the women were teaching, while 27.0 percent worked in research and development.

---

[11] Margaret W. Rossiter, "Quantitative History of Women Scientists in U.S., 1920-1950" (Paper presented at the International Symposium on Quantitative Methods in the History of Science, Berkeley, Califorina, 25-27 August 1976), p. 2 and Table 2.

[12] Betty M. Vetter and Eleanor L. Babco, *Professional Women and Minorities: A Manpower Resource Service* (Washington, D.C.: Scientific Manpower Commission, 1975), pp. 221, 225, Table PS-P-2.

TABLE VII-5
*Number of Physics Degrees Awarded to Women by Degree Level,
1972-73 through 1974-75*

Year	Bachelor		Master		Doctoral	
	Number	Percent of Total	Number	Percent of Total	Number	Percent of Total
1972-73	303	6.2	132	6.7	47	3.3
1973-74	319	6.9	125	7.1	53	4.3
1974-75	406	8.9	115	7.0	53	4.5

Sources: *Physics Manpower Report, Enrollments and Degrees*, No. R-151.11 (New York: American Institute of Physics, 1974), pp. 2, 5, Tables I, VII.
Physics Manpower Report, Enrollments and Degrees, No. R-151.12 (New York: American Institute of Physics, 1975), p. 8, Table VIII.
Physics Manpower Report, Enrollments and Degrees, No. R-151.13 (New York: American Institute of Physics, 1976), p. 7, Table IX.

Women, however, made up only 0.7 percent of the management/administration in the 1970 physics workforce.[13]

PREDICTING THE NUMBERS OF MINORITIES AND WOMEN IN PHYSICS

The review of the past and present status of minorities and women in the physics profession not only documents the small number of black and female physicists, but also the paucity of existing qualitative information. This void in the literature is, perhaps, an indication of the degree of emphasis given to integrating the profession.

The labor supply creation model was implemented to examine the future course of the racial and sexual composition of the profession. The same format used for the other occupations included in this study is followed here: a base line projection and three alternative simulations. The base line projections indicate slow but steady progress in increasing black and female representation among physicists. The simulations show that greater progress could be achieved given the parameters of the labor supply model.

Base Line Projections

The input data used in all the projections of new entrants to the physicist labor force and the labor force itself are provided in Table VII-6. An interesting observation about the data is that black men display a higher separation rate than white men, while the reverse exists for the other occupational classifications examined in this study. The relative size of the separation rates is important because of the impact these rates have on the expected changes in black participation in the physicist labor force. The racial data on the proportion of degrees awarded to blacks and the entry rates used in the calculations were derived from surveys conducted by the American Institute of Physics and from other information supplied by the Institute.[14]

---

13 *Ibid.*, p. 232, Tables PS-P-15, PS-P-16.

14 *Physics Manpower Report, Enrollments and Degrees*, No. R-151.11 (New York: American Institute of Physics, 1974), pp. 2, 6, Tables I, VIII; *Physics Manpower Report, Enrollments and Degrees*, No. R-151.12 (New York: American Institute of Physics, 1975), p. 8, Table VIII; *Physics Manpower Report, Enrollments and Degrees*, No. R-151.13 (New York: American Institute of Physics, 1976), p. 7, Table IX; *Physics Manpower, 1973, op. cit.*, pp. 33-35, 83, 85-87.

TABLE VII-6
Input Data for Simulation
of Physicists in the Labor Force to 1985

	MALE·	FEMALE
SEPARATION RATE		WHITE
1970	0.0096	0.0546
1985	0.0084	0.0564
		BLACK
1970	0.0177	0.0651
1985	0.0162	.0.0661
ENTRY RATE		
BACHELOR	0.3000	0.3000
MASTER	0.4500	0.4500
DOCTOR	0.5500	0.5500
SUPPLY BASE - 1970		
TOTAL	19850	818
BLACK	189	70

	DEGREES AWARDED	
	% FEMALE	% BLACK
BACHELOR		
1969	5.76	1.03
1970	6.15	1.12
1971	6.70	1.57
1972	6.96	1.30
1973	7.16	2.30
1974	8.30	1.52
1975	9.63	2.29
MASTER		
1969	4.90	1.53
1970	6.62	1.62
1971	6.22	2.19
1972	7.18	2.30
1973	5.56	1.68
1974	7.15	1.52
1975	6.72	1.82
DOCTOR.		
1969	2.47	1.00
1970	2.57	1.40
1971	2.90	1.55
1972	3.15·	1.60
1973	3.61	0.37
1974	4.27	.0.57
1975	4.89	1.07

The number of new entrants to the physicist labor pool, shown in Table VII-7, is projected to decline from less than 3,400 in 1970 to less than 2,100 in 1985. This decline will be absorbed by the white male group as the number of entering women and blacks is projected to increase over the period. In 1970, women comprised 5.3 percent of the entering labor pool, and their representation should increase to 11.8 percent in 1985. Black representation in the new entrants pool is projected to be 2.9 percent in 1985, a level that is more than twice the proportion of blacks in 1970, 1.3 percent.

The base line projections of the labor force (Table VII-8) show that the number of physicists in the labor force will continue to increase from 1970 to 1985, but at a decreasing rate. Black and female participation in 1970 was 1.3 percent and 4.0 percent, respectively. If the new entrant projections were achieved, black penetration would increase 0.4 percentage points to 1.7 percent in 1985, and women would make up 4.9 percent of the labor force in that year. In contrast to the experience in other professions, these are absolute gains in representation as opposed to net gains.

These base line projections indicate that with a substantial decline in the number of new labor force entrants being absorbed by white men, black and female representation will increase slowly, but consistently, in the future.

Sensitivity Analysis

In order to assess the sensitivity of the projection calculations of the labor force to changes in the racial and sexual composition of new entrants, three alternative forecasts were implemented. Simulation I dictates a 100 percent increase in the number of degrees awarded to blacks by 1985, while the base line projections of white degree earners are maintained. Simulation II repeats the process for women, while the base line projections for men are maintained. The third simulation doubles the number of projected degrees awarded to women and blacks by 1985, while the projected number of degrees awarded to white men is again maintained.

The results of Simulation I are shown in Table VII-9 for new entrants and in Table VII-10 for the labor force. A doubling of the number of black degree recipients produces an increase in the proportion of blacks among new labor force entrants to

TABLE VII-7
United States
New Labor Force Entrants, by Occupation,
Race, and Sex, 1970 to 1985

PHYSICISTS

YEAR	TOTAL	WHITE		BLACK	
		MALE	FEMALE	MALE	FEMALE
1970	3377	3156	178	42	2
1971	3289	3056	182	48	3
1972	3019	2790	181	46	3
1973	2734	2523	164	45	3
1974	2520	2309	173	35	3
1975	2467	2240	181	43	3
1976	2435	2203	186	43	3
1977	2264	2035	183	42	4
1978	2217	1980	190	43	4
1979	2165	1920	195	45	5
1980	2145	1891	203	46	5
1981	2144	1880	211	48	6
1982	2131	1857	218	49	6
1983	2120	1837	226	51	7
1984	2098	1807	232	52	7
1985	2078	1779	238	53	8

Percentage Distribution of
New Labor Force Entrants, by Occupation,
Race, and Sex, 1970 to 1985

PHYSICISTS.

YEAR	TOTAL	WHITE		BLACK	
		MALE	FEMALE	MALE	FEMALE
1970	100.00	93.44	5.26	1.23	0.07
1971	100.00	92.91	5.54	1.47	0.08
1972	100.00	92.41	5.98	1.51	0.09
1973	100.00	92.27	5.99	1.63	0.10
1974	100.00	91.63	6.86	1.40	0.10
1975	100.00	90.78	7.35	1.73	0.14
1976	100.00	90.47	7.62	1.76	0.15
1977	100.00	89.87	8.10	1.86	0.17
1978	100.00	89.29	8.56	1.98	0.19
1979	100.00	88.69	9.03	2.07	0.22
1980	100.00	88.16	9.44	2.15	0.24
1981	100.00	87.67	9.84	2.23	0.27
1982	100.00	87.16	10.24	2.31	0.29
1983	100.00	86.65	10.64	2.39	0.32
1984	100.00	86.13	11.05	2.47	0.35
1985	100.00	85.63	11.45	2.55	0.37

TABLE VII-8
United States
Projection of Labor Force, by Occupation, Race, and Sex, 1970 to 1985

PHYSICISTS

YEAR	TOTAL	WHITE MALE	WHITE FEMALE	BLACK MALE	BLACK FEMALE
1970	20668	19661	748	189	70
1971	23721	22530	889	234	68
1972	26471	25107	1021	276	67
1973	28905	27395	1129	316	65
1974	31099	29450	1240	345	64
1975	33217	31419	1353	382	63
1976	35280	33335	1463	419	63
1977	37151	35069	1566	454	62
1978	38955	36735	1669	489	63
1979	40689	38329	1771	526	63
1980	42385	39882	1875	563	64
1981	44063	41415	1981	602	66
1982	45711	42914	2088	641	68
1983	47332	44384	2196	682	70
1984	48914	45815	2305	722	73
1985	50461	47209	2413	764	76

Percentage Distribution of
Projection of Labor Force, by Occupation, Race, and Sex, 1970 to 1985

PHYSICISTS

YEAR	TOTAL	WHITE MALE	WHITE FEMALE	BLACK MALE	BLACK FEMALE
1970	100.00	95.13	3.62	0.91	0.34
1971	100.00	94.98	3.75	0.99	0.29
1972	100.00	94.85	3.86	1.04	0.25
1973	100.00	94.78	3.91	1.09	0.23
1974	100.00	94.70	3.99	1.11	0.20
1975	100.00	94.59	4.07	1.15	0.19
1976	100.00	94.49	4.15	1.19	0.18
1977	100.00	94.40	4.21	1.22	0.17
1978	100.00	94.30	4.28	1.26	0.16
1979	100.00	94.20	4.35	1.29	0.16
1980	100.00	94.10	4.42	1.33	0.15
1981	100.00	93.99	4.50	1.37	0.15
1982	100.00	93.88	4.57	1.40	0.15
1983	100.00	93.77	4.64	1.44	0.15
1984	100.00	93.66	4.71	1.48	0.15
1985	100.00	93.56	4.78	1.51	0.15

TABLE VII-9
United States
New Labor Force Entrants, by Occupation,
Race, and Sex, 1970 to 1985

PHYSICISTS

YEAR	TOTAL	WHITE MALE	WHITE FEMALE	BLACK MALE	BLACK FEMALE
1970	3377	3156	178	42	2
1971	3289	3056	182	48	3
1972	3019	2790	181	46	3
1973	2734	2523	164	45	3
1974	2520	2309	173	35	3
1975	2467	2240	181	43	3
1976	2440	2203	186	47	4
1977	2274	2035	183	51	5
1978	2232	1980	190	56	6
1979	2185	1920	195	63	7
1980	2171	1891	203	69	8
1981	2177	1880	211	77	9
1982	2170	1857	218	84	11
1983	2166	1837	226	91	12
1984	2151	1807	232	99	14
1985	2139	1779	238	106	16

Percentage Distribution of
New Labor Force Entrants, by Occupation,
Race, and Sex, 1970 to 1985

PHYSICISTS

YEAR	TOTAL	WHITE MALE	WHITE FEMALE	BLACK MALE	BLACK FEMALE
1970	100.00	93.44	5.26	1.23	0.07
1971	100.00	92.91	5.54	1.47	0.08
1972	100.00	92.41	5.98	1.51	0.09
1973	100.00	92.27	5.99	1.63	0.10
1974	100.00	91.63	6.86	1.40	0.10
1975	100.00	90.78	7.35	1.73	0.14
1976	100.00	90.30	7.61	1.93	0.16
1977	100.00	89.51	8.07	2.23	0.20
1978	100.00	88.72	8.51	2.53	0.25
1979	100.00	87.88	8.95	2.87	0.30
1980	100.00	87.12	9.33	3.19	0.36
1981	100.00	86.37	9.69	3.52	0.42
1982	100.00	85.60	10.05	3.86	0.48
1983	100.00	84.81	10.41	4.21	0.56
1984	100.00	84.00	10.78	4.58	0.64
1985	100.00	83.19	11.12	4.95	0.73

TABLE VII-10
United States
Projection of Labor Force, by Occupation, Race, and Sex, 1970 to 1985

PHYSICISTS

YEAR	TOTAL	WHITE		BLACK	
		MALE	FEMALE	MALE	FEMALE
1970	20668	19661	748	189	70
1971	23721	22530	889	234	68
1972	26471	25107	1021	276	67
1973	28905	27395	1129	316	65
1974	31099	29450	1240	345	64
1975	33217	31419	1353	382	63
1976	35284	33335	1463	423	63
1977	37164	35069	1566	466	63
1978	38983	36735	1669	515	65
1979	40736	38529	1771	569	67
1980	42457	39882	1875	629	71
1981	44165	41415	1981	695	75
1982	45850	42914	2088	767	81
1983	47514	44384	2196	846	88
1984	49146	45815	2305	931	96
1985	50748	47209	2413	1022	105

Percentage Distribution of
Projection of Labor Force, by Occupation, Race, and Sex, 1970 to 1985

PHYSICISTS

YEAR	TOTAL	WHITE		BLACK	
		MALE	FEMALE	MALE	FEMALE
1970	100.00	95.13	3.62	0.91	0.34
1971	100.00	94.98	3.75	0.99	0.29
1972	100.00	94.85	3.86	1.04	0.25
1973	100.00	94.78	3.91	1.09	0.23
1974	100.00	94.70	3.99	1.11	0.20
1975	100.00	94.59	4.07	1.15	0.19
1976	100.00	94.48	4.15	1.20	0.18
1977	100.00	94.36	4.21	1.25	0.17
1978	100.00	94.23	4.28	1.32	0.17
1979	100.00	94.09	4.35	1.40	0.17
1980	100.00	93.94	4.42	1.48	0.17
1981	100.00	93.77	4.49	1.57	0.17
1982	100.00	93.60	4.55	1.67	0.18
1983	100.00	93.41	4.62	1.78	0.18
1984	100.00	93.22	4.69	1.89	0.19
1985	100.00	93.03	4.75	2.01	0.21

5.7 percent in 1985, which is 4.4 percentage points above the 1970 level. The impact of this change on the composition of the labor force is an increase of 0.5 percentage points in black labor force penetration from the 1985 base line projection and less than a 1.0 percentage point increase above the 1970 level of black participation. The carry-over impact on females via black females is minimal—0.1 percentage point increases among new entrants and the labor force from 1985 base line projections.

The effects of a doubling of the number of degrees awarded to women on the new entrants pool are shown in Table VII-11. Female representation among new entrants would reach 21.2 percent in 1985, a 15.9 percentage point increase above the 1970 female representation level. Black representation would increase 1.7 percentage points from the increases in the proportion of black female entrants. Incorporating these changes in the new entrants pool into the labor force calculations reveals that the participation of women in the physicist labor force could increase 2.0 percentage points over the base line projections for 1985 (Table VII-12), or 2.0 percentage points above the 1970 female participation level of 4.0 percent.

Simulation III combines the effects of the separate black and female simulations. The requirements of this third alternative yield a 1985 new entrants pool that would be 20.7 percent female and 5.1 percent black, compared to 5.3 percent female and 1.3 percent black in 1970, as shown in Table VII-13. These changes in the racial and sexual composition of new labor force entrants translates into a 2.8 percentage point increase in female participation in the labor force by 1985 from the 4.0 percent level in 1970. The corresponding change for blacks is an improvement of 0.5 percentage points from the 1985 base line projections, or less than a 1.0 percent point increase in black penetration from the 1970 level. These results are enumerated in Table VII-14.

These simulations show that the projections of the physicist labor force display some degree of flexibility and sensitivity to changes in the composition of new degree recipients. One hundred percent increases in the number of degrees awarded to blacks and women by 1985 would cause the proportion of blacks in the labor force to increase by almost 30 percent, and the proportion of women to increase by almost 40 percent above their respective base line projections.

TABLE VII-11
United States
New Labor Force Entrants, by Occupation,
Race, and Sex, 1970 to 1985

PHYSICISTS

YEAR	TOTAL	WHITE MALE	WHITE FEMALE	BLACK MALE	BLACK FEMALE
1970	3377	3156	178	42	2
1971	3289	3056	182	48	3
1972	3019	2790	181	46	3
1973	2734	2523	164	45	3
1974	2520	2309	173	35	3
1975	2467	2240	181	43	3
1976	2454	2203	204	43	4
1977	2302	2035	220	42	5
1978	2276	1980	247	43	6
1979	2245	1920	274	45	7
1980	2249	1891	304	46	8
1981	2274	1880	338	48	9
1982	2288	1857	371	49	11
1983	2306	1837	406	51	12
1984	2313	1807	440	52	14
1985	2324	1779	476	53	16

Percentage Distribution of
New Labor Force Entrants, by Occupation,
Race, and Sex, 1970 to 1985

PHYSICISTS

YEAR	TOTAL	WHITE MALE	WHITE FEMALE	BLACK MALE	BLACK FEMALE
1970	100.00	93.44	5.26	1.23	0.07
1971	100.00	92.91	5.54	1.47	0.08
1972	100.00	92.41	5.98	1.51	0.09
1973	100.00	92.27	5.99	1.63	0.10
1974	100.00	91.63	6.86	1.40	0.10
1975	100.00	90.78	7.35	1.73	0.14
1976	100.00	89.77	8.32	1.75	0.16
1977	100.00	88.41	9.56	1.83	0.20
1978	100.00	87.00	10.84	1.91	0.24
1979	100.00	85.52	12.19	1.99	0.29
1980	100.00	84.09	13.51	2.05	0.35
1981	100.00	82.66	14.84	2.10	0.40
1982	100.00	81.18	16.21	2.15	0.46
1983	100.00	79.67	17.61	2.20	0.53
1984	100.00	78.12	19.04	2.24	0.60
1985	100.00	76.57	20.48	2.28	0.67

TABLE VII-12
United States
Projection of Labor Force, by Occupation, Race, and Sex, 1970 to 1985

PHYSICISTS

YEAR	TOTAL	WHITE MALE	WHITE FEMALE	BLACK MALE	BLACK FEMALE
1970	20668	19661	748	189	70
1971	23721	22530	889	234	68
1972	26471	25107	1021	276	67
1973	28905	27395	1129	316	65
1974	31099	29450	1240	345	64
1975	33217	31419	1353	382	63
1976	35299	33335	1482	419	63
1977	37206	35069	1620	454	63
1978	39066	36735	1777	489	65
1979	40873	38329	1951	526	67
1980	42663	39882	2146	563	71
1981	44455	41415	2364	602	75
1982	46238	42914	2602	641	81
1983	48015	44384	2862	682	88
1984	49774	45815	3142	722	96
1985	51518	47209	3440	764	105

Percentage Distribution of Projection of Labor Force, by Occupation, Race, and Sex, 1970 to 1985

PHYSICISTS

YEAR	TOTAL	WHITE MALE	WHITE FEMALE	BLACK MALE	BLACK FEMALE
1970	100.00	95.13	3.62	0.91	0.34
1971	100.00	94.98	3.75	0.99	0.29
1972	100.00	94.85	3.86	1.04	0.25
1973	100.00	94.78	3.91	1.09	0.23
1974	100.00	94.70	3.99	1.11	0.20
1975	100.00	94.59	4.07	1.15	0.19
1976	100.00	94.44	4.20	1.19	0.18
1977	100.00	94.26	4.35	1.22	0.17
1978	100.00	94.03	4.55	1.25	0.17
1979	100.00	93.77	4.77	1.29	0.16
1980	100.00	93.48	5.03	1.32	0.17
1981	100.00	93.16	5.32	1.35	0.17
1982	100.00	92.81	5.63	1.39	0.17
1983	100.00	92.44	5.96	1.42	0.18
1984	100.00	92.05	6.31	1.45	0.19
1985	100.00	91.64	6.68	1.48	0.20

TABLE VII-13
United States
New Labor Force Entrants, by Occupation,
Race, and Sex, 1970 to 1985

PHYSICISTS

YEAR	TOTAL	WHITE		BLACK	
		MALE	FEMALE	MALE	FEMALE
1970	3377	3156	178	42	2
1971	3289	3056	182	48	3
1972	3019	2790	181	46	3
1973	2734	2523	164	45	3
1974	2520	2309	173	35	3
1975	2467	2240	181	43	3
1976	2458	2203	204	47	4
1977	2310	2035	220	51	5
1978	2289	1980	247	56	6
1979	2263	1920	274	63	7
1980	2272	1891	304	69	8
1981	2303	1880	338	77	9
1982	2323	1857	371	84	11
1983	2347	1837	406	91	12
1984	2360	1807	440	99	14
1985	2377	1779	476	106	16

Percentage Distribution of
New Labor Force Entrants, by Occupation,
Race, and Sex, 1970 to 1985

PHYSICISTS

YEAR	TOTAL	WHITE		BLACK	
		MALE	FEMALE	MALE	FEMALE
1970	100.00	93.44	5.26	1.23	0.07
1971	100.00	92.91	5.54	1.47	0.08
1972	100.00	92.41	5.98	1.51	0.09
1973	100.00	92.27	5.99	1.63	0.10
1974	100.00	91.63	6.86	1.40	0.10
1975	100.00	90.78	7.35	1.73	0.14
1976	100.00	89.62	8.31	1.92	0.16
1977	100.00	88.08	9.53	2.19	0.20
1978	100.00	86.51	10.78	2.47	0.24
1979	100.00	84.85	12.09	2.77	0.29
1980	100.00	83.24	13.37	3.05	0.34
1981	100.00	81.63	14.65	3.32	0.39
1982	100.00	79.97	15.97	3.60	0.45
1983	100.00	78.29	17.30	3.89	0.52
1984	100.00	76.57	18.66	4.18	0.58
1985	100.00	74.87	20.02	4.46	0.66

TABLE VII-14
United States
Projection of Labor Force, by Occupation,
Race, and Sex, 1970 to 1985

PHYSICISTS

YEAR	TOTAL	WHITE		BLACK	
		MALE	FEMALE	MALE	FEMALE
1970	20668	19661	748	189	70
1971	23721	22530	889	234	68
1972	26471	25107	1021	276	67
1973	28905	27395	1129	316	65
1974	31099	29450	1240	345	64
1975	33217	31419	1353	382	63
1976	35303	33635	1482	423	63
1977	37219	35069	1620	466	63
1978	39091	36735	1777	515	65
1979	40916	38329	1951	569	67
1980	42728	39882	2146	629	71
1981	44548	41415	2364	695	75
1982	46364	42914	2602	767	81
1983	48180	44384	2862	846	88
1984	49983	45815	3142	931	96
1985	51776	47209	3440	1022	105

Percentage Distribution of
Projection of Labor Force, by Occupation,
Race, and Sex, 1970 to 1985

PHYSICISTS

YEAR	TOTAL	WHITE		BLACK	
		MALE	FEMALE	MALE	FEMALE
1970	100.00	95.13	3.62	0.91	0.34
1971	100.00	94.98	3.75	0.99	0.29
1972	100.00	94.85	3.86	1.04	0.25
1973	100.00	94.78	3.91	1.09	0.23
1974	100.00	94.70	3.99	1.11	0.20
1975	100.00	94.59	4.07	1.15	0.19
1976	100.00	94.43	4.20	1.20	0.18
1977	100.00	94.22	4.35	1.25	0.17
1978	100.00	93.97	4.54	1.32	0.17
1979	100.00	93.68	4.77	1.39	0.16
1980	100.00	93.34	5.02	1.47	0.17
1981	100.00	92.97	5.31	1.56	0.17
1982	100.00	92.56	5.61	1.65	0.17
1983	100.00	92.12	5.94	1.76	0.18
1984	100.00	91.66	6.29	1.86	0.19
1985	100.00	91.18	6.64	1.97	0.20

MINORITIES AND WOMEN IN CHEMISTRY

The primary impetus for chemical employers to intensify their efforts to recruit, hire, and promote minority and women scientists was provided by the need for employers to comply with federal laws and executive orders prohibiting job discrimination and by federal regulations requiring government contractors to develop affirmative action programs for women and minorities. Recruiting minority group chemists and chemical engineers is difficult, however, because the supply of minority and women college graduates in those fields is particularly small. Of the 3,167 students who received bachelor's degrees in chemical engineering in 1974-75, only 40, or 1.3 percent, were blacks; only 131, or 4.1 percent, were women. Of the 1,050 students who obtained master's degrees in chemical engineering, only 8, or 0.8 percent, were blacks; 18, or 1.7 percent, were women. And of the 366 who received Ph.D.s in chemical engineering, none were blacks, and only 5, or 1.4 percent, were women. The supply of women graduates is much greater in the field of chemistry. Of the 10,649 students who received bachelor's degrees in chemistry in 1974-75, about 2,130, or 20 percent, were women, but less than 210, or less than 2.0 percent, were black.[15]

Background

In April 1876 when the American Chemical Society (ACS) was founded in New York City, chemistry was just emerging in the United States as a recognized science and profession. As late as 1890, less than 7 percent of the 14 to 17 age group attended high school in this country. Moreover, admission to college at the time was based on the knowledge of Latin, Greek, elementary math, history, and geography. It was not until the turn of the century that colleges began accepting subjects like modern languages, chemistry, and physics as qualifications of entrance. In 1876, the United States had fewer than 600 institutions of higher learning, which enrolled 13,000 students. The curricula were geared to medicine, the military, or the church. Chemistry was then taught as part of the medical education. Dr. John MacLean, who was perhaps the first professor of chemistry in this country, began teaching at Princeton in 1795, and in the

---

[15] "Employers Step Up Programs to Expand Jobs for Women and Minorities," *Chemical and Engineering News*, Vol. 54 (October 25, 1976), p. 40.

early 1800s Yale, Bowdoin, Brown, and Dartmouth followed in offering chemistry courses.[16]

Development of the Chemistry Profession

The first Ph.D. in chemistry was awarded by Harvard College in 1877 to Frank Austin Gooch. As a result of the limited facilities and opportunities to study chemistry in the United States, most of this country's early chemists obtained their advanced degrees in Europe. Early in the 1880s Standard Oil Company hired George Saybolt, who was probably the first full-time chemist in industry. The majority of chemists at the time were concentrated in academe.[17]

Until World War I, Europe was well ahead of the United States in chemical technology and chemical science. Germany, for example, had an excellent system of universities and technical colleges specifically designed to produce scientists. Between 1920 and 1940 the number of American industrial laboratories increased from 300 to 3,500, and their scientific staffs grew from 9,000 to 70,000. The importance of science, chemistry in particular, was not realized in this country, however, until World War II and the development of the atomic bomb.[18]

Space programs and an emphasis on education in the sciences by the federal government during the last 25 years has dramatically increased the popularity of the sciences. The number of bachelor's degrees awarded annually in chemistry increased from 5,500 in 1954 to 12,000 in 1975. The number of Ph.D.s in chemistry awarded each year rose from 1,013 in 1950-51 to 1,733 in 1973-74. Scientists and engineers, however, faced uncertain futures and stiff competition when in 1968 the federal government began cutting its support of research and development programs in government, industry, and academe. During the period from 1969 to 1971, 1,500 industrial chemists and chemical engineers lost their jobs. Furthermore, ACS membership, which had reached its all-time high of 116,816 in 1969, dropped to 110,285 in 1973.[19]

---

16 Kenneth M. Reese, ed., *A Century of Chemistry* (Washington, D.C.: American Chemical Society, 1976), pp. 2, 60.

17 *Ibid.*, pp. 2, 60.

18 *Ibid.*, pp. 11, 29.

19 *Ibid.*, pp. 44-45, 49-50, 70.

Census Data

Table VII-15 provides data from the Bureau of Census on the number of chemists from 1940 through 1970. The Census numbers are a count of those individuals who identify themselves as chemists. Although there is criticism of the methodology and coverage of the Census data, these estimates are generally acceptable as one of the best occupational data sources available.

According to the Census data, the proportion of nonwhites and women in the chemistry labor force has risen over the past 30 years. Between 1940 and 1970 the representation of nonwhite chemists increased from 0.5 percent to 7.3 percent. During the same period, the proportion of women chemists rose from 0.0 percent to 11.9 percent. White males, however, continue to dominate the field. Although their representation among all chemists declined from 99.5 percent in 1940 to 82.1 percent in 1970, white males still hold the largest portion of the chemistry labor force.

National Science Foundation (NSF) Estimate of
Professional Chemists

Table VII-16 presents a summary of the National Science Foundation's (NSF) estimate of the 1974 sexual and racial composition of chemists in the United States. The primary inputs to the estimates given in the report, *U.S. Scientists and Engineers: 1974* (NSF 76-329), originated in the Foundation's Manpower Characteristics System, which consists of the National Sample, the New Entrants Surveys, and the Doctoral Roster. Through these surveys, NSF estimates that in 1974 there were 138,000 chemists in the United States.[20]

BLACKS

It is estimated that between 1876 and 1969, 650 American blacks obtained doctoral degrees in the natural sciences. This is an extremely small number considering that over 84,000 natural science doctorates were awarded by American universities between 1920 and 1962. The recent participation of blacks in science is emphasized by the fact that over 80 percent of all

---

[20] *U.S. Scientists and Engineers: 1974*, NSF 76-329 (Washington, D.C.: Government Printing Office, 1976), pp. 12, 29.

TABLE VII-15

Number of Experienced Civilian Chemists by Sex and Race, 1940-1970

Sex and Race	1940	1950	1960	1970
Chemists Total	55,900	76,590	82,109	111,790
Male Chemists	55,900	69,540	75,414	98,470
White	55,640	68,340	72,986	91,831
Negro	260 [a]	870	1,533	3,350
Other Races		330	895	3,289
Male Chemists with 4 or More Years of College	32,680	43,800	53,094	71,608
White	32,620	43,110	51,280	
Nonwhite	60	690	1,814	2,259 [b]
Female Chemists	—	7,050	6,695	13,320
White	—	6,900	6,209	11,746
Negro	—	150	266	595
Other Races	—	—	220	979
Female Chemists with 4 or More Years of College	—	4,800	4,741	10,053
White	—	4,680	4,418	
Nonwhite	—	120	323	377 [b]

Sources: *Sixteenth Census of the United States: 1940 Population, The Labor Force, Occupational Characteristics* (Washington, D.C.: Government Printing Office, 1943), pp. 59-70 *passim*, Table 3. *United States Census of Population 1950, Occupational Characteristics*, P-E No. 1B (Washington, D.C.: Government Printing Office, 1956), pp. 29, 107, 115, Tables 3, 10, 11. *United States Census of Population 1960, Occupational Characteristics*, PC(2)-7A (Washington, D.C.: U.S. Department of Commerce, 1961), pp. 21, 116, 123, 130, 137, Tables 3, 9, 10. *1970 Census of Population Subject Report, Occupational Characteristics*, PC(2)-7A (Washington, D.C.: U.S. Department of Commerce, 1973), pp. 12, 59, 73, 87, 101.

[a] Only nonwhite data available.
[b] Only Negro data available.

TABLE VII-16

National Science Foundation Estimate of Chemists in the
United States by Sex and Race, 1974[a]

Total		White		Black		Indian		Asian		Other	
138,000		130,800		3,000		300		3,100		900	
Male	Female	Male	Female	Male	Female	Male	Female [b]	Male	Female	Male	Female
122,400	15,600	117,000	13,800	2,400	500	300	—	2,400	700	300	600

Source: *U.S. Scientists and Engineers: 1974*, NSF 76-329 (Washington, D.C.: Government Printing Office, 1976), p. 29, Table B-8.

[a] Detail may not add to total because of rounding.
[b] Too few cases to estimate.

American Negroes who have received science doctorates are still alive.[21]

Education of Black Chemists

The first American Negro to receive the doctorate in chemistry was Saint Elmo Brady who received his Ph.D. from the University of Illinois in 1916. It is estimated that 186 blacks obtained Ph.D.s in chemistry between 1876 and 1969.[22]

Although there are no data on the actual number of chemistry degrees received by blacks, recent surveys by the ACS do indicate the participation of blacks in chemistry degree programs. Of the 1974-75 chemistry graduates responding to the ACS survey, blacks represented 1.6 percent of the bachelor's degrees, 1.6 percent of the master's degrees, and 2.0 percent of the Ph.D. degrees in chemistry.[23]

Participation of Blacks in the Chemistry Profession

The ACS Office of Manpower Studies has been collecting information on the minority status of its members since 1973. The 1975 ACS survey shows that blacks then comprised 0.9 percent of the ACS membership at the bachelor's degree level, 1.5 percent at the master's level, 0.8 percent at the Ph.D. level, and 1.0 percent overall.[24]

OTHER MINORITIES

Most of the data in this section on minorities in chemistry are the results from ACS surveys of their membership and chemistry graduates. In using these surveys it is important to stress the caution of ACS that "the minorities constitute a small fraction of the respondents . . . due to this small number the statistical estimates are necessarily volatile and unreliable." [25]

---

[21] James M. Jay, *Negroes in Science*, pp. vii, 64.

[22] *Ibid.*, pp. 38, 46.

[23] *1975 Survey Report: Starting Salaries and Employment Status of Chemistry and Chemical Engineering Graduates* (Washington, D.C.: Office of Manpower Studies, American Chemical Society, 1976), p. 36, Table T-5.

[24] *Professionals in Chemistry 1975* (Washington, D.C.: Office of Manpower Studies, American Chemical Society, 1976), p. 76, Appendix II, Table 6.

[25] *Ibid.*, p. 13.

Education of Minority Chemists

Data are not available for the actual number of minority graduates in chemistry. Nevertheless, results of the ACS survey of chemistry graduates, which are given in Table VII-17, indicate the participation of minorities at each degree level for 1972-73, 1973-74, and 1974-75.

Participation of Minorities in the Chemistry Profession.

ACS surveys of their membership show the distribution of minority chemists by degree level, which corresponds to the participation of minorities in the chemistry profession. Data from the 1975 and 1976 surveys are provided in Table VII-18.

Orientals constitute the largest minority group participation in the chemistry labor force. The Oriental group's characteristics identified by the survey are, compared both with the ACS membership and other minority groups, a higher percentage of Ph.D.s and a higher percentage of non-United States citizens.[26]

Minorities responding to the ACS membership survey are over-represented in universities and the federal government, but they show little participation in the manufacturing sector. Moreover, their work functions are typically basic and applied research, not management.[27]

WOMEN

The 1870 Census reported no women chemists; however, between 1880 and 1940 the number of women identified as chemists, assayers, or metallurgists increased from 49, which represented 2.4 percent of all those in this occupation, to 1,734, or 2.9 percent. This small representation of women in chemistry is primarily the result of limitations on the scientific training of women that existed during the period.[28]

Education of Women Chemists

The percentage of women receiving degrees in chemistry has increased gradually over the past 30 years. Although the

---

[26] *Ibid.*, p. 15.

[27] *Ibid.*

[28] Janet M. Hooks, *Women's Occupations Through Seven Decades* (Washington, D.C.: Government Printing Office, 1947), p. 177.

TABLE VII-17
Minority Classification of Chemistry Graduates by Degree Level, 1972-73 through 1974-75

Group	Bachelor			Master			Doctoral		
	Percent of Total			Percent of Total			Percent of Total		
	1972-73	1973-74	1974-75	1972-73	1973-74	1974-75	1972-73	1973-74	1974-75
Black	2.3	2.1	1.6	2.1	3.6	1.6	1.4	1.4	2.0
American Indian	0.2	0.2	0.1	—	—	0.5	—	0.2	0.2
Oriental	3.2	2.9	2.4	9.1	8.8	7.1	9.4	9.8	4.4
Spanish-surnamed	0.7	1.2	1.0	0.9	0.3	0.5	1.1	1.0	0.9
Nonminorities	93.6	93.6	94.9	87.8	87.3	90.1	88.1	87.7	92.6

Sources: *1974 Survey Report: Starting Salaries and Employment Status of Chemistry and Chemical Engineering Graduates* (Washington, D.C.: Office of Manpower Studies, American Chemical Society, 1975), p. 23, Table E-2. *1975 Survey Report: Starting Salaries and Employment Status of Chemistry and Chemical Engineering Graduates* (Washington, D.C.: Office of Manpower Studies, American Chemical Society, 1976), p. 36, Table T-5.

TABLE VII-18

Distribution of Minority Chemists by Degree Level,
1975 and 1976

Group	Bachelor		Master		Doctoral		Overall	
	1975	1976	1975	1976	1975	1976	1975	1976
Black	0.9	1.2	1.5	1.8	0.8	1.0	1.0	1.2
American Indian	0.1	0.2	0.1	0.0	0.2	0.2	0.2	0.2
Oriental	1.4	2.1	3.0	2.8	4.9	4.2	3.5	3.3
Spanish-surnamed	0.5	0.7	0.9	0.8	0.7	0.5	0.7	0.6
All minorities	2.9	4.2	5.5	5.4	6.6	5.9	5.3	5.3
Non-minorities	97.1	95.8	94.5	94.6	93.4	94.1	94.7	94.7

Source: Betty M. Vetter and Eleanor L. Babco, *Professional Women and Minorities: A Manpower Resource Service* (Washington, D.C.: Scientific Manpower Commission, 1975), p. 194.1, Table PS-C-21A.

total number of chemistry degrees awarded at each level has been declining since 1970-71, recently both the percentage and absolute number of women receiving degrees at the bachelor and doctoral levels have been increasing. The percentage and absolute number of women receiving master's degrees in chemistry, however, have been declining in recent years. Table VII-19 presents the data on chemistry degrees earned by women from 1960-61 through 1974-75.

Participation of Women in the Chemistry Profession

The 1975 ACS membership survey showed that 835 of the 10,731 respondents were women, or 7.8 percent of the total. Of the 835 female respondents, 7.9 percent of them were minorities and 92.1 percent were nonminorities.[29]

Most female full-time chemists are employed in industry or by educational institutions, but few are self-employed. Furthermore, the work activities performed by the largest proportion of full-time female chemists are research and development or teaching, and the smallest proportion work in marketing, sales, production, and quality control.[30]

A mid-1976 survey of industry shows that 4.7 percent of its chemical professionals are women, which is up from 4.3 percent identified in mid-1975. The proportion is expected to rise to 5.2 in mid-1977.[31]

CURRENT PROGRAMS

Chemical employers, organizations, and professionals are working actively to promote, recruit, and hire women and minority scientists. Because of their need to comply with federal laws and regulations, chemical employers are particularly interested in recruiting more women and minorities into science professions. In one approach, they are urging junior high school students with interest in science or engineering to take the courses that will prepare them for study in these fields. Chemical employers are also encouraging their older employees who are

---

[29] *Professionals in Chemistry 1975*, p. 78, Appendix II, Table 8.

[30] Vetter and Babco, *Professional Women and Minorities*, p. 192, Tables PS-C-17, PS-C-18.

[31] Betty Vetter, ed., *Scientific Engineering, Technical Manpower Comments*, Vol. 13 (November 1976), p. 3.

TABLE VII-19

Distribution of Degrees Awarded in Chemistry by Sex and Degree Level, 1960-61 through 1974-75

Year	Bachelor			Master			Doctoral		
	Total Both Sexes	Women Only	Percent Women	Total Both Sexes	Women Only	Percent Women	Total Both Sexes	Women Only	Percent Women
1960-61 through 1969-70	98,165	18,651	19.0	17,174	3,251	18.9	14,562	931	6.4
1970-71	11,037	2,031	18.4	2,197	464	21.1	1,952	154	7.9
1971-72	10,560	2,052	19.4	2,177	479	22.0	1,852	180	9.7
1972-73	10,099	1,911	18.9	2,130	451	21.2	1,686	153	9.1
1973-74	10,348	2,070	20.0	2,008	438	21.8	1,630	150	9.2
1974-75	10,409	2,310	22.2	1,871	387	20.7	1,660	183	11.0

Sources: Betty M. Vetter and Eleanor L. Babco, *Professional Women and Minorities: A Manpower Resource Service* (Washington, D.C.: Scientific Manpower Commission, 1975), p. 185, Tables PS-C-1, PS-C-2. Data from 1970-71 through 1974-75 provided by National Center for Educational Statistics, Washington, D.C.

women or members of minority groups to obtain on-the-job training or other education that will qualify them for higher-level
jobs.

Chemical Employers

Besides providing financial support to chemistry students and
university research facilities, chemical employers are also hiring
a greater percentage of minority and women students for summer jobs and college co-op programs in hopes that they will
look favorably on industrial employment after graduation. Some
firms have also established visiting instructor programs to improve science and engineering education in minority colleges.[32]

Chemical Organizations

The National Science Foundation (NSF), the American Chemical Society (ACS), and the Manufacturing Chemists Association
(MCA) are working to expand the employment opportunities
for women and minorities in science and engineering. The NSF
Women in Science Program was begun in late 1975 to develop
and to test methods to attract and to retain women in science
careers. Since 1972 NSF has also been sponsoring the Minority
Institutions Science Improvement Program to upgrade science
education at minority colleges and universities.[33]

The ACS conducts a variety of programs to improve the employment status of its members. Moreover, its Women Chemists
Committee has been active since 1926 in improving the status of
women chemists. The ACS Catalyst project, which annually en-
ables about 100 disadvantaged high school students to work for
about 10 weeks during the summer in an academic chemistry
laboratory, has been sponsored by ACS, its members, and its
Corporation Associates since 1968.[34]

The MCA is also involved in promoting job opportunities for
women and minorities. This Association's Industrial Relations
Advisory Committee has had an Equal Employment Opportunity
Subcommittee since 1971, which focuses on affirmative action

---

[32] "Employers Step Up Programs to Expand Jobs for Women and Minorities," p. 43.

[33] *Ibid.*, pp. 43-46.

[34] *Ibid.*, p. 46.

programs.[35] Specific programs of individual employers are too numerous to describe here, but it is evident that chemical employers and organizations, prodded by the federal regulations, are pursuing programs to increase the prospects for chemical professionals who are women or members of minority groups.

PREDICTING THE NUMBER OF MINORITY AND WOMEN CHEMISTS

The review of the past and the current status of minority and women chemists leads now to the projections, as drawn by the labor supply model, of the experience expected in the future. A base line projection and three simulations are presented and discussed in this section.

Base Line Projections

The input data used to produce the projections relevant to the chemistry profession are provided in Table VII-20. Data on the racial characteristics of degree recipients, derived from surveys conducted by the American Chemical Society,[36] and other information supplied by the Society are available for the 4 years 1972 through 1975. The downward sloping trend apparent in the 4 years of data would result in the eventual elimination of black degree earners if extended into the future. The first 3 years of data were synthesized to complete the requirements of the forecasting model and to reverse the trend evident in the available data. The projections of the proportion of black new entrants and of the labor force, therefore, are totally artificial, but still instructive because the situation being created is more favorable than the one that actually exists. Entry rates were also derived from American Chemical Society reports.[37]

Women comprised 16.6 percent of the new entrants to the chemists labor force in 1970, as shown in Table VII-21, and are

---

[35] *Ibid.*

[36] *1974 Survey Report: Starting Salaries and Employment Status of Chemistry and Chemical Engineering Graduates* (Washington, D.C.: Office of Manpower Studies, American Chemical Society, 1975), p. 23, Table E-2; *1975 Survey Report: Starting Salaries and Employment Status of Chemistry and Chemical Engineering Graduates* (Washington, D.C.: Office of Manpower Studies, American Chemical Society, 1976), p. 36, Table T-5.

[37] *1974 Survey Report, op. cit.,* p. 6, Table A-1; *1975 Survey Report, op. cit.,* p. 11, Table E-1.

TABLE VII-20
Input Data for Simulation
of Chemists in the Labor Force to 1985

	MALE	FEMALE
SEPARATION RATE	WHITE	
1970	0.0139	0.0577
1985	0.0124	0.0598
	BLACK	
1970	0.0080	0.0712
1985	0.0069	0.0735
ENTRY RATE		
BACHELOR	0.3000	0.3000
MASTER	0.4500	0.4500
DOCTOR	0.5000	0.5000
SUPPLY BASE - 1970		
TOTAL	71608	10053
BLACK	2259	377

	DEGREES AWARDED	
	% FEMALE	% BLACK
BACHELOR		
1969	18.17	1.60
1970	17.93	1.80
1971	18.40	2.00
1972	19.43	2.30
1973	18.97	2.10
1974	20.00	1.60
1975	22.19	1.90
MASTER		
1969	18.39	1.60
1970	22.41	1.80
1971	21.12	2.00
1972	22.00	2.10
1973	21.17	3.60
1974	21.81	1.60
1975	20.68	2.90
DOCTOR		
1969	8.40	0.80
1970	7.66	1.00
1971	7.89	1.00
1972	9.72	1.40
1973	9.07	1.40
1974	9.20	2.00
1975	11.02	0.60

TABLE VII-21
United States
New Labor Force Entrants, by Occupation,
Race, and Sex, 1970 to 1985

CHEMISTS

YEAR	TOTAL	WHITE		BLACK	
		MALE	FEMALE	MALE	FEMALE
1970	5489	4500	897	76	16
1971	5375	4382	897	79	17
1972	5151	4146	904	82	19
1973	4940	3971	866	84	19
1974	4943	3950	903	73	17
1975	4901	3867	939	75	19
1976	4776	3757	920	79	20
1977	4649	3622	927	79	21
1978	4764	3685	974	83	23
1979	4726	3624	994	84	24
1980	4713	3589	1014	86	25
1981	4705	3561	1032	87	26
1982	4723	3552	1055	89	27
1983	4685	3501	1067	90	28
1984	4620	3432	1070	90	28
1985	4524	3340	1067	90	29

Percentage Distribution of
New Labor Force Entrants, by Occupation,
Race, and Sex, 1970 to 1985

CHEMISTS

YEAR	TOTAL	WHITE		BLACK	
		MALE	FEMALE	MALE	FEMALE
1970	100.00	81.99	16.34	1.38	0.29
1971	100.00	81.53	16.68	1.46	0.32
1972	100.00	80.50	17.54	1.59	0.36
1973	100.00	80.39	17.52	1.69	0.39
1974	100.00	79.91	18.27	1.47	0.34
1975	100.00	78.90	19.17	1.54	0.40
1976	100.00	78.66	19.26	1.65	0.42
1977	100.00	77.91	19.94	1.70	0.45
1978	100.00	77.35	20.44	1.74	0.47
1979	100.00	76.68	21.04	1.78	0.50
1980	100.00	76.15	21.51	1.82	0.52
1981	100.00	75.68	21.93	1.85	0.55
1982	100.00	75.20	22.35	1.88	0.57
1983	100.00	74.72	22.78	1.92	0.59
1984	100.00	74.27	23.17	1.95	0.61
1985	100.00	73.82	23.57	1.98	0.63

projected to increase their representation to 24.2 percent by 1985. In addition to their growth in absolute numbers of new entrants, female representation is aided by the fact that the total number of new entrants is expected to decline from almost 5,500 in 1970 to more than 4,500 in 1985. The projections of the chemists labor force, provided in Table VII-22, indicate that the labor force is expected to continue to increase, but at a decreasing rate. Despite the increases in new entrants, however, female participation in the labor force will decline from 12.3 percent in 1970 to 11.4 percent in 1985. The high separation rate of women, relative to that of men, is responsible for the erosion of female participation in the labor force.

The artificial trend in the proportion of degrees awarded to blacks produces a new entrants pool that is 1.7 percent black in 1970 and increases to 2.6 percent black in 1985. Even with this increase in the proportion of black new labor force entrants, the proportion of blacks in the labor force would decline from 3.2 percent in 1970 to 2.8 percent in 1985. The reason for this decline is that the proportion of black new entrants is less than the proportion of blacks in the labor force.

The prognosis for blacks and women in the chemistry profession is obviously not favorable, but may be improved by several conditions. Concerted efforts to attract more blacks to the study of chemistry is evidently needed and may arrest the downward trend in the proportion of black graduates. Nation-wide trends in the increasing labor force participation of women would probably have very positive effects on the proportion of women chemists because early separations from scientific occupations tend to be more permanent than those from other occupations because of the rapid development of scientific information and the retraining necessary to re-enter the labor force.

Sensitivity Analysis

Three simulations were implemented in order to assess the effects of changes in the racial and sexual composition of new graduates on the composition of the labor force. The first simulation involves a 100 percent increase in the number of degrees awarded to blacks by 1985, while the base line projection of the number of white degree recipients is maintained. The second simulation makes the same adjustment for the number of degrees awarded to women. The final simulation doubles the number of

TABLE VII-22
United States
Projection of Labor Force, by Occupation, Race, and Sex, 1970 to 1985

CHEMISTS

YEAR	TOTAL	WHITE		BLACK	
		MALE	FEMALE	MALE	FEMALE
1970	81661	69349	9676	2259	377
1971	85474	72774	10013	2320	367
1972	89003	75923	10336	2384	360
1973	92265	78862	10601	2449	353
1974	95482	81748	10887	2503	345
1975	98608	84519	11190	2559	339
1976	101562	87153	11455	2619	335
1977	104344	89624	11710	2679	332
1978	107202	92135	11995	2742	330
1979	109979	94561	12282	2806	330
1980	112702	96931	12569	2871	331
1981	115377	99250	12857	2938	332
1982	118031	101542	13148	3006	335
1983	120609	103763	13433	3075	338
1984	123085	105898	13702	3144	341
1985	125430	107924	13949	3211	345

Percentage Distribution of
Projection of Labor Force, by Occupation, Race, and Sex, 1970 to 1985

CHEMISTS

YEAR	TOTAL	WHITE		BLACK	
		MALE	FEMALE	MALE	FEMALE
1970	100.00	84.92	11.85	2.77	0.46
1971	100.00	85.14	11.71	2.71	0.43
1972	100.00	85.30	11.61	2.68	0.40
1973	100.00	85.47	11.49	2.65	0.38
1974	100.00	85.62	11.40	2.62	0.36
1975	100.00	85.71	11.35	2.60	0.34
1976	100.00	85.81	11.28	2.58	0.33
1977	100.00	85.89	11.22	2.57	0.32
1978	100.00	85.95	11.19	2.56	0.31
1979	100.00	85.98	11.17	2.55	0.30
1980	100.00	86.01	11.15	2.55	0.29
1981	100.00	86.02	11.14	2.55	0.29
1982	100.00	86.03	11.14	2.55	0.28
1983	100.00	86.03	11.14	2.55	0.28
1984	100.00	86.04	11.13	2.55	0.28
1985	100.00	86.04	11.12	2.56	0.27

black and female degree earners by 1985, while the base line projection for white men is maintained.

Doubling the number of black degree recipients by 1985, as required by the first simulation, would create a new entrants pool with 5.1 percent blacks in that year. As seen in Table VII-23, the 5.1 percent level is 3 times the 1970 black representation level and, when compared to the baseline projections, is a 2.5 percentage point increase for 1985. The resultant effect on the labor force is a small net gain in black participation. Black penetration in the labor force was 3.2 percent in 1970 and would reach 3.3 percent in 1985 after an initial decline (Table VII-24). No cross-over effects on female participation are evident.

The impact of the second simulation on the new entrants pool can be seen in Table VII-25, and on the resultant labor force in Table VII-26. A doubling of the number of chemistry degrees awarded to women yields a 1985 new entrants pool that is 39 percent female, almost 6.0 percentage points above the 1985 base line projection and almost 2.5 times the 1970 female representation level. The downward trend in female participation in the labor force would be arrested by 1976, and women would improve their relative standing in the labor force by 2.5 percentage points from their 1970 level of participation to 14.8 percent in 1985.

The third and final simulation dictates a doubling of the number of black and female degree recipients by 1985, while the base line projection for white men is maintained. As shown in Table VII-27, the new entrants pool would change from 16.6 percent female and 1.7 percent black in 1970 to 38.4 percent female and 4.1 percent black in 1985. Incorporating the stream of new entrants into the labor force reveals that female participation would reach 14.7 percent in 1985, and that black penetration would reach 3.2 percent in that year (Table VII-28). These end results represent only slight modifications of the separate simulations.

The results of these alternative projections, taken together, indicate a rather bleak future for blacks in chemistry. Efforts, greater than those currently existing, are necessary to increase the proportion of degrees awarded to blacks in order to maintain their relative labor force position. The same holds true for women, except that specialized programs to facilitate labor force re-entry and, therefore, make female separations less permanent may help to maintain or improve their relative status.

TABLE VII-23
United States
New Labor Force Entrants, by Occupation,
Race, and Sex, 1970 to 1985

CHEMISTS

YEAR	TOTAL	WHITE MALE	WHITE FEMALE	BLACK MALE	BLACK FEMALE
1970	5489	4500	897	76	16
1971	5375	4382	897	79	17
1972	5151	4146	904	82	19
1973	4940	3971	866	84	19
1974	4943	3950	903	73	17
1975	4901	3867	939	75	19
1976	4786	3757	920	·87	22
1977	4669	3622	927	95	25
1978	4796	3685	974	108	29
1979	4769	3624	994	118	33
1980	4768	3589	1014	129	37
1981	4773	3561	1032	139	41
1982	4804	3552	1055	151	45
1983	4779	3501	1067	162	50
1984	4727	3432	1070	171	54
1985	4643	3340	1067	179	57

Percentage Distribution of
New Labor Force Entrants, by Occupation,
Race, and Sex, 1970 to 1985

CHEMISTS

YEAR	TOTAL	WHITE MALE	WHITE FEMALE	BLACK MALE	BLACK FEMALE
1970	100.00	81.99	16.34	1.38	0.29
1971	100.00	81.53	16.68	1.46	0.32
1972	100.00	80.50	17.54	1.59	0.36
1973	100.00	80.39	17.52	1.69	0.39
1974	100.00	79.91	18.27	1.47	0.34
1975	100.00	78.90	19.17	1.54	0.40
1976	100.00	78.50	19.22	1.82	0.46
1977	100.00	77.57	19.85	2.04	0.54
1978	100.00	76.84	20.30	2.25	0.61
1979	100.00	75.99	20.85	2.47	0.69
1980	100.00	75.27	21.26	2.70	0.78
1981	100.00	74.60	21.62	2.92	0.86
1982	100.00	73.93	21.97	3.15	0.95
1983	100.00	73.25	22.33	3.38	1.04
1984	100.00	72.60	22.64	3.62	1.13
1985	100.00	71.94	22.97	3.86	1.23

TABLE VII-24
United States
Projection of Labor Force, by Occupation, Race, and Sex, 1970 to 1985

CHEMISTS

YEAR	TOTAL	WHITE		BLACK	
		MALE	FEMALE	MALE	FEMALE
1970	81661	69349	9676	2259	377
1971	85474	72774	10013	2320	367
1972	89003	75923	10336	2384	360
1973	92265	78862	10601	2449	353
1974	95482	81748	10837	2503	345
1975	98608	84519	11190	2559	339
1976	101572	87153	11455	2627	337
1977	104374	89624	11710	2702	338
1978	107263	92135	11995	2790	343
1979	110082	94561	12282	2888	351
1980	112858	96931	12569	2995	362
1981	115597	99250	12857	3113	377
1982	118327	101542	13148	3242	395
1983	120993	103763	13433	3381	416
1984	123568	105898	13702	3529	439
1985	126021	107924	13949	3684	464

Percentage Distribution of
Projection of Labor Force, by Occupation, Race, and Sex, 1970 to 1985

CHEMISTS

YEAR	TOTAL	WHITE		BLACK	
		MALE	FEMALE	MALE	FEMALE
1970	100.00	84.92	11.85	2.77	0.46
1971	100.00	85.14	11.71	2.71	0.43
1972	100.00	85.30	11.61	2.68	0.40
1973	100.00	85.47	11.49	2.65	0.38
1974	100.00	85.62	11.40	2.62	0.36
1975	100.00	85.71	11.35	2.60	0.34
1976	100.00	85.80	11.28	2.59	0.33
1977	100.00	85.87	11.22	2.59	0.32
1978	100.00	85.90	11.18	2.60	0.32
1979	100.00	85.90	11.16	2.62	0.32
1980	100.00	85.89	11.14	2.65	0.32
1981	100.00	85.86	11.12	2.69	0.33
1982	100.00	85.81	11.11	2.74	0.33
1983	100.00	85.76	11.10	2.79	0.34
1984	100.00	85.70	11.09	2.86	0.36
1985	100.00	85.64	11.07	2.92	0.37

TABLE VII-25
United States
New Labor Force Entrants, by Occupation,
Race, and Sex, 1970 to 1985

CHEMISTS

| YEAR | TOTAL | WHITE | | BLACK | |
		MALE	FEMALE	MALE	FEMALE
1970	5489	4500	897	76	16
1971	5375	4382	897	79	17
1972	5151	4146	904	82	19
1973	4940	3971	866	84	19
1974	4943	3950	903	73	17
1975	4901	3867	939	75	19
1976	4871	3757	1012	79	22
1977	4839	3622	1112	79	25
1978	5063	3685	1266	83	29
1979	5133	3624	1392	84	33
1980	5232	3589	1520	86	37
1981	5339	3561	1651	87	41
1982	5481	3552	1794	89	45
1983	5561	3501	1921	90	50
1984	5609	3432	2034	90	54
1985	5620	3340	2133	90	57

Percentage Distribution of
New Labor Force Entrants, by Occupation,
Race, and Sex, 1970 to 1985

CHEMISTS

| YEAR | TOTAL | WHITE | | BLACK | |
		MALE	FEMALE	MALE	FEMALE
1970	100.00	81.99	16.34	1.38	0.29
1971	100.00	81.53	16.68	1.46	0.32
1972	100.00	80.50	17.54	1.59	0.36
1973	100.00	80.39	17.52	1.69	0.39
1974	100.00	79.91	18.27	1.47	0.34
1975	100.00	78.90	19.17	1.54	0.40
1976	100.00	77.15	20.78	1.62	0.46
1977	100.00	74.86	22.99	1.64	0.52
1978	100.00	72.78	25.00	1.64	0.58
1979	100.00	70.60	27.12	1.64	0.64
1980	100.00	68.60	29.06	1.64	0.71
1981	100.00	66.68	30.92	1.63	0.77
1982	100.00	64.81	32.74	1.62	0.83
1983	100.00	62.95	34.54	1.62	0.89
1984	100.00	61.18	36.26	1.61	0.96
1985	100.00	59.43	37.96	1.59	1.02

TABLE VII-26
United States
Projection of Labor Force, by Occupation, Race, and Sex, 1970 to 1985

CHEMISTS

YEAR	TOTAL	WHITE MALE	WHITE FEMALE	BLACK MALE	BLACK FEMALE
1970	81661	69349	9676	2259	377
1971	85474	72774	10013	2320	367
1972	89003	75923	10336	2384	360
1973	92265	78862	10601	2449	353
1974	95482	81748	10887	2503	345
1975	98608	84519	11190	2559	339
1976	101656	87153	11547	2619	337
1977	104622	89624	11982	2679	338
1978	107763	92135	12543	2742	343
1979	110913	94561	13195	2806	351
1980	114100	96931	13936	2871	362
1981	117326	99250	14761	2938	377
1982	120621	101542	15679	3006	395
1983	123920	103763	16666	3075	416
1984	127186	105898	17706	3144	439
1985	130380	107924	18780	3211	464

Percentage Distribution of
Projection of Labor Force, by Occupation, Race, and Sex, 1970 to 1985

CHEMISTS

YEAR	TOTAL	WHITE MALE	WHITE FEMALE	BLACK MALE	BLACK FEMALE
1970	100.00	84.92	11.85	2.77	0.46
1971	100.00	85.14	11.71	2.71	0.43
1972	100.00	85.30	11.61	2.68	0.40
1973	100.00	85.47	11.49	2.65	0.38
1974	100.00	85.62	11.40	2.62	0.36
1975	100.00	85.71	11.35	2.60	0.34
1976	100.00	85.73	11.36	2.58	0.33
1977	100.00	85.66	11.45	2.56	0.32
1978	100.00	85.50	11.64	2.54	0.32
1979	100.00	85.26	11.90	2.53	0.32
1980	100.00	84.95	12.21	2.52	0.32
1981	100.00	84.59	12.58	2.50	0.32
1982	100.00	84.18	13.00	2.49	0.33
1983	100.00	83.73	13.45	2.48	0.34
1984	100.00	83.26	13.92	2.47	0.35
1985	100.00	82.78	14.40	2.46	0.36

TABLE VII-27
United States
New Labor Force Entrants, by Occupation,
Race, and Sex, 1970 to 1985

CHEMISTS

| YEAR | TOTAL | WHITE | | BLACK | |
		MALE	FEMALE	MALE	FEMALE
1970	5489	4500	897	76	16
1971	5375	4382	897	79	17
1972	5151	4146	904	82	19
1973	4940	3971	866	84	19
1974	4943	3950	903	73	17
1975	4901	3867	939	75	19
1976	4878	3757	1012	87	22
1977	4854	3622	1112	95	25
1978	5088	3685	1266	108	29
1979	5167	3624	1392	118	33
1980	5275	3589	1520	129	37
1981	5392	3561	1651	139	41
1982	5543	3552	1794	151	45
1983	5633	3501	1921	162	50
1984	5690	3432	2034	171	54
1985	5709	3340	2133	179	57

Percentage Distribution of
New Labor Force Entrants, by Occupation,
Race, and Sex, 1970 to 1985

CHEMISTS

| YEAR | TOTAL | WHITE | | BLACK | |
		MALE	FEMALE	MALE	FEMALE
1970	100.00	81.99	16.34	1.38	0.29
1971	100.00	81.53	16.68	1.46	0.32
1972	100.00	80.50	17.54	1.59	0.36
1973	100.00	80.39	17.52	1.69	0.39
1974	100.00	79.91	18.27	1.47	0.34
1975	100.00	78.90	19.17	1.54	0.40
1976	100.00	77.02	20.74	1.78	0.45
1977	100.00	74.61	22.91	1.96	0.52
1978	100.00	72.43	24.88	2.12	0.58
1979	100.00	70.14	26.94	2.28	0.64
1980	100.00	68.04	28.82	2.44	0.70
1981	100.00	66.04	30.62	2.59	0.76
1982	100.00	64.08	32.37	2.73	0.82
1983	100.00	62.15	34.10	2.87	0.88
1984	100.00	60.31	35.74	3.01	0.94
1985	100.00	58.50	37.36	3.14	1.00

TABLE VII-28
United States
Projection of Labor Force, by Occupation,
Race, and Sex, 1970 to 1985

CHEMISTS

YEAR	TOTAL	WHITE MALE	WHITE FEMALE	BLACK MALE	BLACK FEMALE
1970	81661	69349	9676	2259	377
1971	85474	72774	10013	2320	367
1972	89003	75923	10336	2384	360
1973	92265	78862	10601	2449	353
1974	95482	81748	10887	2503	345
1975	98608	84519	11190	2559	339
1976	101664	87153	11547	2627	337
1977	104646	89624	11982	2702	338
1978	107811	92135	12343	2790	343
1979	110995	94561	13195	2888	351
1980	114224	96931	13936	2995	362
1981	117501	99250	14761	3113	377
1982	120858	101542	15679	3242	395
1983	124226	103763	16666	3381	416
1984	127571	105898	17706	3529	439
1985	130852	107924	18780	3684	464

Percentage Distribution of
Projection of Labor Force, by Occupation,
Race, and Sex, 1970 to 1985

CHEMISTS

YEAR	TOTAL	WHITE MALE	WHITE FEMALE	BLACK MALE	BLACK FEMALE
1970	100.00	84.92	11.85	2.77	0.46
1971	100.00	85.14	11.71	2.71	0.43
1972	100.00	85.30	11.61	2.68	0.40
1973	100.00	85.47	11.49	2.65	0.38
1974	100.00	85.62	11.40	2.62	0.36
1975	100.00	85.71	11.35	2.60	0.34
1976	100.00	85.73	11.36	2.58	0.33
1977	100.00	85.64	11.45	2.58	0.32
1978	100.00	85.46	11.63	2.59	0.32
1979	100.00	85.19	11.89	2.60	0.32
1980	100.00	84.86	12.20	2.62	0.32
1981	100.00	84.47	12.56	2.65	0.32
1982	100.00	84.02	12.97	2.68	0.33
1983	100.00	83.53	13.42	2.72	0.33
1984	100.00	83.01	13.88	2.77	0.34
1985	100.00	82.48	14.35	2.82	0.35

CHAPTER VIII

Minorities and Women in
Medicine and Dentistry

In recent years, industry has been employing an increasing number of doctors as a result of legislative acts to improve employee health and product safety. Medical trade and professional groups estimate there are 4,000 full-time corporate physicians in the United States, which represents less than 2 percent of the physician population. More than 10,000 other doctors, however, serve in similar positions on a part-time basis. Some 1,200 doctors work in the pharmaceutical field, and about 800 are employed as company medical underwriters and claims consultants. In addition to these major categories, a few physicians are chairmen or executive officers of large companies, especially in the drug industry.[1] Furthermore, the dental insurance plans currently being incorporated in employee benefits packages may create an industrial demand for dentists.

This chapter examines the past and present participation of minorities and women in the medical and dental professions, and the labor supply model is implemented to project the representation of minorities and women in these fields between 1970 and 1985.

MINORITIES AND WOMEN IN MEDICINE

Between academic years 1964-65 and 1974-75, the number of students applying for admission into medical schools in the United States increased 122 percent, from 19,168 to 42,624; 27 new medical schools became operational; and the number of graduates with M.D. degrees increased 72 percent, from 7,409

---

[1] William Abrams, "Industry Beckons M.D.'s," *New York Times*, 28 November 1975, Sec. 3, pp. 1, 4.

to 12,714.[2] Women and members of minority groups during the 1975-76 academic year represented 28 percent of the total medical school enrollment, which is a higher percentage than ever in the past.[3]

Background

In 1968 the Association of American Medical Colleges (AAMC) took its first official action to increase the minority representation in United States medical schools. At the initial annual meeting of the AAMC Assembly, the following recommendation was adopted: "Medical schools must admit increased numbers of students from geographic areas, economic backgrounds and ethnic groups that are now inadequately represented." [4]

During 1969 the AAMC obtained its first of several grants from the United States Office of Economic Opportunity to "increase educational opportunities for minorities in the health professions." These grants totaled $1.5 million, and they were used to help fund the national AAMC Office of Minority Affairs, the Medical Minority Applicant Registry, the publication "Minority Student Opportunities in U.S. Medical Schools," and AAMC Regional Workshops on Minority Student Programs. An AAMC task force investigated the poor representation of racial minority groups in medical education during 1969-70. The task force, which was funded by the Alfred P. Sloan Foundation, issued a report in 1970. The report recommended that United States medical schools increase the proportion of minorities entering M.D. programs with the aim of raising the percentage of black freshmen enrolled to at least 12 percent by 1975-76, and this aim was endorsed by the AAMC, the American Hospital Association (AHA), the American Medical Association (AMA), and the National Medical Association (NMA). Consequently, nation-wide recruitment programs were begun to interest minority students

---

[2] Anne E. Crowley, ed., "Medical Education in the United States 1974-75," *Journal of the American Medical Association*, Vol. 234 (December 29, 1975), pp. 1336-38.

[3] Travis L. Gordon and W. F. Dubé, "Medical Student Enrollment, 1971-72 Through 1975-76," *Journal of Medical Education*, Vol. 51 (February 1976), p. 144.

[4] Davis G. Johnson, Vernon C. Smith, Jr., and Stephen L. Tarnoff, "Recruitment and Progress of Minority Medical School Entrants 1970-72," *Journal of Medical Education*, Vol. 50 (July 1975), p. 721.

in medicine, to inform them of opportunities available, and to increase the enrollment of traditionally underrepresented groups.[5]

History

AMA reports that the total number of physicians in the United States as of December 1974 was 379,748, and that of this total, 32,976 (8.7 percent) were women.[6] Presently blacks comprise 2 percent of the nation's physicians.[7]

Table VIII-1 shows the distribution of experienced physicians in the United States by sex and race, 1940-1970. During the 30 years shown, the percentage of male physicians has decreased slightly, from 95.4 percent to 91.0 percent. The number of students and graduates of United States medical schools between 1935-36 and 1974-75 are listed in Table VIII-2.

BLACKS

The total number of blacks enrolled in United States medical schools increased 68 percent 1971-72 and 1975-76.[8] Black medical professionals are concerned, however, because admissions of blacks to medical schools declined in the fall of 1975. At the annual meeting of the National Medical Association (NMA) in August 1976, Dr. Lloyd C. Elam, president of Meharry College, stressed that although the number of blacks entering Meharry School of Medicine had risen, the number entering schools across the country had declined. Dr. Elam cautioned, "The kind of progress that was heralded by the improvement of health services in recent years is going to be less if this type of situation prevails." [9] Reference for the following historical account of blacks in medicine was provided by *Blacks, Medical Schools, and Society.*[10]

---

[5] *Ibid.*

[6] James R. Cantwell, ed., *Profile of Medical Practice* (Chicago: American Medical Association, 1976), pp. 75, 77.

[7] Leonard A. Eiserer, ed., "Black Medical Professionals See Decrease in Training Opportunities for Blacks," *Fair Employment Report*, Vol. 14 (August 23, 1976), p. 132.

[8] Gordon, "Medical School Enrollment," p. 146, Table 3.

[9] Reginald Stuart, "Health Training of Blacks Drops," *New York Times*, 2 August 1976, p. 20.

[10] James L. Curtis, *Blacks, Medical Schools, and Society* (Ann Arbor: University of Michigan Press, 1971), pp. 1-27 *passim.*

TABLE VIII-1

Number of Experienced Civilian Physicians by Sex and Race,
1940-1970

Sex and Race	1940	1950	1960	1970 [a]
Physicians Total	164,760	179,610	230,307	280,557
Male Physicians	157,120	168,000	214,830	255,424
White	153,100	164,010	206,190	239,677
Negro		3,360	4,551	5,258
Other Races	4,020 [b]	630	4,089	10,489
Male Physicians with 5 or More Years of College [c]	147,060	157,050	198,737	240,183
White	143,440	153,120	190,930	
Nonwhite	3,620	3,930	7,807	4,607 [d]
Female Physicians	7,640	11,610	15,477	25,133
White	7,500	11,070	14,072	21,321
Negro		300	487	786
Other Races	140 [b]	240	918	3,026

TABLE VIII-1 (continued)

Sex and Race	1940	1950	1960	1970ᵃ
Female Physicians with 5 or More Years of College ᶜ	5,920	8,940	12,553	18,949
White	5,800	8,550	11,350	
Nonwhite	120	390	1,203	422ᵈ

Sources: *Sixteenth Census of the United States: 1940 Population, The Labor Force, Occupational Characteristics* (Washington, D.C.: Government Printing Office, 1943), pp. 59-70 passim, Table 3.
United States Census of Population 1950, Occupational Characteristics, P-E No. 1B (Washington, D.C.: Government Printing Office, 1956), pp. 29, 107, 115, Tables 3, 10, 11.
United States Census of Population 1960, Occupational Characteristics, PC(2)-7A (Washington, D.C.: U.S. Department of Commerce, 1961), pp. 22, 116, 123, 130, 137, Tables 3, 9, 10.
1970 Census of Population Subject Report, Occupational Characteristics, PC(2)-7A (Washington, D.C.: U.S. Department of Commerce, 1973), pp. 12, 59, 73, 87, 101, Tables 2, 5, 6.

ᵃ Includes medical and osteopathic physicians.
ᵇ Only nonwhite data available.
ᶜ Data only available for four or more years of college completed in 1940 and 1950.
ᵈ Only Negro data available.

TABLE VIII-2
Students and Graduates in Medical and Basic Science Schools, 1935-1975 [a]

Year	No. Schools	Total Enrollment	First-Year	Intermediate Years	Graduates
1935-1936	77	22,564	6,605	10,776	5,183
1940-1941	77	21,379	5,837	10,267	5,275
1945-1946	77	23,216	6,060	11,330	5,826
1950-1951	79	26,186	7,177	12,874	6,135
1955-1956	82	28,639	7,686	14,108	6,845
1956-1957	85	29,130	8,014	14,320	6,796
1957-1958	85	29,473	8,030	14,582	6,861
1958-1959	85	29,614	8,128	14,626	6,860
1959-1960	85	30,084	8,173	14,830	7,081
1960-1961	86	30,288	8,298	14,996	6,994
1961-1962	87	31,078	8,483	15,427	7,168
1962-1963	87	31,491	8,642	15,585	7,264
1963-1964	87	32,001	8,772	15,893	7,336
1964-1965	88	32,428	8,856	16,163	7,409
1965-1966	88	32,835	8,759	16,502	7,574
1966-1967	89	33,423	8,964	16,716	7,743
1967-1968	94	34,538	9,479	17,086	7,973
1968-1969	99	35,833	9,863	17,911	8,059
1969-1970	101	37,669	10,401	18,901	8,367
1970-1971	103	40,487	11,348	20,165	8,974
1971-1972	108	43,650	12,361	21,738	9,551
1972-1973	112	47,546	13,726	23,429	10,391
1973-1974	114	50,886	14,185	25,088	11,613
1974-1975	114	54,074	14,963	26,397	12,714
1975-1976	114	56,244	15,351	27,332	13,561

Source: Sylvia I. Etzel and John J. Fauser, eds., "Medical Education in the United States 1975-1976," *Journal of the American Medical Association*, Vol. 236 (December 27, 1976), p. 2961, Table 9.
[a] Prior to 1956-57, schools in development were not included.

Early American Period: 1619-1812

At the time of the American Revolution there were 3,500 practitioners of medicine in this country. Of the total, 3,100 were apprentice-trained, and 400 were university-educated physicians. Lucas Santomee Peters, a Dutch-educated physician who practiced during the late 1600s in New York colony, is considered to be the first African physician in the colonies. In 1792 the first medical publication by a Negro appeared in the *Massachusetts Magazine*.

Philadelphia's James Derham, born in 1762, is thought to be the best-trained and most successful Negro practitioner of the era. Abolitionists of the period frequently cited Derham as proof that blacks were potentially as capable as whites.

Cotton Mather learned a technique of smallpox inoculation, which had originated in Africa, from his slave Onesimus. This method was used in the colonies with success in the 1721 small-pox epidemic and throughout the Revolutionary War period, several years before 1798 when Edward Jenner's work on the vaccination was published in England.

Pre-Civil War through World War II: 1812-1944

In 1816 the American Colonization Society was founded by those proposing to resolve the Negro-white American problem by sending free Negroes from the United States to the west coast of Africa. Although exorbitant costs stifled the venture, the American Colonization Society was the first major source of encouragement for the training of Negro doctors. Those planning the colonization reasoned that Negro physicians would be needed to go to Africa to care for their race.

David J. Peck became the first black to receive the M.D. degree from an American medical school, Rush Medical College, in 1847. Two years later Bowdoin College conferred M.D. degrees on John V. DeGrasse and Thomas J. White. DeGrasse studied several additional years in Europe and, after returning to the United States, became the first Negro member of a medical society; furthermore, during the Civil War, DeGrasse was the first Negro surgeon to be commissioned by the United States Army. By 1860 at least nine United States medical schools had admitted one or more Negroes.

Howard University, which opened in 1866, started its medical school in 1868 as an attempt to meet the need for emergency health, education, job placement, and welfare services in Washington, D.C. Another medical school for Negroes, Meharry Medical College, was founded in 1866 as part of the Central Tennessee College, but it was not operative until 1876. A Negro medical society was formed in 1895 after Negro faculty members of Howard Medical College were refused membership to the Washington, D.C., local AMA branch on several occasions between 1869 and 1884.

More than 360,000 Negro troops served during World War I, and 356 Negro officers were commissioned in the United States Medical Corps to operate a segregated hospital. One of these men held the rank of major. There were 3,855 Negro physicians in the United States at the time, most of whom had graduated from Howard or Meharry.

During 1943, 582,861 Negroes were serving in World War II. The number of black commissioned officers exceeded 4,000 by this time; however, the total number of commissioned medical officers was only 395 in the Medical Corps and 67 in the Dental Corps. Although throughout World War II black medical personnel operated a larger segregated hospital than in World War I, there was only one Negro medical officer serving as lieutenant colonel and ten as majors.

It became clear during the 1940s that segregated medical education could not serve the health needs of the Negro. At that time the yearly production of black physicians, which was about 100, was running below the number of black physicians who died each year. As W. Montague Cobb, editor of the *Journal of the National Medical Association,* wrote in 1947:

> The present indication is for Howard and Meharry to open their doors to more white students and for the other 75 medical schools to admit such qualified applicants as might appear. It is only through a program of intelligent integration that the health needs of the Negro, which are inseparable from those of the general population, can be met.[11]

Integration: 1944-1970

Since the late 1940s, United States Supreme Court decisions have attempted to undo the separatist rulings from the turn of the century. In 1956 the Imhotep National Conference on Hospital Integration was formed to press for laws to end segregated hospital services, to promote lawsuits to prevent public funds from supporting the construction or operation of segregated services, and to advise governmental bureaus and administrations on methods to remove racially discriminatory practices and policies. Not until 1964, however, did the American Hospital Association issue a statement that medical and hospital care should be made available to everyone without qualification of any kind.

During the 1950s the federal government outlawed segregation and discrimination in governmental health facilities by accepting Negro patients and staff in hospitals operated by the Armed Forces, the Public Health Service, and the Veterans Administration. The Hill-Burton Act of 1964 provided states with financial support to build nursing homes, hospitals, and rehabilitation centers; however, the clause allowing states to build "separate-but-equal" facilities was deleted. By virtue of

---

11 *Ibid.,* pp. 18-19.

the 1964 Civil Rights Act's Title VI, no federal funds can now
be given any program from which anyone is excluded for reasons
of race, color, or national origin. The Office of Equal Health
Opportunity was established to monitor hospitals and insure that
their practices were in compliance with the law. The enrollment
of black students in United States medical schools for this
period, 1938-39 through 1969-70, is shown in Table VIII-3.

Since 1970

One of every 560 white Americans becomes a doctor, but for
blacks the same ratio is 1 of 3,800.[12] As shown in Table VIII-
4, in the fall of 1975 black Americans made up 6.8 percent of
the first-year medical school students in the United States and
they represented 6.2 percent of the total United States medical
school enrollments of about 56,000.

Future

Growth in the population, increase in the age group over 65,
and extension of hospitalization and medical care programs such
as Medicare and Medicaid will create a need for more physicians.
Increases in graduates from existing and developing United
States medical schools combined with foreign medical graduate
entrants suggest a greatly improved supply situation. This
improved supply could bring about the movement of physicians
into rural and other areas which have experienced shortages
of doctors in the past.[13]

A report released in September 1976 by the Carnegie Council
on Policy Studies for Higher Education concludes that graduates
of medical schools under development in the United States,
combined with the number of foreign medical school graduates,
could lead to an overpopulation of physicians in the United
States. The Council estimates there may be 477,000 practicing
physicians in the United States by 1985 compared with about
350,000 in 1973. Consequently, the Council recommends that

---

[12] George Blue Spruce, Jr., "Development of Minority Health Manpower—
Setting the Goals," *Quarterly of the National Dental Association, Inc.*, Vol.
31 (January 1973), p. 28.

[13] U.S. Department of Labor, *Occupational Outlook Handbook: 1974-75
Edition*, Bulletin 1785 (Washington, D.C.: Government Printing Office, 1974),
pp. 480-81.

TABLE VIII-3
*Black Student Enrollment in
U.S. Medical Schools for Selected Years
1938-39 to 1969-70*

Year	Total Enrollment	Number of Black Students	% Black Students	% of Total Black Enrollment in Predominantly White Schools
1938-1939	21,302	350	1.64	12.9
1947-1948	22,739	588	2.59	15.8
1948-1949	23,670	612	2.59	19.1
1949-1950	25,103	651	2.59	21.2
1950-1951	26,186	661	2.52	21.6
1951-1952	27,076	697	2.57	23.2
1952-1953	27,135	715	2.63	26.7
1955-1956	28,639	761	2.66	31.0
1968-1969	35,828	782	2.18	37.3
1969-1970	37,756	1,042	2.75	52.4

Source: James L. Curtis, *Blacks, Medical Schools, and Society* (Ann Arbor: University of Michigan Press, 1971), p. 34, Table III.

only 1 of 13 planned medical schools is necessary.[14] This may be interpreted to mean that opportunities for blacks to study medicine will not expand.

The country's third black medical school will be established in the fall of 1978 at Morehouse College, which is one of six institutions making up Atlanta University in Atlanta, Georgia. The school will begin as a two-year program with students transferring to other medical schools for their final years of study. Morehouse is, however, expected to become a four-year, degree-granting institution by 1983.[15]

---

[14] "New Medical Schools, Foreign Graduates May Cause U.S. Doctor Excess, Panel Says," *Wall Street Journal*, 3 September 1976, n. 4.

[15] Thomas A. Johnson, "Nation's 3rd Black Medical School to be Established at Atlanta's Morehouse College, Stressing Care of Poor," *New York Times*, 18 January 1977, p. 11.

TABLE VIII-4
First-Year and Total Enrollment of Blacks in
U.S. Medical Schools, 1971-72 through 1975-76

Black Enrollment	1971-72		1972-73		1973-74		1974-75		1975-76	
	Number	Percentage	Number	Percentage	Number	Percentage	Number	Percentage	Number	Percentage
First-Year										
Black Americans	882	7.1	957	7.0	1,027	7.2	1,106	7.5	1,036	6.8
Total										
Black Americans	2,055	4.7	2,582	5.4	3,049	6.0	3,355	6.3	3,456	6.2

Source: Travis L. Gordon and W. F. Dubé, "Medical Student Enrollment, 1971-72 Through 1975-76," *Journal of Medical Education*, Vol. 51 (February 1976), pp. 145-46, Tables 2, 4.

OTHER MINORITIES

It has been only since 1969-70 that medical schools have reported minority enrollment statistics in the Annual Report on Medical Education, which is published in the *Journal of the American Medical Association.* During 1975-76 minority students enrolled in United States medical schools numbered 5,928, which represents 10.6 percent of the total enrollment. First-year and total enrollment figures for minority students from 1971-72 through 1975-76 appear in Table VIII-5. After a 6-year surge in the percentage of minorities constituting first-year medical school enrollments, enrollments in 1975-76 and 1976-77 show a drop in the proportion of entering minority students. There is a growing concern that the national mood that supported special programs to recruit minority medical students is changing and that court decisions and charges of reverse discrimination will make it difficult to continue similar efforts in the future.[16]

Minority Student Recruitment

The past efforts of individual medical schools to recruit minority students has been thwarted by three factors: the small number of minority applicants; competition among schools for minority students; and cutbacks in federal loan and scholarship funds.

Constraints that limit the size of the minority pool and the number of minority students enrolling in medical school was the subject of a study by a task force of the Association of American Medical Colleges, the American Hospital Association, AMA, and NMA. The task force was supported by a grant from the Alfred P. Sloan Foundation. The report of this task force identifies major efforts necessary to increase the representation of minorities in the medical profession on a nation-wide basis.

Recommendations of the task force fall into four areas of emphasis: retention, financial aid, counseling, and class size. Major efforts should be focused on retention of minority students. The most important factors in retention during pre-medical education are the availability of financial aid at the undergraduate level and the student's perception of its avail-

---

[16] Gene I. Maeroff, "Proportion of Minority Students Entering Medical Schools Drops Again, Creating Concern About Future," *New York Times,* 15 November 1976, p. 19.

TABLE VIII-5

First-Year and Total Enrollment of U.S. Minorities and Foreign Students in U.S. Medical Schools,[a] *1971-72 through 1975-76*

Minorities	1971-72		1972-73		1973-74		1974-75		1975-76	
	No.	Percentage	No.	Percentage	No.	Percentage	No.	Percentage	No.	Percentage
First-Year										
Selected U.S. Minorities										
Black American	882	7.1	957	7.0	1,027	7.2	1,106	7.5	1,036	6.8
American Indian	23	0.2	34	0.3	44	0.3	71	0.5	60	0.4
Mexican American	118	1.0	137	1.0	174	1.2	227	1.5	224	1.5
Puerto Rican-Mainland	40	0.3	44	0.3	56	0.4	69	0.5	71	0.5
Subtotal	1,063	8.6	1,172	8.6	1,301	9.2	1,473	10.0	1,391	9.1
Other U.S. Minorities										
Oriental American	217	1.8	231	1.7	259	1.8	275	1.9	282	1.8
Cuban American									41	0.3
Other			34	0.2	71	0.5	91	0.6	73	0.5
Subtotal	217	1.8	265	1.9	330	2.3	366	2.5	396	2.6
Total U.S. Minorities	1,280	10.4	1,437	10.5	1,631	11.5	1,839	12.5	1,787	11.7
Foreign Students										
Non-U.S. Black	57	0.4	38	0.6	77	0.5	90	0.6	65	0.4

	No.	%[a]	No.	%[a]	No.	%[a]	No.	%[a]	No.	%[a]
Other	182	1.5	153	1.1	140	1.0	129	.9	162	1.1
Total	239	1.9	241	1.7	217	1.5	219	1.5	227	1.5
Total										
Selected U.S. Minorities										
Black American	2,055	4.7	2,582	5.4	3,049	6.0	3,355	6.3	3,456	6.2
American Indian	42	0.1	69	0.2	97	0.2	159	0.3	172	0.3
Mexican American	252	0.6	361	0.8	496	1.0	638	1.2	699	1.3
Puerto Rican-Mainland	76	0.2	90	0.2	123	0.2	172	0.3	197	0.4
Subtotal	2,425	5.6	3,102	6.6	3,765	7.4	4,324	8.1	4,524	8.1
Other U.S. Minorities										
Oriental American	647	1.5	718	1.5	883	1.7	959	1.8	1,022	1.8
Cuban American									144	0.3
Other			98	0.2	192	0.4	277	0.5	238	0.4
Subtotal	647	1.5	816	1.7	1,075	2.1	1,236	2.3	1,404	2.5
Total U.S. Minorities	3,072	7.1	3,918	8.3	4,840	9.5	5,560	10.4	5,928	10.6
Foreign Students										
Non-U.S. Black	210	0.5	275	0.6	296	0.6	287	0.5	249	0.4
Other	505	1.1	461	1.0	509	1.0	532	1.0	554	1.0
Total	715	1.6	736	1.6	805	1.6	819	1.5	803	1.4

Source: Travis L. Gordon and W. F. Dubé, "Medical Student Enrollment, 1971-72 Through 1975-76," *Journal of Medical Education*, Vol. 51 (February 1976), pp. 145-46, Tables 2, 4.

[a] Percentage of total U.S. medical school enrollment (percentages may not add because of rounding).

ability at the medical school level. It is important to reverse the trend of inadequate financial aid and to establish a better mechanism for utilizing available funds. Counseling should be directed to those efforts which help students fully realize their potential and gain the confidence needed to pursue careers in medicine. Existing medical school class size presents a major obstacle to increasing the production of physicians; because of this obstacle, many capable students are not permitted to study medicine.[17]

WOMEN

Between 1964 and 1974 the percentage of United States physicians who were women increased from 8 percent to 10 percent.[18] Table VIII-6 shows the participation of women in medical school education for selected years from 1949-50 to 1974-75.

Early Years

Nineteenth century women were considered mentally and physically inferior to men. Few believed it possible for a woman to engage successfully in a business or profession. Moreover, Victorian concepts of modesty and morality complicated the possibility of men and women participating together in physiological discussion and dissection of the human body.[19] In his 1871 presidential address to the AMA, Dr. Alfred Stillé said:

> On the whole, then, we believe that all experience teaches that woman is characterized by a combination of distinctive qualities, of which the most striking are uncertainty of rational judgement, capriciousness of sentiment, fickleness of purpose, and indecision of action, which totally unfit her for professional pursuits.[20]

Graduating from Geneva Medical College of Syracuse, New York, in 1849, Elizabeth Blackwell became the first woman to

---

[17] Bernard W. Nelson, Richard A. Bird, and Gilbert M. Rogers, "Expanding Educational Opportunities in Medicine for Blacks and Other Minority Students," *Journal of Medical Education*, Vol. 45 (October 1970), pp. 731-36.

[18] "A Close-up of Women in U.S.—and Ways their Status is Changing," *U.S. News & World Report* (December 8, 1975), p. 57.

[19] Mrs. Harold Keegan, ed., "Women in Medicine," *Illinois Medical Journal*, Vol. 147 (April 1975), pp. 382-83.

[20] Martha Johnson, "Struggle and Triumph for Illinois' First Women Physicians," *Illinois Medical Journal*, Vol. 149 (March 1976), p. 291.

TABLE VIII-6
Women in U.S. Medical Schools,
Selected Years 1949-50 through 1975-76 [a]

Academic Year	Women Applicants		Women in Entering Class		Total Women Enrolled		Women Graduates	
	No.	%	No.	%	No.	%	No.	%
1949-1950	1,390	5.7	387	5.5	1,806	7.2	595	10.7
1959-1960	1,026	6.9	494	6.0	1,710	5.7	405	5.7
1964-1965	1,731	9.0	786	8.9	2,503	7.7	503	6.8
1969-1970	2,289	9.4	952	9.2	3,390	9.0	700	8.4
1970-1971	2,734	10.9	1,256	11.1	3,894	9.6	827	9.2
1971-1972	3,737	12.8	1,693	13.7	4,755	10.9	860	9.0
1972-1973	5,480	15.2	2,315	16.9	6,099	12.8	924	8.9
1973-1974	7,202	17.8	2,743	19.6	7,731	15.4	1,264	11.1
1974-1975	8,712	20.4	3,260	22.3	9,786	18.1	1,706	13.4
1975-1976	9,575	22.6	3,656	23.8	11,527	20.5	2,200	16.2

Source: Sylvia I. Etzel and John J. Fauser, eds., "Medical Education in the United States 1975-76," *Journal of the American Medical Association*, Vol. 236 (December 27, 1976), p. 2962, Table 13.

[a] Harvard did not provide enrollment figures for 1973-74.

receive a diploma from an accredited medical school.[21] Many prominent physicians opposed medical education for women; however, they gradually approved separate colleges for female instruction. Physicians also fought the admission of women to the AMA until 1876 when Dr. Sarah Hackett Stevenson became the first woman to belong.

Today's Female Physicians

During the past 5 years, the number of women entering United States medical schools has increased 115 percent. Table VIII-7 shows the first-year and total enrollments for women at United States medical schools from 1971-72 through 1975-76.

The most common complaint of young female medical students is a feeling of loneliness and isolation, which is experienced most strongly during the first year of study. Those feelings, however, usually disappear during the second year with the establishment of closer bonds, joint interests, shared complaints, and anxieties.[22]

During 1974, the American Medical Women's Association sponsored a survey to find why women study medicine. The surveys

---

[21] *Ibid.*

[22] Helen Tausend, "Women in Medicine and Their Identity," *Journal of the American Medical Women's Association*, Vol. 31 (March 1976), p. 109.

TABLE VIII-7
First-Year and Total Enrollment of Men and Women in U.S. Medical Schools, 1971-72 through 1975-76

Male and Female Enrollment	1971-72 (108 schools)		1972-73 (112 schools)		1973-74 (114 schools)		1974-75 (114 schools)		1975-76 (114 schools)	
	Number	Percentage	Number	Percentage	Number	Percentage	Number	Percentage	Number	Percentage
First-Year										
Men	10,668	86.3	11,377	83.2	11,369	80.3	11,488	77.8	11,648	76.2
Women	1,693	13.7	2,300	16.8	2,790	19.7	3,275	22.2	3,647	23.8
Total	12,361	100.0	13,677	100.0	14,159	100.0	14,763	100.0	15,295	100.0
Total										
Men	38,895	89.1	41,284	87.2	42,923	84.6	43,893	82.0	44,401	79.5
Women	4,755	10.9	6,082	12.8	7,828	15.4	9,661	18.0	11,417	20.5
Total	43,650	100.0	47,366	100.0	50,751	100.0	53,554	100.0	55,818	100.0

Source: Travis L. Gordon and W. F. Dubé, "Medical Student Enrollment, 1971-72 Through 1975-76," *Journal of Medical Education*, Vol. 51 (February 1976), pp. 145-46, Tables 1, 3.

were sent to 115 deans of United States medical schools, and responses were returned by 95 percent. The factor identified most frequently by the deans as being important in the decision of women to study medicine was the changing attitudes of society, which encourage women to aspire to a career as well as to marriage.[23]

AMA figures show that at the end of 1974 female physicians numbered 32,976, which represents 8.7 percent of the total physicians labor force.[24] The female physicians most commonly specialize in psychiatry, pediatrics, or general family practice. The distribution of male and female physicians in the various specialties is given in Table VIII-8.

CURRENT PROGRAMS

The National Chicano Health Organization sponsors minority recruitment, admission, and retention programs for Chicanos studying one of the health professions. The National Boricua Health Organization, acting on behalf of disadvantaged mainland Puerto Ricans, and the Association of American Indian Physicians, working with American Indians, operate similar programs to increase the proportion of those minorities' students in medicine.

The Office of Health Manpower Opportunity, which was established in the early 1970s within the Department of Health, Education and Welfare, is authorized to award Special Health Careers Opportunity Grants to nonprofit health and educational entities to perform two functions. One function is to establish and operate projects to identify and to enroll in health training individuals likely to practice in shortage areas. Another function is to establish and to operate projects that will identify disadvantaged students with a potential for health training, encourage and assist them in enrolling in health schools, and facilitate and insure the completion of their training.[25]

---

[23] Laura E. Morrow, "Preliminary Report: Why Women Study Medicine," *Journal of the American Medical Women's Association*, Vol. 30 (March 1975), p. 141.

[24] Cantwell, ed., *Profile*, p. 77.

[25] Spruce, "Development of Minority Health Manpower," pp. 32-34.

TABLE VIII-8

Specialty Distribution of Male and Female Physicians

Specialty	Percent of Male Physicians in Specialty	Percent of Female Physicians in Specialty
All Specialties	100.0	100.0
General and Family Practice	22.9	15.8
Internal Medicine	16.3	9.7
Pediatrics	5.8	17.6
Obstetrics-Gynecology	7.3	9.0
Surgery	24.5	5.1
Psychiatry	5.8	18.3
Radiology	4.2	3.0
Anesthesiology	4.8	10.6
Other Specialties	8.4	10.9

Source: Judith Warner and Phil Aherne, eds., *Profile of Medical Practice* (Chicago: American Medical Association, 1974), p. 40.

The Josiah Macy, Jr. Foundation

In 1966 the Josiah Macy, Jr. Foundation established a program aimed at increasing the number of minorities in medicine. The Foundation's first grant was to support the Post-Baccalaureate Premedical Fellowship Program. Participants in this program were graduates from black colleges who were selected to enroll in summer programs at Haverford and Oberlin Colleges and to follow with a fifth academic year at participating liberal arts colleges. This additional academic experience was to prepare the students more fully for medical school study. Since 1966 the Foundation has made grants totalling over $4,000,000 to 33 medical schools for programs to recruit, prepare, and retain minority group students for the study of medicine.

During 1971 the Macy Foundation initiated a program to strengthen black students' preparation for medical study and to improve health profession advisory services at black colleges. This program funded two summer institutes and awarded grants to thirteen black colleges.

The Macy Foundation Faculty Fellowship Program, begun in 1970, sponsored thirty minority group members on faculties of schools of medicine and public health. Selection of recipients of the eight fellowships was made each year by a national committee. Final appointments were made in 1974. The Foundation has convened nine national and regional conferences, which are principally aimed at strengthening communication, cooperation, and confidence between black colleges in the South and medical schools of the area.

The Macy Foundation is currently sponsoring a study, "Minority Groups for Medicine," which is being directed by Charles E. Odegaard, president emeritus of the University of Washington. The objective is to review various programs developed on campuses of colleges with private and public institutional support intended to facilitate the professional education of more students from minority backgrounds for entry into the practice of medicine. Thus study will examine the strengths and weaknesses of past efforts and suggest the most promising types of efforts for the future.[26]

---

[26] "Macy Foundation Study—'Minority Groups for Medicine'," *Journal of the National Medical Association*, Vol. 67 (March 1975), p. 177.

PREDICTING THE NUMBERS OF MINORITIES AND WOMEN IN MEDICINE

The preceding review of the past and present status of minorities and women in medicine explains their current position in the profession and identifies efforts being made to increase the participation of these groups in medicine. The labor supply model was implemented to produce some estimates of the future participation of minorities and women as doctors. Four sets of projections of new labor force entrants and the resulting labor force were produced for the 1970 to 1985 period. The first of these, a base line forecast, represents a continuation of current trends in the composition of medical school graduates. Three alternative projections were produced to examine the impact of alterations in the racial and sexual composition of medical school graduates on the labor force of physicians.

The projections indicate that substantial progress can be expected in the participation of minorities and women in the medical profession in spite of the historical domination of the field by white males.

Base Line Projections

Table VIII-9 summarizes the input data used to generate all 4 projections for doctors. Data from the American Medical Association as published in *Professional Women and Minorities: A Manpower Data Resource Service* provided information on the information on the racial composition of medical school degree earners.[27] The base line projections of new entrants to the labor force and of the labor force are based on a continuation of current trends in the racial and sexual composition of medical school graduates. New entrants to the labor force with medical school degrees should increase from 8,300 in 1970 to 17,920 in 1985. As shown in Table VIII-10, the proportion of female and black entrants will increase from 8.2 percent and 1.8 percent in 1970 to 19.4 percent and 10.1 percent, respectively, in 1985.

The projections of the labor force, which are given in Table VIII-11, show the impact that new entrants have on the labor force of physicians. In 1970 women and blacks comprised 6.8 percent and 2.0 percent, respectively, of the doctors in the labor

---

[27] Betty M. Vetter and Eleanor L. Babco, *Professional Women and Minorities: A Manpower Resource Service* (Washington, D.C.: Scientific Manpower Commission, 1975), p. 446, Tables LS-M-16B, LS-M-16E.

TABLE VIII-9
Input Data for Simulation
of Medical Doctors in the Labor Force to 1985

	MALE	FEMALE
SEPARATION RATE		WHITE
1970	0.0309	0.0532
1985	0.0284	0.0542
		BLACK
1970	0.0312	0.0538
1985	0.0287	0.0554
ENTRY RATE		
FIRST PROFESSIONAL	1.0000	1.0000
SUPPLY BASE — 1970		
TOTAL	237427	17406
BLACK	4607	422

	DEGREES AWARDED	
FIRST PROFESSIONAL	.% FEMALE	% BLACK
1969	7.60	1.36
1970	8.41	1.97
1971	9.07	2.01
1972	8.97	2.40
1973	8.91	3.28
1974	11.27	3.90
1975	13.09	5.02

TABLE VIII-10
United States
New Labor Force Entrants, by Occupation,
Race, and Sex, 1970 to 1985

PHYSICIANS — MEDICAL

YEAR	TOTAL	WHITE		BLACK	
		MALE	FEMALE	MALE	FEMALE
1970	8314	7490	671	140	13
1971	8919	7946	782	174	17
1972	9253	8172	838	220	23
1973	10310	9001	963	313	34
1974	11210	9557	1210	393	50
1975	12447	10365	1485	522	75
1976	13810	11431	1670	619	90
1977	14260	11631	1816	702	110
1978	14710	11824	1967	789	131
1979	15230	12063	2130	881	156
1980	15490	12090	2260	960	180
1981	15990	12298	2428	1056	208
1982	16500	12505	2600	1154	240
1983	17160	12816	2801	1266	277
1984	17540	12909	2960	1360	312
1985	17920	12996	3121	1454	349

Percentage Distribution of
New Labor Force Entrants, by Occupation,
Race, and Sex, 1970 to 1985

PHYSICIANS — MEDICAL

YEAR	TOTAL	WHITE		BLACK	
		MALE	FEMALE	MALE	FEMALE
1970	100.00	90.09	8.07	1.68	0.15
1971	100.00	89.10	8.76	1.95	0.19
1972	100.00	88.32	9.06	2.38	0.25
1973	100.00	87.30	9.34	3.03	0.33
1974	100.00	85.26	10.79	3.51	0.44
1975	100.00	83.28	11.93	4.19	0.60
1976	100.00	82.77	12.09	4.48	0.65
1977	100.00	81.57	12.74	4.93	0.77
1978	100.00	80.38	13.37	5.36	0.89
1979	100.00	79.21	13.99	5.78	1.02
1980	100.00	78.05	14.59	6.20	1.16
1981	100.00	76.91	15.18	6.60	1.30
1982	100.00	75.79	15.76	7.00	1.45
1983	100.00	74.68	16.32	7.38	1.61
1984	100.00	73.59	16.88	7.75	1.78
1985	100.00	72.52	17.41	8.12	1.95

TABLE VIII-11
United States
Projection of Labor Force, by Occupation,
Race, and Sex, 1970 to 1985

PHYSICIANS — MEDICAL

YEAR	TOTAL	WHITE MALE	WHITE FEMALE	BLACK MALE	BLACK FEMALE
1970	254833	232820	16984	4607	422
1971	255526	233611	16861	4638	416
1972	256573	234642	16800	4715	417
1973	258686	236510	16866	4883	427
1974	261671	238917	17174	5127	454
1975	265835	242098	17739	5493	504
1976	271262	246291	18458	5945	567
1977	276998	250599	19284	6469	646
1978	283034	255013	20215	7064	742
1979	289428	259579	21258	7735	857
1980	295909	264080	22373	8467	989
1981	302713	268702	23594	9274	1143
1982	309840	273442	24920	10157	1321
1983	317420	278401	26374	11128	1524
1984	325181	283356	27907	12166	1752
1985	333095	288305	29515	13271	2004

Percentage Distribution of
Projection of Labor Force, by Occupation,
Race, and Sex, 1970 to 1985

PHYSICIANS — MEDICAL

YEAR	TOTAL	WHITE MALE	WHITE FEMALE	BLACK MALE	BLACK FEMALE
1970	100.00	91.36	6.66	1.81	0.17
1971	100.00	91.42	6.60	1.82	0.16
1972	100.00	91.45	6.55	1.84	0.16
1973	100.00	91.43	6.52	1.89	0.17
1974	100.00	91.30	6.56	1.96	0.17
1975	100.00	91.07	6.67	2.07	0.19
1976	100.00	90.79	6.80	2.19	0.21
1977	100.00	90.47	6.96	2.34	0.23
1978	100.00	90.10	7.14	2.50	0.26
1979	100.00	89.69	7.34	2.67	0.30
1980	100.00	89.24	7.56	2.86	0.33
1981	100.00	88.76	7.79	3.06	0.38
1982	100.00	88.25	8.04	3.28	0.43
1983	100.00	87.71	8.31	3.51	0.48
1984	100.00	87.14	8.58	3.74	0.54
1985	100.00	86.55	8.86	3.98	0.60

force. Between 1970 and 1985 female physicians will show a net gain less than 3 percentage points in their participation in the labor force, increasing from 6.8 percent to 9.5 percent. The 11-fold increase in black entrants translates into just more than a 2-fold increase in labor force penetration as black doctors increase their representation from 2.0 percent in 1970 to 4.6 percent in 1985.

These projections of the labor force indicate that both women and blacks will make substantial progress in increasing their participation in the medical profession as a result of their increasing representation among medical school graduates. The projection for blacks is favorable, but less so than that of women. Even though black representation among new medical school graduates is growing at a faster average annual rate than female representation, the number of black medical school graduates is still less than that of women. Moreover, the base of black doctors in the labor force in 1970 is less than that of females.

Sensitivity Analysis

Three alternative projections were developed by simulating the effects of changes in the racial and sexual composition of degree earners and calculating the resultant labor force. For the first simulation, the number of black degree recipients by 1985 was doubled, while the base line projection of degrees awarded to whites was maintained. The second simulation repeated the procedure for female degree recipients. The third exercise doubled by 1985 the number of blacks and women receiving degrees, while the base line number of white male degree recipients was maintained.

Tables VIII-12 and VIII-13 record the results of the black degree recipient manipulation. Doubling the number of degrees awarded to blacks and its effect on the supply of new entrants is presented in Table VIII-12. This doubling results in an increase of 4.6 percentage points in the proportion of black physicians from 1970 to 1985 (shown in Table VIII-13), or an additional 2.0 percentage points over the base line projection for 1985. The impact on the female labor force through the increase of black female degree recipients is minimal.

The results of the second simulation, which provides a 100 percent increase in the number of female degree earners, are shown in Tables VIII-14 and VIII-15. If these results were

TABLE VIII-12
United States
New Labor Force Entrants, by Occupation, Race, and Sex, 1970 to 1985

PHYSICIANS – MEDICAL

YEAR	TOTAL	WHITE MALE	WHITE FEMALE	BLACK MALE	BLACK FEMALE
1970	8314	7490	671	140	13
1971	8919	7946	782	174	17
1972	9253	8172	838	220	23
1973	10310	9001	963	313	34
1974	11210	9557	1210	393	50
1975	12447	10365	1485	522	75
1976	13881	11431	1670	680	99
1977	14422	11631	1816	843	132
1978	14986	11824	1967	1025	171
1979	15645	12063	2130	1233	218
1980	16060	12090	2260	1440	269
1981	16748	12298	2428	1689	333
1982	17476	12505	2600	1962	408
1983	18394	12816	2801	2279	498
1984	19044	12909	2960	2583	592
1985	19724	12996	3121	2909	698

Percentage Distribution of New Labor Force Entrants, by Occupation, Race, and Sex, 1970 to 1985

PHYSICIANS – MEDICAL

YEAR	TOTAL	WHITE MALE	WHITE FEMALE	BLACK MALE	BLACK FEMALE
1970	100.00	90.09	8.07	1.68	0.15
1971	100.00	89.10	8.76	1.95	0.19
1972	100.00	88.32	9.06	2.38	0.25
1973	100.00	87.30	9.34	3.03	0.33
1974	100.00	85.26	10.79	3.51	0.44
1975	100.00	83.28	11.93	4.19	0.60
1976	100.00	82.35	12.03	4.90	0.72
1977	100.00	80.65	12.59	5.84	0.91
1978	100.00	78.90	13.12	6.84	1.14
1979	100.00	77.11	13.62	7.88	1.39
1980	100.00	75.28	14.07	8.97	1.68
1981	100.00	73.43	14.50	10.09	1.99
1982	100.00	71.56	14.88	11.23	2.33
1983	100.00	69.67	15.23	12.39	2.71
1984	100.00	67.78	15.54	13.57	3.11
1985	100.00	65.89	15.82	14.75	3.54

TABLE VIII-13
United States
Projection of Labor Force, by Occupation,
Race, and Sex, 1970 to 1985

PHYSICIANS — MEDICAL

YEAR	TOTAL	WHITE MALE	WHITE FEMALE	BLACK MALE	BLACK FEMALE
1970	254833	232820	16984	4607	422
1971	255526	233611	16861	4638	416
1972	256573	234642	16800	4715	417
1973	258686	236510	16866	·4883	427
1974	261671	238917	17174	5127	454
1975	265835	242098	17739	5493	504
1976	271332	246291	18458	6007	576
1977	277229	250599	19284	6669	676
1978	283533	255013	20215	7495	810
1979	290326	259579	21258	8506	984
1980	297347	264080	22373	9695	1199
1981	304862	268702	23594	11099	1466
1982	312893	273442	24920	12737	1794
1983	321614	278401	26374	14646	2193
1984	330733	283356	27907	16806	2664
1985	340267	288305	29515	19232	3215

Percentage Distribution of
Projection of Labor Force, by Occupation,
Race, and Sex, 1970 to 1985

PHYSICIANS — MEDICAL

YEAR	TOTAL	WHITE MALE	WHITE FEMALE	BLACK MALE	BLACK FEMALE
1970	100.00	91.36	6.66	1.81	0.17
1971	100.00	91.42	6.60	1.82	0.16
1972	100.00	91.45	6.55	1.84	0.16
1973	100.00	91.43	6.52	1.89	0.17
1974	100.00	91.30	6.56	1.96	0.17
1975	100.00	91.07	6.67	2.07	0.19
1976	100.00	90.77	6.80	2.21	.0.21
1977	100.00	90.39	6.96	2.41	0.24
1978	100.00	89.94	7.13	2.64	0.29
1979	100.00	89.41	7.32	2.93	0.34
1980	100.00	88.81	7.52	3.26	0.40
1981	100.00	88.14	7.74	3.64	0.48
1982	100.00	87.39	7.96	4.07	0.57
1983	100.00	86.56	8.20	4.55	0.68
1984	100.00	85.68	8.44	5.08	0.81
1985	100.00	84.73	8.67	5.65	0.94

TABLE VIII-14
United States
New Labor Force Entrants, by Occupation,
Race, and Sex, 1970 to 1985

PHYSICIANS — MEDICAL

YEAR	TOTAL	WHITE		BLACK	
		MALE	FEMALE	MALE	FEMALE
1970	8314	7490	671	140	13
1971	8919	7946	782	174	17
1972	9253	8172	838	220	23
1973	10310	9001	963	313	34
1974	11210	9557	1210	393	50
1975	12447	10365	1485	522	75
1976	13986	11431	1837	619	99
1977	14645	11631	2180	702	132
1978	15339	11824	2557	789	171
1979	16144	12063	2983	881	218
1980	16710	12090	3391	960	269
1981	17572	12298	3884	1056	333
1982	18488	12505	4421	1154	408
1983	19622	12816	5042	1266	498
1984	20485	12909	5624	1360	592
1985	21390	12996	6241	1454	698

Percentage Distribution of
New Labor Force Entrants, by Occupation,
Race, and Sex, 1970 to 1985

PHYSICIANS — MEDICAL

YEAR	TOTAL	WHITE		BLACK	
		MALE	FEMALE	MALE	FEMALE
1970	100.00	90.09	8.07	1.68	0.15
1971	100.00	89.10	8.76	1.95	0.19
1972	100.00	88.32	9.06	2.38	0.25
1973	100.00	87.30	9.34	3.03	0.33
1974	100.00	85.26	10.79	3.51	0.44
1975	100.00	83.28	11.93	4.19	0.60
1976	100.00	81.73	13.13	4.42	0.71
1977	100.00	79.42	14.88	4.80	0.90
1978	100.00	77.08	16.67	5.14	1.11
1979	100.00	74.72	18.47	5.46	1.35
1980	100.00	72.35	20.29	5.75	1.61
1981	100.00	69.99	22.11	6.01	1.90
1982	100.00	67.64	23.91	6.24	2.21
1983	100.00	65.31	25.70	6.45	2.54
1984	100.00	63.02	27.45	6.64	2.89
1985	100.00	60.76	29.18	6.80	3.27

TABLE VIII-15
United States
Projection of Labor Force, by Occupation,
Race, and Sex, 1970 to 1985

PHYSICIANS - MEDICAL

YEAR	TOTAL	WHITE MALE	WHITE FEMALE	BLACK MALE	BLACK FEMALE
1970	254833	232820	16984	4607	422
1971	255526	233611	16861	4638	416
1972	256573	234642	16800	4715	417
1973	258686	236510	16866	4883	427
1974	261671	238917	17174	5127	454
1975	265835	242098	17739	5493	504
1976	271438	246291	18625	5945	576
1977	277550	250599	19806	6469	676
1978	284185	255013	21298	7064	810
1979	291432	259579	23135	7735	984
1980	299025	264080	25279	8467	1199
1981	307243	268702	27800	9274	1466
1982	316113	273442	30720	10157	1794
1983	325823	278401	34101	11128	2193
1984	336066	283356	37879	12166	2664
1985	346858	288305	42067	13271	3215

Percentage Distribution of
Projection of Labor Force, by Occupation,
Race, and Sex, 1970 to 1985

PHYSICIANS - MEDICAL

YEAR	TOTAL	WHITE MALE	WHITE FEMALE	BLACK MALE	BLACK FEMALE
1970	100.00	91.36	6.66	1.81	0.17
1971	100.00	91.42	6.60	1.82	0.16
1972	100.00	91.45	6.55	1.84	0.16
1973	100.00	91.43	6.52	1.89	0.17
1974	100.00	91.30	6.56	1.96	0.17
1975	100.00	91.07	6.67	2.07	0.19
1976	100.00	90.74	6.86	2.19	0.21
1977	100.00	90.29	7.14	2.33	0.24
1978	100.00	89.73	7.49	2.49	0.29
1979	100.00	89.07	7.94	2.65	0.34
1980	100.00	88.31	8.45	2.83	0.40
1981	100.00	87.46	9.05	3.02	0.48
1982	100.00	86.50	9.72	3.21	0.57
1983	100.00	85.45	10.47	3.42	0.67
1984	100.00	84.32	11.27	3.62	0.79
1985	100.00	83.12	12.13	3.83	0.93

achieved, the percentage of females in the medical labor force would increase to 13.1 percent in 1985 from 6.8 percent in 1970 (Table VIII-15). This represents an increase of 3.6 percentage points over the base line projection for 1985. The change in the proportion of labor force that would be black because of the changes for black females is not material.

Doubling the number of degrees awarded to both blacks and women in the third simulation produces a new entrants pool that is 30.4 percent female and 15.8 percent black in 1985 (Table VIII-16). Within the labor force, which is presented in Table VIII-17, women would make up 12.8 percent of all doctors in 1985, and blacks would comprise 6.4 percent of the labor force. These projections of the labor force represent an increase of 3.3 percentage points for women and 1.8 percentage points for blacks over the initial base line projections for 1985.

These simulations indicate that both minorities and women can make substantial gains in their participation in medicine because of their representation in the profession in 1970 and the increasing number of medical degrees earned by them. The penetration of blacks in this occupation, however, will occur more slowly than that of women. This is due to the smaller representation of black physicians in the 1970 labor force and their smaller representation among medical school graduates.

MINORITIES AND WOMEN IN DENTISTRY

During the 1975-76 academic year, 20,767 students were enrolled in the 59 dental schools in the United States. Of that total, 2,020 students, or 9.7 percent, were from minority groups, and 1,861, or 9.0 percent, were women.[28] Currently 2 percent, or 2,400, of the nation's 120,000 dentists are black,[29] and in 1970, 3.5 percent were women.[30]

The increasing proportion of minorities attending institutions of higher education since the late 1960s has produced a larger pool of minorities from which entrants to health professional

---

[28] "Annual Report 1975-76, Dental Education Supplement 11, Trend Analysis," report of the American Dental Association, 1975-76, pp. 3, 13, 14, Tables VIII, XII, XIII.

[29] Spruce, "Development of Minority Health Manpower—Setting the Goals," p. 28.

[30] Randi Sue Tillman, "Women in Dentistry—A Review of the Literature," *Journal of the American Dental Association*, Vol. 91 (December 1975), p. 1214.

TABLE VIII-16
United States
New Labor Force Entrants, by Occupation,
Race, and Sex, 1970 to 1985

PHYSICIANS — MEDICAL

YEAR	TOTAL	WHITE		BLACK	
		MALE	FEMALE	MALE	FEMALE
1970	8314	7490	671	140	13
1971	8919	7946	782	174	17
1972	9253	8172	838	220	23
1973	10310	9001	963	313	34
1974	11210	9557	1210	393	50
1975	12447	10365	1485	522	75
1976	14048	11431	1837	680	99
1977	14786	11631	2180	843	132
1978	15576	11824	2557	1025	171
1979	16497	12063	2983	1233	218
1980	17190	12090	3391	1440	269
1981	18205	12298	3884	1689	333
1982	19296	12505	4421	1962	408
1983	20635	12816	5042	2279	498
1984	21708	12909	5624	2583	592
1985	22844	12996	6241	2909	698

Percentage Distribution of
New Labor Force Entrants, by Occupation,
Race, and Sex, 1970 to 1985

PHYSICIANS — MEDICAL

YEAR	TOTAL	WHITE		BLACK	
		MALE	FEMALE	MALE	FEMALE
1970	100.00	90.09	8.07	1.68	0.15
1971	100.00	89.10	8.76	1.95	0.19
1972	100.00	88.32	9.06	2.38	0.25
1973	100.00	87.30	9.34	3.03	0.33
1974	100.00	85.26	10.79	3.51	0.44
1975	100.00	83.28	11.93	4.19	0.60
1976	100.00	81.37	13.08	4.84	0.71
1977	100.00	78.67	14.74	5.70	0.89
1978	100.00	75.91	16.42	6.58	1.09
1979	100.00	73.12	18.08	7.48	1.32
1980	100.00	70.33	19.72	8.38	1.57
1981	100.00	67.55	21.34	9.28	1.83
1982	100.00	64.81	22.91	10.17	2.11
1983	100.00	62.11	24.43	11.04	2.41
1984	100.00	59.46	25.91	11.90	2.73
1985	100.00	56.89	27.32	12.73	3.06

TABLE VIII-17
United States
Projection of Labor Force, by Occupation, Race, and Sex, 1970 to 1985

PHYSICIANS — MEDICAL

YEAR	TOTAL	WHITE MALE	WHITE FEMALE	BLACK MALE	BLACK FEMALE
1970	254833	232820	16984	4607	422
1971	255526	233611	16861	4638	416
1972	256573	234642	16800	4715	417
1973	258686	236510	16866	4883	427
1974	261671	238917	17174	5127	454
1975	265835	242098	17739	5493	504
1976	271499	246291	18625	6007	576
1977	277750	250599	19806	6669	676
1978	284616	255013	21298	7495	810
1979	292203	259579	23135	8506	984
1980	300253	264080	25279	9695	1199
1981	309068	268702	27800	11099	1466
1982	318692	273442	30720	12737	1794
1983	329341	278401	34101	14646	2193
1984	340706	283356	37879	16806	2664
1985	352820	288305	42067	19232	3215

Percentage Distribution of
Projection of Labor Force, by Occupation, Race, and Sex, 1970 to 1985

PHYSICIANS — MEDICAL

YEAR	TOTAL	WHITE MALE	WHITE FEMALE	BLACK MALE	BLACK FEMALE
1970	100.00	91.36	6.66	1.81	0.17
1971	100.00	91.42	6.60	1.82	0.16
1972	100.00	91.45	6.55	1.84	0.16
1973	100.00	91.43	6.52	1.89	0.17
1974	100.00	91.30	6.56	1.96	0.17
1975	100.00	91.07	6.67	2.07	0.19
1976	100.00	90.71	6.86	2.21	0.21
1977	100.00	90.22	7.13	2.40	0.24
1978	100.00	89.60	7.48	2.63	0.28
1979	100.00	88.84	7.92	2.91	0.34
1980	100.00	87.95	8.42	3.23	0.40
1981	100.00	86.94	8.99	3.59	0.47
1982	100.00	85.80	9.64	4.00	0.56
1983	100.00	84.53	10.35	4.45	0.67
1984	100.00	83.17	11.12	4.93	0.78
1985	100.00	81.71	11.92	5.45	0.91

schools can be drawn. Even dramatic increases in first-year and total enrollments in dental schools, however, will not lead to immediate and substantial changes in the composition of active practitioners. The change will be very gradual since new graduates each year constitute such a small segment of the total practitioner supply.

History

Census data on experienced dentists from 1940-1970 are shown in Table VIII-18. Figures from the 1940 Census are misleading because the numbers for female dentists include pharmacists, osteopaths, and veterinarians.

It is important to note that there is reason to question the accuracy of Census occupational data, which are self-reported by individuals or by members of their families. Data compiled by the Bureau of Census on the number of dentists in the United States include a considerable number of persons who are only partially active as dentists and exclude some who have been trained as dentists, but are not active as such. Furthermore, because occupational data reported in the 1970 Census are based on a 5 percent sample of the population, the sampling errors may be substantial.

Table VIII-19 shows the number of dentists for selected years between 1950 and 1972 as reported by the Division of Health Manpower and Facilities within the U.S. Department of Health, Education and Welfare.

BLACKS

There is 1 dentist for every 1,750 Americans, but only 1 black dentist for every 11,500 black Americans.[31] Participation of blacks in dentistry is increasing. In 1971-72 black enrollment in United States dental schools represented 3.5 percent of the total enrollment, and black graduates represented 2 percent of the total dental school graduates.[32] During the 1975-76 academic year, black enrollment constituted 4.7 percent of the total enrollment in the nation's dental schools, and black graduates

---

[31] Spruce, "Development of Minority Health Manpower," p. 28.

[32] U.S. Department of Health, Education and Welfare, *Minorities and Women in the Health Fields: Applicants, Students, and Workers* (Washington, D.C.: Government Printing Office, 1975), pp. 22, 26.

TABLE VIII-18

Number of Experienced Civilian Dentists by Sex and Race,
1940-1970

Sex and Race	1940 [a]	1950 [a]	1960	1970
Dentists Total	75,520	68,730	87,110	92,776
Male Dentists	69,320	66,540	85,273	89,974
White	67,700	64,650	82,110	86,426
Negro		1,620	2,261	2,218
Other Races	1,620 [b]	270	902	1,330
Male Dentists with 5 or more Years of College [c]	58,140	60,090	64,392	79,627
White	56,860	58,380	62,003	
Nonwhite	1,280	1,710	2,389	1,998 [d]
Female Dentists [a]	6,200	2,190	1,837	2,802
White	6,080	2,130	1,757	2,590
Negro		60	80	166
Other Races	120 [b]	—	—	46

TABLE VIII-18 (continued)

Sex and Race	1940 [a]	1950 [a]	1950	1970
Female Dentists with 5 or more Years of College [c]	3,800	930	639	1,079
White	3,680	930	619	
Nonwhite	120	—	20	95 [d]

Sources: *Sixteenth Census of the United States: 1940 Population, The Labor Force, Occupational Characteristics* (Washington, D.C.: Government Printing Office, 1943), pp. 59-70 passim, Table 3.
United States Census of Population 1950, Occupational Characteristics, P-E No. 1B (Washington, D.C.: Government Printing Office, 1956), pp. 29, 107, 115, Tables 3, 10, 11.
United States Census of Population 1960, Occupational Characteristics, PC(2)-7A (Washington, D.C.: U.S. Department of Commerce, 1961), pp. 21, 116, 123, 130, 187, Tables 3, 9, 10.
1970 Census of Population Subject Report, Occupational Characteristics, PC(2)-7A (Washington, D.C.: U.S. Department of Commerce, 1973), pp. 12, 59, 73, 87, 101, Tables 2, 5, 6.

[a] Female data for 1940 includes pharmacists, osteopaths, and veterinarians.
[b] Only nonwhite data available.
[c] Data only available for four or more years of college completed in 1940 and 1950.
[d] Only Negro data available.

TABLE VIII-19

Total Dentists and Active Dentists in the United States for Selected Years 1950-1972

Total and Active Dentists	1950	1960	1970	1972
Total Dentists	89,440	102,940	116,280	119,700
Active Dentists	76,940	90,040	102,220	105,400

Source: U.S. Department of Health, Education, and Welfare, *Health Resources Statistics, 1974* (Washington, D.C.: Government Printing Office, 1974), p. 71.

accounted for 3.8 percent of the total number of dental school graduates.[33]

Past

As recently as 1951, black applicants were not considered for admission to 16 of the 40 accredited dental schools.[34] In 1964, 8 United States dental schools had blacks enrolled; in 1966 the number of schools with black students was 11; in 1970 it had increased to 37.[35] By 1975-76, 55 of the 59 accredited dental schools had black students enrolled; however, Meharry Medical College and Howard University accounted for 44 percent of the total black student enrollment. Meharry Medical College and Howard University produced 50 percent of the total number of black dental school graduates in 1975-76.[36] In fact, over the past century less than 2 percent of all black dentists have been trained at schools other than Meharry and Howard.[37]

Present

Meharry Medical College and Howard University, which have for years trained 80 to 90 percent of all black dentists, are now having difficulty recruiting qualified applicants. The difficulty is a result of 3 factors: high cost and time commitment for obtaining a dental education; problems that average students have in meeting admission standards; and competition with industry in recruiting potential dental students.[38]

During a meeting of the Student National Dental Association in 1972, Joseph L. Henry, Dean of Howard University's College

---

[33] "Annual Report 1975-76, Dental Education Supplement 3, Minority Report," report of the American Dental Association, 1975-76, pp. 6-7, Tables 6, 7.

[34] Louis J. P. Calisti and Joseph L. Hozid, "Recruiting Minority Group Students for the Health Professions," *Journal of the American Dental Association*, Vol. 82 (May 1971), p. 1094.

[35] Joseph L. Henry and Jeanne C. Sinkford, "Minority Recruitment is a Major Project," *Dental Student*, Vol. 51 (May 1973), p. 55.

[36] A.D.A., "Supplement 3," pp. 6-7, Tables 6, 7.

[37] Joseph L. Henry, "Letter to the Editor," *Journal of the American Dental Association*, Vol. 78 (February 1968), p. 234.

[38] M. R. Holland, "Need for More Racial Minority People in Dentistry," *Northwest Dentistry*, Vol. 50 (May-June 1971), p. 213.

of Dentistry, talked to black students about the difficulties they faced in dental school. Blacks defined their problems as the following: inadequate or no special programs to meet their needs; inadequate scholarship and loan funds; covert and sometimes overt unfriendliness from other students in manner, words, and actions; failure of students, faculty, and administration to extend a helping hand of warmth, welcome, and acceptance; failure of other students to share student-accumulated education aids, including old exam files and information banks; the feeling of an uneasy truce and virtually total exclusion from all but the formal social life of the college; and fear of survival to graduation related to the high failure and dropout rate of blacks.[39] Even though most admission barriers have fallen for blacks interested in attending dental school, attitudinal bias continues to be a problem with some students, faculty, and administrators involved in dental education.

Although minority enrollments in United States dental schools increased in the early 1970s, undergraduate college enrollments indicate a leveling off or decline in entering minority students. The enrollment of black students in colleges rose from less than 3 percent in the mid 1960s to 8.7 percent in 1972. Between 1962 and 1972, black enrollment in the nation's colleges increased 248 percent; however, the high of 8.7 percent in 1972 had fallen to 7.4 percent by the 1974-75 academic year.[40] The decreasing number of minority college graduates will reduce the pool of minorities available as entrants to health professional schools. Dental schools may experience this decline several years from now when present minority students near graduation.

Future

Recruitment programs play a major role in the future development of more black dentists. Effective programs will use the resources of dental schools, dental professional organizations, minority groups, and minority dentists. Dental schools currently using successful recruitment programs operate on five basic levels: to find the potential students; to gain their interest in the

---

[39] Joseph L. Henry, "Minority Group Students Need a Helping Hand," *Dental Student*, Vol. 51 (December 1972), pp. 30, 35.

[40] James E. Mulvihill, "Barriers to Identification and Motivation of Minority Group Members for Dentistry," *Journal of Dental Education*, Vol. 40 (March 1976), pp. 142-46.

dental profession; to identify the individual's potential; to provide financial support; and to reinforce the student academically.[41]

MINORITY GROUPS

In academic year 1975-76 minority group students (including blacks, Puerto Ricans, Mexican-Americans, American Indians, Orientals, and other minorities) constituted 11.1 percent of first-year enrollments, 9.7 percent of total enrollments, and 7.5 percent of graduates from United States dental schools.[42] This represents quite an improvement considering that in 1969 only 2.2 percent of all enrolled dental students were minorities.[43]

Present

Data for minority group members' participation in dentistry are only available since 1970-71, and these are listed in Table VIII-20. Although these data show a continuous increase in the number of minority dental students, this is not the case in all dental schools. During the 1975-76 academic year, Howard University and Meharry Medical College accounted for 23 percent of the total minority enrollment. Consequently, the remaining 57 dental schools had a minority enrollment of only 7.6 percent. Seven of the 59 currently operating dental schools had less than 5 minority students in their entire student population in 1975-76. These 7 schools had 1,779 students of whom only 19 were minorities. In 25 of the 59 dental schools, minority students represented less than 5 percent of the total student enrollment. Only 16 dental schools had minority enrollments greater than 10 percent; furthermore, several schools achieved this percentage by enrolling a large number of Oriental students, many of whom were not disadvantaged. Of the total 1975-76 enrollment of 2,020, there were 588 Orientals.

Minority Group Barriers

As identified by James E. Mulvihill, the major barriers to the identification and motivation of minority group members for dental education are education, psychosocial background, counsel-

---

[41] Henry and Sinkford, "Minority Recruitment is a Major Project," p. 55.

[42] A.D.A., "Supplement 3," pp. 1, 6, 7, Tables 1, 6, 7.

[43] Mulvihill, "Barriers to Identification," p. 142.

TABLE VIII-20

Number of Graduates from U.S. Dental Schools
by Racial/Ethnic Category, 1972-1976

Year	Total Graduates	Racial/Ethnic Category						
		Minority	Black	Puerto Rican	Mexican American	American Indian	Oriental	Other
		Number of graduates						
1972	3,961	167	74	3	9	1	61	19
1973	4,230	241	110	3	22	1	73	32
1974	4,515	335	154	—	31	2	113	35
1975	4,969	368	187	6	33	5	107	30
1976	5,336	467	213	1	49	3	158	43

Sources: *Annual Report 1972-73* Dental Education (Chicago: American Dental Association, n.d.), p. 4, Figure 2.
Annual Report 1973-74 Dental Education (Chicago: American Dental Association, n.d.), p. 4, Figure 3.
Annual Report 1974-75 Dental Education (Chicago: American Dental Association, n.d.), p. 4, Figure 3.
Annual Report 1975-76 Dental Education (Chicago: American Dental Association, n.d.), p. 4, Figure 3.
Annual Report 1976-77 Dental Education (Chicago: American Dental Association, n.d.), p. 4, Figure 3.

ing, and finances.[44] The following is an explanation of these four factors which limit minority group participation in dental education.

Minority Group Students' Education. In the United States there exist two systems of primary and secondary education with two standards of operation. The differences in the operation of these two systems are reflected in the quality and quantity of the faculty, physical facilities, and fiscal resources of the two systems. These differences are seen in the variety of educational programs and opportunities offered to youth at the primary and secondary levels; they are perceived in the differing degrees of preparation in fundamental quantitative, reading, and verbal skills, in the motivation, and in the attainment of the students participating in the two educational systems.

Minority Group Students' Background. Members of minority groups currently have a lower economic status, and a disproportionately high percentage of minority families exist at the poverty level. Poverty creates in people damaged and uncertain self-concepts, as indicated in the following description of the poverty culture from the *Journal of Rehabilitation:*

> The culture of poverty is characterized by its members' lack of adequate education, long-term experience of powerlessness, lack of self esteem, a sense of hopelessness regarding improvement of their socio-economic status, and willingness to accept immediate gain rather than postpone satisfaction. They are concerned most with the present, taking their satisfaction on a moment-to-moment basis, and their goals are short-term. Typically, they have learned it is futile to think of the future.[45]

When students from the poverty environment move to the campus of a predominantly white college, they are often frustrated as they are confronted with the choice of absorption into the prevailing middle class culture or of withdrawal into a separate minority society. At the same time, students are faced with the academic challenges of a college curriculum.

Minority Group Students' Counseling. A well-organized, accessible system of effective academic and psychosocial counseling and remediation could help minority students overcome educational and psychosocial barriers. Even though such help is avail-

---

[44] *Ibid.,* pp. 142-45.

[45] Vivian M. Johnson, "Counselor Preparation for Serving Culturally Deprived Persons," *Journal of Rehabilitation,* Vol. 36 (November-December 1970), p. 19.

able occasionally, more often, the counseling that a minority student receives, or the lack of counseling, constitutes a further barrier in effect. Counselors frequently do not know the facts about health professions; consequently, it is not uncommon for a counselor to steer counselees to occupations with which he is more familiar, such as teaching. Moreover, in order to be effective with minority group students, counselors also need to be familiar with the needs of disadvantaged individuals.

Minority Group Students' Finances. Most minority students and their families cannot afford a dental education: the extensive educational period and related costs are prohibitive. Prospective students frequently opt for the least costly college education that gives opportunity for gainful employment immediately after graduation with a bachelor's degree.

Civil rights legislation of 1964 prompted compliance efforts by business, industry, labor, and government and resulted in the availability of numerous attractive job opportunities to minority group members. Many of these also carried respectable income levels and fringe benefits of additional schooling or on-the-job training. The result of this was a marked decrease in the quality and size of the dental school minority applicant pool.[46]

WOMEN

Legislation forbidding sex discrimination and the changing role of women in recent years are contributing factors to the increase of women entering dental schools. Table VIII-21 shows the first-year and total enrollment figures for women in United States dental schools from 1967-68 through 1975-76.

Past

The percentage of women in dentistry has not changed significantly in the past 50 years. One source reports that: in 1920 women dentists represented 3 percent of the profession; in 1968 they represented 1.2 percent of the total number of dentists; and in 1970 women constituted 3.5 percent of all dentists in the United States. As recently as 1950, Harvard University, Georgetown University, and St. Louis University did not admit

---

[46] Joseph L. Henry, "The Problems Facing Negroes in Dental Education," *Journal of the American College of Dentists*, Vol. 36 (October 1969), p. 237.

TABLE VIII-21
First-Year and Total Enrollments in U.S. Dental Schools by Sex,
1967-68 through 1975-76

Academic Year	Both Sexes	Male	Female
	Number of Students		
First Year			
1967-68	4,200	4,154	46
1968-69	4,203	4,157	46
1969-70	4,355	4,299	56
1970-71	4,565	4,471	94
1971-72	4,745	4,598	147
1972-73	5,337	5,113	224
1973-74	5,445	5,054	391
1974-75	5,617	4,986	631
1975-76	5,763	5,056	707
Total			
1967-68	14,955	14,778	177
1968-69	15,408	15,241	167
1969-70	16,008	15,834	174
1970-71	16,553	16,322	231
1971-72	17,305	16,971	334
1972-73	18,376	17,865	511
1973-74	19,369	18,533	836
1974-75	20,146	18,785	1,361
1975-76	20,767	18,906	1,861

Source: "Annual Report 1975-76, Dental Education Supplement 11, Trend Analysis," report of the American Dental Association, 1975-76, pp. 3, 9, 12, 13, Tables II, VIII, IX, XII.

women as dental students.[47] Moreover, that same year the total number of women enrolled in United States dental schools was 94.[48]

[47] Randi Sue Tillman, "Women in Dentistry—A Review of the Literature," *Journal of the American Dental Association*, Vol. 91, No. 6 (December 1975), p. 1215.

[48] A.D.A., "Supplement 11," p. 13, Table XII.

Present

Studies in the late 1960s show that women tend to do better scholastically and are more highly motivated than their male counterparts. Women do not have trouble handling academics or clinical responsibilities, but they often have difficulty in non-scholastic areas. Male peers accuse women of receiving preferential treatment from instructors; instructors often limit women students' career options by advising them to go into "female" specialties; and women are left out of after-school groups and informal gatherings.[49]

After graduating from dental school, the majority of female dentists are professionally active. According to a study published in 1970, 85 percent of all female dentists are actively employed. Female dentists are more likely to specialize than males: 31 percent of all females specialize as opposed to 10 percent of males. The most popular specialities for male dentists are orthodontics and oral surgery; however, women dentists most frequently choose pedodontics and orthodontics.[50]

There are several reasons that women do not select professions in dentistry: it is considered a masculine profession because it is practiced primarily by men in this country; it involves science and mechanical ability, which are both considered masculine subjects; and there are currently few role models with whom prospective female dental students can identify.

Future

Recruitment is the key to increasing the number of female dentists. These recruitment programs must be directed at the high school, junior high school, and elementary school levels; furthermore, they must reach not only students, but also educators, counselors, and parents. Half of the women who had chosen dentistry as a career reported in 1972 that they made that decision before entering college. In addition, 25 percent of women dentists surveyed in 1960 reported that their parents had opposed their choice of dentistry as a career.[51]

---

[49] Tillman, "Women in Dentistry," p. 1215.

[50] *Ibid.*, p. 1216.

[51] *Ibid.*, pp. 1215, 1218.

CURRENT PROGRAMS

In 1968 the W. K. Kellogg Foundation contributed a $177,500 3-year grant to establish a scholarship program for black dental students. An additional grant of $172,500 was made in 1970 by the Kellogg Foundation to broaden the scholarship program to include other minority students underrepresented in the dental profession. The funds are administered by the American Fund for Dental Education (AFDE), which is located in Chicago.[52]

During 1972 the Robert Wood Johnson Foundation presented a $4 million student aid grant, which is also administered by AFDE, to American dental schools. The purpose of this grant is to increase the number of dentists in areas that have inadequate access to dental care. Dental schools must use the money for scholarships or loan awards to women students, students from rural areas, and black, Mexican-American, American Indian, and mainland Puerto Rican students. The data indicate these groups are most likely to practice dentistry in rural and inner-city communities that do not have an adequate supply of dentists.[53]

Career Planning Programs

The National Chicano Health Organization, which is active primarily in the Southwest, sponsors minority recruitment, admission, and retention programs to increase the number of Chicanos in medical, dental, pharmacy, nursing, and public health schools. The National Boricua Health Organization has a similar program for disadvantaged mainland Puerto Ricans.[54]

Several universities in the country sponsor programs to prepare high school and college students for health professions. Examples of such programs are Harvard University's Health Careers Summer Program, Howard University's Academic Reinforcement Program, University of Illinois' Medical Opportunities Program, the Harvard-Yale-Columbia Intensive Summer Study Program, and Haverford College's Post-Baccalaureate Program.

---

[52] "AFDE Plans More Aid to Minority Students," *Journal of the American Dental Association*, Vol. 83 (July 1971), p. 83.

[53] "Johnson Foundation Announces $4 Million Student Grant," *Journal of the American Dental Association*, Vol. 85 (December 1972), p. 1244.

[54] Spruce, "Development of Minority Health Manpower," p. 32.

The Junior Dental Institute of the University of Oregon and the public school-based health career orientation program in Boston are characteristic of the programs to improve basic skills and motivation of junior and senior high school students.

The Long Island Jewish-Hillside Medical Center operates two programs concerning health careers. The Alternative Education Program gives junior high school students the opportunity to spend two hours a day at the Medical Center. Students are exposed to numerous health occupations as they rotate through the various departments to hear lectures and observe the departments' functions. The second program, which is held at the Medical Center's Main Campus, is an information workshop acquainting junior and senior high school counselors from local New York City public schools with health careers. In addition, special grants are available for counselors to study health careers at the Medical Center during vacation periods.[55]

PREDICTING THE NUMBERS OF MINORITIES AND WOMEN IN DENTISTRY

The review of the past and present status of minorities and women in dentistry explains the present efforts to increase the participation of these groups in the profession. The labor supply model was implemented to produce some estimates of the future participation of minorities and women in dentistry. Four sets of projections for new labor force entrants and the resulting dental labor force were produced for the 1970 to 1985 period. The first of these is a base line projection, which represents the continuation of current trends in the composition of dental school graduates. Three simulations were implemented to show the effect of altering the racial and sexual distributions of degree recipients on the labor force. This analysis indicates that female representation will increase slowly in the coming years, while blacks will be in a better position because of their relative status in the initial supply base and among degree earners.

Base Line Projections

The basic input data necessary to exercise the model for the dental occupation appear in Table VIII-22. The base line projections of new entrants to the labor force and of the labor force

---

[55] Mulvihill, "Barriers to Identification," p. 145.

TABLE VIII-22
*Input Data for Simulation
of Dentists in the Labor Force to 1985*

	MALE	FEMALE	
SEPARATION RATE	WHITE		
1970	0.0364	0.0686	
1985	0.0336	0.0690	
	BLACK		
1970	0.0355	0.0513	
1985	0.0326	0.0329	
ENTRY RATE			
FIRST PROFESSIONAL	1.0000	1.0000	
SUPPLY BASE - 1970			
TOTAL	79627	1079	
BLACK	1998	95	

	DEGREES AWARDED	
	% FEMALE	% BLACK
FIRST PROFESSIONAL		
1969	0.94	0.26
1970	0.91	0.88
1971	1.12	1.47
1972	1.11	2.01
1973	1.36	2.80
1974	1.91	3.44
1975	3.06	3.76

are based on a continuation of current trends in the racial and sexual composition of dental school graduates. American Dental Association data, published in the Bureau of Health Manpower's *Minorities & Women in the Health Fields: Applicants, Students, and Workers,* provided information on the racial characteristics of degree earners.[56] New entrants to the labor force with dental school degrees should increase from 3,700 in 1970 to 5,700 in 1985, an increase in the proportion of female and black entrants from 0.9 percent each in 1970 to 5.4 percent and 9.7 percent, respectively, in 1985. These figures are presented in Table VIII-23.

The projections of the labor force, provided in Table VIII-24, show the impact that new entrants have on the labor force. In 1970 women and blacks comprised 1.3 percent and 2.6 percent, respectively, of dentists in the labor force. Given the trends in the new entrants pool, female participation should increase to 2.2 percent in 1985, which is a net improvement of less than 1 percentage point over the 1970 level. Black penetration should increase to 4.8 percent, a level that is almost double black participation in 1970.

These projections indicate that blacks will make substantial progress in increasing their participation in the dental profession as a result of increasing their representation among new graduates. The projection for women is favorable, but less so than that for blacks. This is primarily because the initial base of female dentists in the labor force in 1970 is less than that of blacks, and female representation among new graduates is growing at a slower average annual rate than black representation.

Sensitivity Analysis

Three alternative projections were produced in order to assess the sensitivity of the racial and sexual composition of the dental labor force to changes in black and female representation among new dental school graduates. The first simulation altered the stream of black graduates from 1975 to 1985 in order to achieve a 100 percent increase in their numbers above the base line projection in 1985. The number of white degree recipients was maintained at the base line level. The second simulation followed

---

[56] U.S. Department of Health, Education and Welfare, *Minorities & Women in the Health Fields: Applicants, Students, and Workers* (Washington, D.C.: Government Printing Office, 1975), p. 26, Table 9.

TABLE VIII-23
United States
New Labor Force Entrants, by Occupation,
Race, and Sex, 1970 to 1985

DENTISTRY

YEAR	TOTAL	WHITE		BLACK	
		MALE	FEMALE	MALE	FEMALE
1970	3718	3652	33	32	0
1971	3745	3647	43	55	1
1972	3862	3734	49	78	1
1973	4050	3876	62	110	2
1974	4440	4204	86	147	3
1975	4723	4418	124	176	5
1976	5400	5018	140	236	7
1977	5210	4796	149	256	8
1978	5150	4697	161	282	10
1979	5490	4961	187	350	12
1980	5540	4960	203	363	15
1981	5680	5038	222	402	18
1982	5740	5044	239	436	21
1983	5750	5006	254	467	24
1984	5750	4960	268	496	27
1985	5750	4914	281	525	30

Percentage Distribution of
New Labor Force Entrants, by Occupation,
Race, and Sex, 1970 to 1985

DENTISTRY

YEAR	TOTAL	WHITE		BLACK	
		MALE	FEMALE	MALE	FEMALE
1970	100.00	98.23	0.89	0.87	0.01
1971	100.00	97.38	1.13	1.46	0.02
1972	100.00	96.67	1.28	2.02	0.03
1973	100.00	95.71	1.54	2.71	0.04
1974	100.00	94.69	1.94	3.30	0.07
1975	100.00	93.54	2.63	3.72	0.10
1976	100.00	92.92	2.59	4.36	0.12
1977	100.00	92.06	2.87	4.92	0.15
1978	100.00	91.21	3.13	5.47	0.19
1979	100.00	90.36	3.40	6.01	0.23
1980	100.00	89.52	3.66	6.55	0.27
1981	100.00	88.69	3.91	7.08	0.31
1982	100.00	87.87	4.16	7.60	0.36
1983	100.00	87.06	4.41	8.12	0.41
1984	100.00	86.25	4.66	8.63	0.47
1985	100.00	85.45	4.89	9.13	0.52

TABLE VIII-24
United States
Projection of Labor Force, by Occupation,
Race, and Sex, 1970 to 1985

DENTISTRY

YEAR	TOTAL	WHITE		BLACK	
		MALE	FEMALE	MALE	FEMALE
1970	80706	77629	984	1998	95
1971	81499	78465	959	1982	93
1972	82396	79371	942	1991	91
1973	83464	80403	940	2031	90
1974	84899	81741	962	2107	90
1975	86581	83259	1020	2210	92
1976	88895	85340	1090	2370	96
1977	90951	87141	1164	2546	100
1978	92890	88796	1245	2741	107
1979	95115	90674	1346	2979	116
1980	97327	92502	1456	3242	127
1981	99617	94363	1578	3536	141
1982	101903	96183	1709	3855	157
1983	104135	97922	1844	4194	175
1984	106306	99573	1985	4553	196
1985	108418	101140	2129	4929	220

Percentage Distribution of
Projection of Labor Force, by Occupation,
Race, and Sex, 1970 to 1985

DENTISTRY

YEAR	TOTAL	WHITE		BLACK	
		MALE	FEMALE	MALE	FEMALE
1970	100.00	96.19	1.22	2.48	0.12
1971	100.00	96.28	1.18	2.43	0.11
1972	100.00	96.33	1.14	2.42	0.11
1973	100.00	96.33	1.13	2.43	0.11
1974	100.00	96.28	1.13	2.48	0.11
1975	100.00	96.16	1.18	2.55	0.11
1976	100.00	96.00	1.23	2.67	0.11
1977	100.00	95.81	1.28	2.80	0.11
1978	100.00	95.59	1.34	2.95	0.12
1979	100.00	95.33	1.42	3.13	0.12
1980	100.00	95.04	1.50	3.33	0.13
1981	100.00	94.73	1.58	3.55	0.14
1982	100.00	94.39	1.68	3.78	0.15
1983	100.00	94.03	1.77	4.03	0.17
1984	100.00	93.67	1.87	4.28	0.18
1985	100.00	93.29	1.96	4.55	0.20

the same specification, but altered the stream of women graduating from dental schools, while the base line projections for men were maintained. The third simulation achieved a doubling of black and female graduates by 1985, while the number of degrees awarded to men was maintained.

Tables VIII-25 and VIII-26 record the results of the black degree recipient manipulation. According to this simulation, in 1985 blacks would comprise 17.6 percent of new labor force entrants, as shown in Table VIII-25. This represents an increase of 16.7 percentage points over their 1970 share and an increase of 7.9 percentage points above the base line projection for 1985. Incorporating these results into the supply calculations yields a labor force that is 6.7 percent black in 1985, a gain of 4.1 percentage points above the 1970 figure and an increase of 1.9 percentage points from the base line projection. These results are presented in Table VIII-26. The gain for females as a result of the increased proportion of degrees granted to black females is not material.

The output of the second simulation, which doubled the number of degrees earned by women, appears in Tables VIII-27 and VIII-28. Increasing the number of female degree recipients in this manner translates into an improvement of 9.4 percentage points over the 1970 level of 0.9 percent for female new entrants by 1985. The participation of women in the dental labor force would be 3.2 percent in 1985, an improvement of 1.9 percentage points over the 1970 situation, but an increase of only 1 percentage point above the base line projection for 1985. The gain for blacks by way of the increased number of degrees earned by black women would not be substantial.

The third and final simulation involved increasing the numbers of both black and female degree earners by 100 percent from their base line levels, while the number of degrees awarded to white males was maintained. This manipulation produces a pool of new labor force entrants in 1985 that is 9.5 percent female and 16.9 percent black, as shown in Table VIII-29. This represents increases of 8.6 percentage points for women and 16 percentage points for blacks over their participation in the new entrants group in 1970. If these changes were achieved, women and blacks would comprise 3.2 percent and 6.7 percent, respectively, of the 1985 labor force, as the figures in Table VIII-30 reveal. These results represent improvements of 1.9 percentage points for women and 4.1 percentage points for blacks over

TABLE VIII-25
United States
New Labor Force Entrants, by Occupation,
Race, and Sex, 1970 to 1985

DENTISTRY

YEAR	TOTAL	WHITE MALE	WHITE FEMALE	BLACK MALE	BLACK FEMALE
1970	3718	3652	33	32	0
1971	3745	3647	43	55	1
1972	3862	3734	49	78	1
1973	4050	3876	62	110	2
1974	4440	4204	86	147	3
1975	4723	4418	124	176	5
1976	5424	5018	140	259	7
1977	5263	4796	149	308	10
1978	5237	4697	161	366	13
1979	5627	4961	187	462	17
1980	5729	4960	203	544	22
1981	5932	5038	222	643	28
1982	6060	5044	239	742	35
1983	6142	5006	254	840	43
1984	6221	4960	268	942	51
1985	6305	4914	281	1050	60

Percentage Distribution of
New Labor Force Entrants, by Occupation,
Race, and Sex, 1970 to 1985

DENTISTRY

YEAR	TOTAL	WHITE MALE	WHITE FEMALE	BLACK MALE	BLACK FEMALE
1970	100.00	98.23	0.89	0.87	0.01
1971	100.00	97.38	1.13	1.46	0.02
1972	100.00	96.67	1.28	2.02	0.03
1973	100.00	95.71	1.54	2.71	0.04
1974	100.00	94.69	1.94	3.30	0.07
1975	100.00	93.54	2.63	3.72	0.10
1976	100.00	92.50	2.58	4.78	0.13
1977	100.00	91.13	2.84	5.85	0.18
1978	100.00	89.68	3.08	6.99	0.24
1979	100.00	88.16	3.32	8.21	0.31
1980	100.00	86.57	3.54	9.50	0.39
1981	100.00	84.93	3.75	10.85	0.48
1982	100.00	83.23	3.95	12.24	0.58
1983	100.00	81.50	4.13	13.68	0.69
1984	100.00	79.73	4.30	15.15	0.82
1985	100.00	77.93	4.46	16.65	0.95

TABLE VIII-26
United States
Projection of Labor Force, by Occupation,
Race, and Sex, 1970 to 1985

DENTISTRY

| YEAR | TOTAL | WHITE | | BLACK | |
		MALE	FEMALE	MALE	FEMALE
1970	80706	77629	984	1998	95
1971	81499	78465	959	1982	93
1972	82396	79371	942	1991	91
1973	83464·	80403	940	2031	90
1974	84899	81741	962	2107	90
1975	86581	83259	1020	2210	92
1976	88919	85340	1090	2394	96
1977	91027	87141	1164	2620	103
1978	93051	88796	1245	2897	112
1979	95408	90674	1346	3262	126
1980	97799	92502	1456	3697	144
1981	100325	94363	1578	4216	168
1982	102907	96183	1709	4818	197
1983	105499	97922	1844	5499	233
1984	108095	99573	1985	6261	·277
1985	110704	101140	2129	7107	328

Percentage Distribution of
Projection of Labor Force, by Occupation,
Race, and Sex, 1970 to 1985

DENTISTRY

| YEAR | TOTAL | WHITE | | BLACK | |
		MALE	FEMALE	MALE	FEMALE
1970	100.00	96.19	1.22	2.48	0.12
1971	100.00	96.28	1.18	2.43	0.11
1972	100.00	96.33	1.14	2.42	0.11
1973	100.00	96.33	1.13	2.43	0.11
1974	100.00	96.28	1.13	2.48	0.11
1975	100.00	96.16	1.18	2.55	0.11
1976	100.00	95.97	1.23	2.69	0.11
1977	100.00	95.73	1.28	2.88	0.11
1978	100.00	95.43	1.34	3.11	0.12
1979	100.00	95.04	1.41	3.42	0.13
1980	100.00	94.58	1.49	3.78	0.15
1981	100.00	94.06	1.57	4.20	0.17
1982	100.00	93.47	1.66	4.68	0.19
1983	100.00	92.82	1.75	5.21	0.22
1984	100.00	92.12	1.84	5.79	0.26
1985	100.00	91.36	1.92	6.42	0.30

TABLE VIII-27
United States
New Labor Force Entrants, by Occupation,
Race, and Sex, 1970 to 1985

DENTISTRY

YEAR	TOTAL	WHITE		BLACK	
		MALE	FEMALE	MALE	FEMALE
1970	3718	3652	33	32	0
1971	3745	3647	43	55	1
1972	3862	3734	49	78	1
1973	4050	3876	62	110	2
1974	4440	4204	86	147	3
1975	4723	4418	124	176	5
1976	5415	5018	154	236	7
1977	5241	4796	179	256	10
1978	5201	4697	210	282	13
1979	5570	4961	261	330	17
1980	5649	4960	304	363	22
1981	5824	5038	356	402	28
1982	5922	5044	406	436	35
1983	5972	5006	457	467	43
1984	6015	4960	509	496	51
1985	6061	4914	563	525	60

Percentage Distribution of
New Labor Force Entrants, by Occupation,
Race, and Sex, 1970 to 1985

DENTISTRY

YEAR	TOTAL	WHITE		BLACK	
		MALE	FEMALE	MALE	FEMALE
1970	100.00	98.23	0.89	0.87	0.01
1971	100.00	97.38	1.13	1.46	0.02
1972	100.00	96.67	1.28	2.02	0.03
1973	100.00	95.71	1.54	2.71	0.04
1974	100.00	94.69	1.94	3.30	0.07
1975	100.00	93.54	2.63	3.72	0.10
1976	100.00	92.67	2.85	4.35	0.13
1977	100.00	91.51	3.42	4.89	0.18
1978	100.00	90.31	4.04	5.42	0.24
1979	100.00	89.07	4.69	5.93	0.31
1980	100.00	87.80	5.38	6.42	0.39
1981	100.00	86.50	6.11	6.90	0.49
1982	100.00	85.18	6.86	7.37	0.59
1983	100.00	83.82	7.65	7.82	0.71
1984	100.00	82.45	8.46	8.25	0.85
1985	100.00	81.06	9.29	8.66	0.99

TABLE VIII-28
United States
Projection of Labor Force, by Occupation,
Race, and Sex, 1970 to 1985

DENTISTRY

YEAR	TOTAL	WHITE MALE	WHITE FEMALE	BLACK MALE	BLACK FEMALE
1970	80706	77629	984	1998	95
1971	81499	78465	959	1982	93
1972	82396	79371	942	1991	91
1973	83464	80403	940	2031	90
1974	84899	81741	962	2107	90
1975	86581	83259	1020	2210	92
1976	88910	85340	1104	2370	96
1977	90996	87141	1207	2546	103
1978	92983	88796	1334	2741	112
1979	95282	90674	1503	2979	126
1980	97592	92502	1704	3242	144
1981	100008	94363	1942	3536	168
1982	102450	96183	2215	3855	197
1983	104868	97922	2519	4194	233
1984	107255	99573	2853	4553	277
1985	109616	101140	3219	4929	328

Percentage Distribution of
Projection of Labor Force, by Occupation,
Race, and Sex, 1970 to 1985

DENTISTRY

YEAR	TOTAL	WHITE MALE	WHITE FEMALE	BLACK MALE	BLACK FEMALE
1970	100.00	96.19	1.22	2.48	0.12
1971	100.00	96.28	1.18	2.43	0.11
1972	100.00	96.33	1.14	2.42	0.11
1973	100.00	96.33	1.13	2.43	0.11
1974	100.00	96.28	1.13	2.48	0.11
1975	100.00	96.16	1.18	2.55	0.11
1976	100.00	95.98	1.24	2.67	0.11
1977	100.00	95.76	1.33	2.80	0.11
1978	100.00	95.50	1.43	2.95	0.12
1979	100.00	95.16	1.58	3.13	0.13
1980	100.00	94.79	1.75	3.32	0.15
1981	100.00	94.36	1.94	3.54	0.17
1982	100.00	93.88	2.16	3.76	0.19
1983	100.00	93.38	2.40	4.00	0.22
1984	100.00	92.84	2.66	4.24	0.26
1985	100.00	92.27	2.94	4.50	0.30

TABLE VIII-29
United States
New Labor Force Entrants, by Occupation, Race, and Sex, 1970 to 1985

DENTISTRY

YEAR	TOTAL	WHITE		BLACK	
		MALE	FEMALE	MALE	FEMALE
1970	3718	3652	33	32	0
1971	3745	3647	43	55	1
1972	3862	3734	49	78	1
1973	4050	3876	62	110	2
1974	4440	4204	86	147	3
1975	4723	4418	124	176	5
1976	5438	5018	154	259	7
1977	5293	4796	179	308	10
1978	5286	4697	210	366	13
1979	5702	4961	261	462	17
1980	5830	4960	304	544	22
1981	6065	5038	356	643	28
1982	6227	5044	406	742	35
1983	6345	5006	457	840	43
1984	6461	4960	509	942	51
1985	6586	4914	563	1050	60

Percentage Distribution of
New Labor Force Entrants, by Occupation, Race, and Sex, 1970 to 1985

DENTISTRY

YEAR	TOTAL	WHITE		BLACK	
		MALE	FEMALE	MALE	FEMALE
1970	100.00	98.23	0.89	0.87	0.01
1971	100.00	97.38	1.13	1.46	0.02
1972	100.00	96.67	1.28	2.02	0.03
1973	100.00	95.71	1.54	2.71	0.04
1974	100.00	94.69	1.94	3.30	0.07
1975	100.00	93.54	2.63	3.72	0.10
1976	100.00	92.27	2.83	4.77	0.13
1977	100.00	90.62	3.39	5.81	0.18
1978	100.00	88.86	3.97	6.93	0.24
1979	100.00	87.01	4.58	8.11	0.30
1980	100.00	85.07	5.21	9.34	0.38
1981	100.00	83.06	5.86	10.61	0.47
1982	100.00	81.00	6.53	11.91	0.56
1983	100.00	78.89	7.20	13.24	0.67
1984	100.00	76.76	7.87	14.59	0.79
1985	100.00	74.60	8.55	15.94	0.91

TABLE VIII-30
United States
Projection of Labor Force, by Occupation,
Race, and Sex, 1970 to 1985

DENTISTRY

| YEAR | TOTAL | WHITE | | BLACK | |
		MALE	FEMALE	MALE	FEMALE
1970	80706	77629	984	1998	95
1971	81499	78465	959	1982	93
1972	82396	79371	942	1991	91
1973	83464	80403	940	2031	90
1974	84899	81741	962	2107	90
1975	86581	83259	1020	2210	92
1976	88933	85340	1104	2394	96
1977	91070	87141	1207	2620	103
1978	93139	88796	1334	2897	112
1979	95565	90674	1503	3262	126
1980	98046	92502	1704	3697	144
1981	100689	94363	1942	4216	168
1982	103414	96183	2215	4818	197
1983	106173	97922	2519	5499	233
1984	108964	99573	2853	6261	277
1985	111794	101140	3219	7107	328

Percentage Distribution of
Projection of Labor Force, by Occupation,
Race, and Sex, 1970 to 1985

DENTISTRY

| YEAR | TOTAL | WHITE | | BLACK | |
		MALE	FEMALE	MALE	FEMALE
1970	100.00	96.19	1.22	2.48	0.12
1971	100.00	96.28	1.18	2.43	0.11
1972	100.00	96.33	1.14	2.42	0.11
1973	100.00	96.33	1.13	2.43	0.11
1974	100.00	96.28	1.13	2.48	0.11
1975	100.00	96.16	1.18	2.55	0.11
1976	100.00	95.96	1.24	2.69	0.11
1977	100.00	95.69	1.33	2.88	0.11
1978	100.00	95.34	1.43	3.11	0.12
1979	100.00	94.88	1.57	3.41	0.13
1980	100.00	94.35	1.74	3.77	0.15
1981	100.00	93.72	1.93	4.19	0.17
1982	100.00	93.01	2.14	4.66	0.19
1983	100.00	92.23	2.37	5.18	0.22
1984	100.00	91.38	2.62	5.75	0.25
1985	100.00	90.47	2.88	6.36	0.29

their levels of participation in 1970, with increases of 1.0 percentage point and 1.9 percentage points, respectively, over the base line projection.

These simulations indicate that blacks can make substantial gains in their penetration of the dental labor force as a result of their representation in the profession in 1970 and of their increasing number among dental school graduates. The projection for females is promising, but because of their small representation in the 1970 dental labor force and among new dental school graduates, their penetration of the profession will happen slowly.

CHAPTER IX

Concluding Remarks

The preceding chapters document the past and present status of minorities and women in several white-collar occupations. This documentation is based on a comprehensive search and review of the literature pertaining to this experience and of the current programs in operation to assist minorities and women to enter these fields. Included in each chapter is an assessment of the future representation of minorities and women in the occupation. The assessment is based on the results of a model of the labor supply creation process which incorporates the current trends in minority and female presence among potential labor force entrants and entry and separation rates.

These concluding remarks are addressed to the future experience and include a summary and comparison of the findings. Highlights of the analyses of the projections of new entrants into the labor force and of the projections of the resultant labor force are discussed and are followed by some limited generalizations about the rate of progress of increasing minority and female representation in these occupations.

SUMMARY OF CHANGES, 1970-1985

It is first of all obvious that minority and female participation in the various professions studied will continue to vary significantly. The differences in new entrants will be reflected in the participation ratios of 1985. Although the latter will be higher for most groups studied, some will actually be lower.

New Entrants

In the occupations examined in this study, mechanical engineering saw the smallest proportion of new female entrants in 1970. That same year the largest share of new female en-

268

trants went to chemistry. Between 1970 and 1985, however, the proportion of women entering the labor force as chemists will increase by only 150 percent, which represents the smallest proportional increase for female entrants during the 15 year period in the occupations studied. Increases in female entrants of 5-fold or larger are found in law, engineering, mechanical engineering, chemical engineering, industrial engineering, and dentistry. The largest proportional increase in new female entrants between 1970 and 1985 will occur in industrial engineering where women will increase their representation from 0.7 percent to 5.1 percent, which translates into an increase of over 7-fold. In 1985 the model's projections show women to hold their smallest representation among new entrants in mechanical engineering with 2.2 percent and to have their largest representation in accounting with 28.3 percent.

Our data show that in 1970 the smallest proportion of new black entrants was in chemical engineering. Their highest representation among new entrants that year was in law. The smallest proportional increase for black entrants to the labor force between 1970 and 1985 will be in chemistry and chemical engineering. Increases of 5-fold or larger in the proportion of black entrants to the labor force for the 15 year period are found in engineering, industrial engineering, electrical engineering, mechanical engineering, other engineering, accounting, other business and management, medicine, and dentistry. The largest proportional increase in new black entrants between 1970 and 1985 will be in dentistry, where blacks will raise their representation among new entrants from 0.9 percent to 9.7 percent, or 11-fold. The model shows that in 1985 the smallest representation of black entrants will be in chemical engineering where they will comprise 0.6 percent of new entrants. Blacks will make up 12.3 percent of those entering other business and management, which is the occupation in which their largest representation among new entrants occurs.

Participation

In the professions discussed in this study, women had their smallest proportional labor force representation in 1970 in mechanical engineering. During that same year, females constituted 12.3 percent of all chemists, their largest representation in any profession studied in this volume. Between 1970 and 1985 a drop in the proportion of female participation will occur in electrical engineering and chemistry. The labor supply model shows a doubling in the representation of female chemical engineers and a tripling of female lawyers during the same 15 year period. In 1985 women will hold the smallest share of the labor force in the field of mechanical engineering, where they will comprise only 0.8 percent of the work force. Their largest representation will be in accounting where they will constitute 12.9 percent of all accountants.

In 1970, black participation in the field of chemical engineering was the lowest in any profession studied; in dentistry, the highest. In those professions examined in this study, the proportion of blacks will decrease in only one field between 1970 and 1985. That involves those working as chemists; their participation will decline from 3.2 percent to 2.8 percent. The labor supply model shows at least a doubling between 1970 and 1985 in the proportion of blacks in chemical engineering, mechanical engineering, accounting, other business and management, law, and medicine. According to the model, in 1985 blacks will hold their smallest representation in chemical engineering with 1.1 percent, and they will hold their largest proportion in other business and management with 5.7 percent.

RATE OF PROGRESS

The results of this analysis show that progress in increasing black and female representation in these occupations obviously varies from one occupation to another. Some generalizations may be made about the rate of progress, and these are concerned with the relationships between the parameters of the labor supply model.

Black or female penetration of the labor force of an occupation will usually increase as long as the proportion of new black or female entrants to an occupation exceeds their proportion in that occupation's existing labor force. This relationship describes the condition for increasing black representation, but is not the only condition necessary for increasing female representation. In an occupation, the rate of increase in black representation is limited by the initial white dominance of the associated labor force, the rate of increase in black representation among potential new labor force entrants, and the relative size of the new entrants pool to the existing labor force. For the professions included in this study, the relative sizes of black and white separation rates do not have major effects on the rate of black progress because, in most cases, they are very close in magnitude.

The only exception can be found for physicists where the black separation rate exceeds the white separation rate by a factor of two, but black representation in the labor force is projected, by the model, to increase over time nonetheless.

In only one occupation, chemistry, will black representation decrease despite increasing black representation among new entrants. The reason for this decline is that the proportion of blacks among new entrants is less than their representation in the labor force throughout the projection period. A possible explanation for the existence of this situation may be that the initial supply base contains individuals who identify themselves as chemists but who entered the labor force with a degree in some field other than chemistry; therefore, the proportion of blacks in the profession's labor force is not consistent with the graduate chemists population.

Progress in increasing female representation in the professions discussed herein adheres to the general rule described above, but is complicated by the differences in male and female separation rates. In those occupations in which female separation rates greatly exceed the rates for men, the rate of progress is constrained because the number of female new entrants only marginally exceeds the number of female separations. Female participation in a profession's labor force will not increase unless the difference between entrants and separations is substantial, and the proportional increase in the size of the female component of the labor force is greater than the proportional increase in the male segment.

This problem is most apparent in chemistry, physics, and several of the engineering subfields. In several of the other occupations, the high female separation rate intensifies the differences in the proportion of women among new entrants and the proportion of women in the labor force and limits progress in female representation even further. These discrepancies may be attributable to the problem in the initial supply base explained above in regard to blacks—that is, the differences between those women who identify themselves as a member of a profession and those who are actually trained in that profession.

THE SITUATION FOR NONBLACK MINORITIES

Because of the limited data available on the educational experience of nonblack minorities, it is impossible to implement the labor supply model to project the future participation of these groups in the occupations studied herein. Some generalizations can be made, however, using information on occupational characteristics of the labor force from the 1970 Census and data on degrees awarded gathered from various professional organizations.

Nonblack minorities show a greater participation than blacks in the technical professions: chemistry, physics, engineering, and medicine. In each of these fields except medicine, nonblack minorities represent a significantly larger proportion of degree earners than blacks; consequently, the representation of such minorities in the chemist, physicist, and engineer labor forces would increase if these trends continued. The large projection of the nonblack minority group degree earners in chemistry and engineering is attributable in part to the large representation of Orientals in these two fields.

The participation of nonblack minorities in medicine is not easy to predict. Even though their representation in medical schools is increasing, it is still below their proportion in the 1970 physician labor force and would, therefore, cause a decline in their proportion of the physician labor force. Furthermore, doctors immigrating to the United States must be considered because they heavily affect the representation of these minorities in the physician labor force.

In the occupations of accounting, other business, and dentistry, black representation is higher than that of other minorities, according to the 1970 Census. Data on degrees awarded in law, other business, and accounting are limited; therefore, it is difficult to make any predictions on the future participation of nonblack minorities in these occupations. Statistics on dental school graduates show that the proportion of degrees earned by nonblack minorities has more than doubled. In the future this should translate into a larger representation in the dental labor force.

FINAL COMMENT

In summary, this analysis indicates that the potential is great for increased participation of blacks, other minorities, and women in these selected professions. The rate of increase in representation, however, will be slow and is limited by the white male's traditional dominance of these occupations, the relative size of the entrants pool relative to the existing supply of persons already in the professions, and the high rates at which women leave these occupations.

Index

Racial Policies of American Industry Series

1. *The Negro in the Automobile Industry,*
   by Herbert R. Northrup.   1968
2. *The Negro in the Aerospace Industry,*
   by Herbert R. Northrup.   1968
3. *The Negro in the Steel Industry,* by Richard L. Rowan.   1968
4. *The Negro in the Hotel Industry,* by Edward C. Koziara
   and Karen S. Koziara.   1968
5. *The Negro in the Petroleum Industry,* by Carl B. King
   and Howard W. Risher, Jr.   1969
6. *The Negro in the Rubber Tire Industry,* by Herbert R.
   Northrup and Alan B. Batchelder.   1969
7. *The Negro in the Chemical Industry,*
   by William Howard Quay, Jr.   1969
8. *The Negro in the Paper Industry,* by Herbert R. Northrup.   1969
9. *The Negro in the Banking Industry,*
   by Armand J. Thieblot, Jr.   1970
10. *The Negro in the Public Utility Industries,*
    by Bernard E. Anderson.   1970
11. *The Negro in the Insurance Industry,* by Linda P. Fletcher.   1970
12. *The Negro in the Meat Industry,* by Walter A. Fogel.   1970
13. *The Negro in the Tobacco Industry,*
    by Herbert R. Northrup.   1970
14. *The Negro in the Bituminous Coal Mining Industry,*
    by Darold T. Barnum.   1970
15. *The Negro in the Trucking Industry,* by Richard D. Leone.   1970
16. *The Negro in the Railroad Industry,*
    by Howard W. Risher, Jr.   1971
17. *The Negro in the Shipbuilding Industry,* by Lester Rubin.   1970
18. *The Negro in the Urban Transit Industry,*
    by Philip W. Jeffress.   1970
19. *The Negro in the Lumber Industry,* by John C. Howard.   1970
20. *The Negro in the Textile Industry,* by Richard L. Rowan.   1970
21. *The Negro in the Drug Manufacturing Industry,*
    by F. Marion Fletcher.   1970
22. *The Negro in the Department Store Industry,*
    by Charles R. Perry.   1971
23. *The Negro in the Air Transport Industry,*
    by Herbert R. Northrup et al.   1971
24. *The Negro in the Drugstore Industry,* by F. Marion Fletcher. 1971
25. *The Negro in the Supermarket Industry,*
    by Gordon F. Bloom and F. Marion Fletcher.   1972
26. *The Negro in the Farm Equipment and Construction
    Machinery Industry,* by Robert Ozanne.   1972
27. *The Negro in the Electrical Manufacturing Industry,*
    by Theodore V. Purcell and Daniel P. Mulvey.   1971
28. *The Negro in the Furniture Industry,* by William E. Fulmer.   1973
29. *The Negro in the Longshore Industry,* by Lester Rubin
    and William S. Swift.   1974
30. *The Negro in the Offshore Maritime Industry,*
    by William S. Swift.   1974
31. *The Negro in the Apparel Industry,* by Elaine Gale Wrong.   1974

Order from: Kraus Reprint Co., Route 100, Millwood, New York 10546

OTHER COLLECTIVE BARGAINING STUDIES

Open Shop Construction, by Herbert R. Northrup and Howard G. Foster. Major Study No. 54.   1975. $15.00

Coalition Bargaining, by William N. Chernish. Major Study No. 45.
                                                                      1969. $7.95

Restrictive Labor Practices in the Supermarket Industry, by Herbert R. Northrup and Gordon R. Storholm. Major Study No. 44.   1967. $7.50

INDUSTRY STUDIES

Prescription Drug Pricing in Independent and Chain Drugstores, by Jonathan P. Northrup.   1975. $5.95

Market Restraints in the Retail Drug Industry, by F. Marion Fletcher. Major Study No. 43.   1967. $10.00

The Carpet Industry: Present Status and Future Prospects, by Robert W. Kirk. Miscellaneous Report Series No. 17.   1970. $5.95

The Economics of Carpeting and Resilient Flooring: An Evaluation and Comparison, by George M. Parks. Major Study No. 41.   1966. $2.95